"*Superior Street was a mere trail cut through the woods, so rough that sledges and wagons, which constituted traffic, had to wind their way carefully around tree stumps and boulders... Wolves, bears, and deer living in the surrounding woods used to come to the edge of town to peer curiously at the usurping humans, and at night the cries of wild animals could be heard...*"

-E.A. Silberstein
Duluth, 1870

THIS IS DULUTH

By

Dora Mary Macdonald

PARADIGM PRESS - 1999

Printed by Morris Publishing of Kearney, Nebraska

First printing

ISBN: 1-889924-03-2
Library of Congress Catalog Card Number: 98-94255
Cover photo and frontispiece ©1999 by Jared Glovsky.

Frontispiece: Superior Street, Duluth, Minnesota - 1998

Cover photo: View from the Hill; Radisson Hotel, Duluth
Entertainment and Convention Center, Aerial Lift-Bridge,
and Park Point stretching out to Lake Superior.

INTRODUCTION

In 1950, Dora Mary Macdonald wrote of reviewing the past and taking inventory of the present. As we draw ever closer to the end of this - the greatest century in human history - it seems appropriate, and increasingly important, to continue doing so.

We at Paradigm Press agree with the saying, "*The past remains present.*" Indeed, the more things change, the more they stay the same. The city of Duluth has been through some momentous changes in the last 150 years. It has witnessed times of stellar prosperity and times of crunching depression.

Some aspects, however, of the city's character have never changed: doggedness and determination, strength of spirit, striving to keep looking forward and at the same time never forgetting where it's been. Dora Mary Macdonald appreciated this, and in writing this volume, created an entertaining, informative, and complete chronicle.

It is the hope of Paradigm Press that the reader as well comes to appreciate the virtues prevalent in Duluth's history, and endeavors to incorporate them into his or her own life.

-Jared Glovsky
Paradigm Press

TABLE OF CONTENTS

FOREWORD   i

CHAPTER I *"Millions of Years Ago"*   1

CHAPTER II *"Indians"*   5

CHAPTER III *"Explorers and Traders"*   18

CHAPTER IV *"Missionaries"*   31

CHAPTER V *"The Village of Duluth"*   42

CHAPTER VI *"The City of Duluth"*   71

CHAPTER VII *"Village and City Again"*   99

CHAPTER VIII *"The Nineties"*   122

CHAPTER IX *"Twentieth Century 1900-1920"*   149

CHAPTER X *"Twentieth Century - To Mid-Century"* 206

Appendix
About the Author

TO MY HUSBAND
Alexander Paul (Sandy) Macdonald

FOREWORD

In the mid-century we pause to review the past and to take inventory of the present. I have gathered together bits of information and stories here and there about Duluth, and have endeavored to weave them together to give a chronicle of the city. This volume started out to be a serious, factual, informative account of the growth of the city, but as Duluthians contributed anecdotes, the tone changed, and the book has become a story of and stories about Duluth. Sometimes a sprightly anecdote did not fit into the picture very well, but if it helped to interpret the personality of the city, it was included in the book.

It was O. Henry who once declared that every city has a civic voice, an oral expression of its personality. It this be true, it seems to me the voice of Duluth has a vigorous ring resounding from lake to rock-bound hills, a voice embodying the spirit of the hardy men and women who founded the community. This Duluth has never been a soft and gentle city; its voice reflects its spirit of challenge. There is an overtone of culture worthy of Daniel de Greysolon Sieur du Luth; there is magnificence in its generosity; and there is compassion for the unfortunate. Here is a lusty city, but a city that has its dreams and the capacity to make those dreams come true.

In writing this book, I have incurred many obligations. I gratefully acknowledge research done by Mrs. Anne N. Dyrdahl, who, because of love for her city, spent years gathering information about it. Mrs. Dyrdahl generously lent me her material, so that I have benefited from her work.

My thanks are also due to Hugh M. Roberts, geologist, for his critical work on the first chapter of the book. Since my study of geology deals entirely with the rocks I overturn in my garden, it is Mr. Roberts' valuable assistance which gives authenticity to that portion of the book.

I also acknowledge with appreciation the help of Mrs. Eugene S. Orren, for her criticisms and copy reading; Miss Ruth O'Malley and Mrs. Cornelia Peters of the reference department of the public library and Miss Cora Colbraith of the St. Louis Historical Society, who gave such efficient and cheerful assistance in gathering material; and Mrs. William Swanberg, whose enthusiasm first interested me in the project and whose encouragement kept me at work. I am also under obligation to many men and women who contributed material. Sources are listed in the bibliography at the end of the book.

Here a word of thanks should be given to members of clubs and organizations who encouraged me in this work; and to my long-suffering friends and family, who patiently coped with me when I interrupted conversations about the hydrogen bomb or welfare state with vital information about the Chippewas or Duluth's first fire department.

Publication of the book has been made possible by Alvin T. Stolen, superintendent of schools, and by the Duluth Board of Education.

To all those who have helped in building this story, I give my sincere thanks.

-DORA MARY MACDONALD

CHAPTER I

Millions of Years Ago

DULUTH, the "zenith city of the unsalted seas," clings to the side of its hills and overlooks the waters of Lake Superior, St. Louis Bay, and St. Louis River. Situated between the water and a ridge of rocks, the city extends nearly east and west. It is about 30 miles long, one mile wide, and at its highest point, 880 feet high.

The ridge or escarpment above Duluth is high owing to the fact that it is composed of a massive gabbro rock formation which has resisted erosion. It is here that Skyline Parkway drive is built. Robert Ingersoll is reported to have said, as he stood on this boulevard drive overlooking the city, "Duluth is the only city I know where a fellow can stand on a city street and spit a mile and a half - straight down."

Duluth's outcropping rocks are among the oldest known, rocks of the Keweenawn Age, which have lain here more than 700 million years, since before there was any record of life on the globe. Lava flows in the vicinity poured out of volcanoes from fissures believed to have been in existence where Lake Superior now lies. In molten condition, the lavas flowed out on the surface in broad sheets and then cooled to form extensive flows, followed by widespread intrusives which cooled into masses known as the Duluth gabbro. This rock formation extends from Mesaba Avenue to West Duluth.

During the latter part of the Archean period in the early Algonkian time, at least three great mountain ranges were uplifted and eroded away in the part of Canada that lies north of here, where the roots of these mountains may be seen along the height of the land.

Above the Archean and Algonkian rocks are found rocks of the ancient Keweenawn System, which are comprised of lavas, intrusives and conglomerates. The flows extend for 300 miles from the tip of Keweenawn Point to within a few miles of Minneapolis, and also along the north shore of Lake Superior. There was no lake at that time, the present basin being a desert, similar to the deserts of Arizona and Nevada. During the period preceding the Keweenawn, iron formations were laid down in the Mesabi and Cuyuna districts; this took place in seas that covered these areas at the time.

The Cambrian Age came next after the Keweenawn, when the highest forms of animal life were species of crustaceans similar to our modern crab. But at least, there was life in this region. Sedimentary rocks are also found in the next period, the Ordovician Age, which dates back a mere 500 million years. Through an interval of some 600 million years, the Lake Superior region has been raised above the sea and lowered beneath it several times, but as a unit and with slight deformation of the rocks.

The last great period which helped to shape the physiographic features of Duluth was the Glacial Period or Ice age, which extended from a time a few hundred thousand years ago up to about 7,000 years ago. It was much colder around Duluth then. Year after year more snow fell than could melt. After many centuries, the great weight of snow turned into an ice sheet several thousands of feet thick. In this glacial form it slowly moved over the region. Three successive ice sheets have moved down over this territory, advancing and retreating, filling up valleys, gouging out lakes, wearing down rocks, and leaving glacial drift to form ridges and hills. As the ice finally melted, Lake Superior and the Duluth shore line began to take somewhat their present outlines.

Lake Superior is a remnant of glacial Lake Namadji, later called Lake Duluth. The former lake was much larger, extending up to the present Boulevard Drive, which formed a gravel beach. However, the present Lake Superior is a good-sized remnant, being the largest known body of fresh water in the world - 383 miles long, 160 miles wide, and 1290 feet deep.

Regardless of the geologic history of the area, the average property owner is more concerned with the problem of dealing with the rocks as they are now found. Dynamite must be used to excavate basements, and the gardener each spring agrees with the old Pennsylvania Dutchman who averred, "Rocks grow every winter, so in the spring there's a new crop to dig out of the garden." Duluth has some splendid rock gardens.

In contrast to the rock-bound hills upon which the city is built, there is Park Point, formerly called Minnesota Point, a sandy spit of land extending out between the lake and bay and forming a natural harbor. It was originally attached to the mainland, the canal being cut through by local inhabitants. The Point is seven miles long and between 300 and 750 feet wide. It has been formed by wave action, shore currents, and strong winds blowing in from Lake Superior. One authority suggests that some sediment was also deposited there during an early post-glacial period.

According to rumor, George Sherwood, one of the old-time real estate men, stood on the barren hills one day with an Easterner, expounding on the charms of the village and the advantages to be gained by investing in Duluth real estate. Pointing to the sandy stretch of land curving out into the water, he said, "There lies Minnesota Point. It looks like God's arm protecting the town of Duluth."

The Easterner, unimpressed by the rock hills, sand, or sentiment, replied, "It looks to me more like God's finger pointing the way out of town."

Even the loyal Duluthians must admit that during the glacial period this region must have been too cold for real comfort. Contrary to general belief, the city has warmed up considerably since those days. The average temperature for the winter months is 13; for spring, 37; for summer, 63; and for autumn, 43. The highest temperature recorded is 106 in July 1906; the lowest is -41 in January 1885. The winters are indubitably cold, but since the air is very dry, the cold is not so penetrating as in localities with greater humidity. In the summers, when heat waves occur in other sections of the country, burning up vegetation and enervating mankind, hordes of people come here to enjoy the comfortable days and cool nights. Duluth has become known as the "air conditioned city."

The cool summers, however, have led to many anecdotes about the Duluth climate. Mark Twain, for instance, once remarked, "The coldest winter I ever spent was a summer in Duluth." There is also the story about the controversy between two groups of citizens following a winter carnival. One group wanted to tear down the ice palace, while the other side wanted to leave it up so it would be ready for the next winter's carnival. And there is the story about the tourist who asked the street car motorman what the summers were like in Duluth. "I don't know," replied the motorman. "I've just lived here fourteen months."

Duluthians may laugh and repeat such stories, but they are inordinately proud of the climate of their city.

This is Duluth.

CHAPTER II

Indians

MUCH has been written in Minnesota history about the Easterners who came to this region to make their fortunes. The Indians, however, first followed Horace Greeley's advice "Go west, young man, go west" - followed it some hundreds of years before it was given.

The Sioux or Dakota Indians were around the Head of the Lakes more or less minding their own business when the Chippewas came on tour, chased them out, and took over the social and industrial life of the region.

The original name of the tribe is Ojibway, but the white men called it Chippewa. The Indians themselves have not adopted the name, but "Chippewa" it stands in treaties and negotiations of the United States government. Some say the word comes from a root meaning "pucker" and was given the tribe because of their moccasins, which had a puckered seam extending up the front. However, this explanation should probably be taken with a grain of salt - a commodity, by the way, unknown to the early Indians.

The Chippewas, of which the Ottawa and Pottawattomie are branches, had been driven back from the eastern seacoast by the warlike Iroquois. They went first to Ottawa, and then to the Sault. About the time Columbus made his first voyage, they set up housekeeping on Madelaine Island. This village was the assembling point for the tribe for about 120 years before it was broken up, probably by disease and famine.

William Whipple Warren, author of a history of his native Chippewas, relates this tradition as given him by an old man of the tribe; "While our forefathers were living on the great salt water toward the rising sun, the great Megis (sea shell) showed itself above the surface of the great water, and the rays of the sun for a long period were reflected from its glossy back. It gave warmth and light to the An-ish-in-aub-ag (red race). All at once it sank into the deep, and for a time our ancestors were not blessed with light. It rose to the surface and appeared again on a great river which drains the waters of the Great Lakes, and again for a long time it gave life to our forefathers, and reflected back the rays of the sun. Again it disappeared from sight and it rose not till it appeared to the eyes of the An-ish-in-aub-ag on the shores of the first great lake. Again it sank from sight, and death daily visited the wigwams of our forefathers till it showed its back and reflected the rays of the sun once more at Bow-e-ting (Sault Ste. Marie). Here it remained for a long time, but once more, and for the last time, it disappeared, and the An-ish-in-aub-ag were left in darkness and misery till it floated and once more showed its bright back at Mo-ning-wun-a-kaun-ing (La Pointe Island), where it has ever since reflected back the rays of the sun and blessed our ancestors with life, light, and wisdom. Its rays reach the remotest village of the widespread Ojibways."

About 1620 when the Pilgrim fathers were parking the Mayflower at Plymouth Rock and unloading their clocks and chests and escritoires, the Chippewas pitched their permanent camp on the present site of Fond du Lac, "the end of the river". Wa-me-gis-ng-o is said to have been the first permanent settler of whom there is a record. His post office address was Wi-ah-quah ke che gume eng. The Chippewas then completely controlled the basin of Lake Superior. Many of the tribe lived in what is now Duluth proper, their wigwams straggling up the hills and along Park Point. An Indian village once stood at the present intersection of Mesaba Avenue and Superior Street.

Even before this time, the Chippewas had met the French white men. Before the fur traders came west, the Indians would go to Montreal to trade their furs for cloth and beads, and knives and guns. The guns, especially, were important, for with these superior weapons, the Chippewas had a distinct advantage over the Sioux, who had only bows and arrows, and could thus drive them out of the northeastern part of this region.

The Chippewas and Sioux seem to have felt no trace of brotherly love toward each other. In fact, a deadly enmity existed between the two nations. However, there were exceptions to the feud.

A legend tells that at one time Chaska, son of a Sioux chief, became so engrossed in the hunt that he unwittingly entered Chippewa territory along the St. Louis River. Hearing a splash in the water, he stealthily parted the bushes, expecting to see a beaver - but there was an Indian girl staring at him. She was Wetona, the daughter of Buckado, a chief of the Chippewas, down at the edge of the river gathering reeds and rushes for weaving baskets. Chaska was handsome; Wetona was beautiful; they were both young; and they soon forgot the enmity between their nations.

The story goes that frequently after that first encounter, as their love deepened, Wetona and Chaska would secretly meet at the highest peak in the hills, where they could see down into the valley and for miles along the shores of the lake and bay. This peak then was known as

Maintou-Ah-Ge-Bik, but the white man today calls it Bardon's Peak.

The Chippewas were planning a surprise attack upon the Sioux, and at night, in the midst of wild preparations for battle, the Chippewa maiden and the Sioux brave fled to a small island in the river, which Wetona called her island.

Buckado and his warriors drove back the Sioux that night. When the battle was over, amid the dancing and feasting, the chief promised Gray Fox, a mighty warrior, a reward - the hand of Wetona in marriage. He ordered Loon Feathers, the grandmother, to prepare the maid for the ceremony and bring her to his presence.

Loon Feathers said that Wetona had disappeared. Then, being a garrulous soul, she told that on that day she had visited Manitou-Ah-Ge-Bik, the high peak, and had hidden in bushes to observe the camp of the Sioux. She said she had heard Chaska and Wetona declaring their love and planning to flee to some place where they might live together in peace.

In great anger, Buckado vowed that his daughter should not take an enemy son for her husband, and he called his warriors together to find Wetona. At the river's edge, they found that Wetona's canoe was gone; then they saw a flickering light on the small island. The warriors embarked in their canoes, and, approaching the island, discovered Wetona's canoe beached there. They surrounded the island, and some kept watch so that no one could escape, and others searched every foot of the little island. All they could find were two pairs of moccasins - the puckered Chippewa moccasins of Wetona and the Sioux moccasins of Chaska. The lovers could not escape, but they were never found.

Loon Feathers cried out, "I am brave and strong, but now a great fear comes over me. I hear strange sounds like music. This is the voice of the Love Spirit, who has carried the lovers to the Moon of Perpetual Honey in his sky canoe."

Fearful to offend the Love Spirit, whose magic is stronger than death, Buckado and his men returned to their camp to mourn the loss of Wetona.

Since then, the scene of the tragedy has been called Spirit Island. The Chippewas are superstitious about the place and say they hear weird music there; but the steel workers at Morgan Park look out on the island just off shore from the steel plant and think it is a very quiet little place.

Another Chippewa legend gives the story background for the state flower - the moccasin flower.

Once on a lovely autumn day, a little Indian girl, Minneopa, who loved to hunt, begged her brothers to take her with them to hunt the red deer. In the manner of elder brothers, they laughed at the idea of a girl hunting with the big boys, and departed from her. After they had gone, Minneopa put on her best moccasins, took her bow and arrow, and started out along to shoot a red deer. She wandered far from home and became so engrossed in trailing a deer that she did not notice that the woods were burning until she was completely surrounded by forest fire. She perished in the flames.

Minneopa's father and mother searched throughout the forest, but they could not find a trace of the little girl. The mother was inconsolable. The next spring she again began her search, and came to a spot where a new kind of plant was growing, with two flowers such as she had never seen before. The blossoms were the same shape and color as the moccasins Minneopa had worn. Then the mother knew these flowers marked the grave of her daughter. The plant is called the moccasin flower.

Credit goes to the Sioux for the name of the state. From Minne, meaning water, and sota, meaning sky-tinted, comes the name sky-tinted water - Minnesota.

9

The Chippewas had four principal types of dwellings: the wigwam (in Chippewa, "wigiwam"), peaked lodge, bark house, and tepee. The wigwam was dome shaped; the peaked lodge had a ridgepole and slanting sides; the bark house had a framework like a low house; and the tepee had a conical framework. The poles or framework were covered with mats of bulrushes tied together with green basswood bark, over which were thrown sheets of elm and cedar bark, or rolls of birch bark. The later tepee might be covered with cloth. No nails were used in construction. There was an opening for a doorway, with a hanging of skins, which had a heavy pole at the lower edge. When a family moved to another territory, it left the framework of the abode but carried along the covering to use again.

All dwellings had a fireplace in the center of the one big room, with logs to mark it off. Some of the long bark houses had two or three fireplaces ranged down the center. Without windows or doors, the interior of the houses was dark and smoky. Cedar boughs were arranged around the room on the hard-packed earth floor, and covered with rush mats. Here, at night, was spread the bedding, which was rolled up during the day and stacked by the wall. The bedding consisted of blankets and tanned deer or bear hides, with the hair still on them. Everyone in the family took off moccasins at night, loosened his clothing, and slept with his feet toward the fire.

Two or three generations of a family would live in one dwelling. The mother and father had their beds on either side of the entrance, and the youngest persons were situated where they must pass their elders in entering or leaving the room.

Cooking was done over the fireplace, and the food was eaten from the clay vessel in which it was cooked, the family sitting around it on the earth floor. A few dishes were fashioned from birch bark, and knives were made of the bones of animals. One peculiar utensil was a narrow wooden stick used for scooping out marrow from bones.

Indians generally ate two meals a day, early in the morning and evening. They made a bread of flour and water, kneaded into hard, round, flat loaves, which they baked by holding the loaves on the end of a stick over the fire. Most of their food consisted of meat of the animals of the forest, fish from the lakes and streams, potatoes, wild rice, corn, maple syrup, and berries. The Chippewas claim to have had pumpkin and squash before the coming of the white man.

When it came time for harvesting wild rice, squaws would collect perhaps thirty bushels a day in their canoes. They would spread it out to dry for a few days and then heat it in kettles until it was thoroughly dry. In a bowl-shaped cavity of the earth, beaten hard and smooth, barefoot Indians would trample the rice and then take it out of the bowl to let the wind blow away the chaff.

Pemmican was another delicacy of the Indians. They would boil buffalo meat, shred it, and pack it into sacks made of buffalo skin. They would pound this until the meat was hard and then pour over it boiling hot buffalo fat, so that no air could get to it. They stored these sacks, which sometimes held ninety pounds, in holes in the ground, and dug out chunks of the pemmican as they wanted it.

As a rule, the Indians did not prepare for the future by growing food or acquiring possessions. Everything was shared, so that if a man had been ambitious and stored up the equivalent of a deep freeze locker of food, he would have to give from it to the improvident members of his neighborhood.

The Reverend Joseph A. Gilfillan, who did missionary work among the Indians from 1877 to 1897, says that while the Indian men had a beautiful, graceful, springing step, the women "trudge along with a heavy, plodding tread, devoid of all beauty of motion." He

11

attributes this to the fact that the squaw had to carry the heavy packs. On a journey the brave strode ahead, carrying his bow and arrows or gun, while his squaw clumped along behind him carrying a pack weighing up to 200 pounds. On her back would be birch bark mats for the tepee, rush mats for the beds, cooking utensils, food, and a papoose.

Besides doing the housework, preparing the meals, and rearing her children, the Indian woman obtained much of the food for her family, raising a bit of corn, supplying the maple syrup, picking blueberries and cranberries, and harvesting wild rice. She stripped skins from animals her husband had killed, tanned them, and fashioned them into articles of clothing - moccasins and dress; she cut wood for the fireplace and lugged it into camp; she built the wigwam. While she was resting, she would bring to camp the deer or bear that her loving husband had tracked down and killed in the forest. He would tell her where to find it.

Indian braves did the hunting, fishing, and fighting for their families. They also met together in conference to determine the action of the tribe - conferences that were the forerunner of executive meetings in smoke-filled rooms. The council began when the chief took a few whiffs from the peace pipe or calumet, an article fashioned from blood-red pipestone. He would then pass the pipe around the circle, and each man would solemnly and silently take a puff. At the end of the council, the procedure was repeated, and the agreement was considered binding. Before they were introduced to tobacco, Indians smoked dried leaves of dogwood, which they called "kinnikinik".

With the coming of the French traders, the Chippewas changed their customs rapidly. They soon became dependent upon the French for arms, ammunition, food, and clothing, and they adopted many of the white man's ways.

In making a study of the Chippewas for the Smithsonian Institute, Miss Frances Densmore wrote in

1929, "Their industrial life is marked by a cooperation of men and women, the men taking the heavier part of the women's work and the women assisting in the lighter part of the men's work, as in the making of canoes." By then, the red man was civilized.

As a sidelight on the Chippewas, Edmund Franklin Ely, missionary to the Indians in Fond du Lac in 1833 and one of the founders of Duluth, says in his diary, "If anyone lends an article to an Indian, he must expect to be at the trouble of following it up till he gets it again." He gives several instances of the Indians borrowing articles with seemingly no intention of returning them. However, when he walked into a wigwam and picked up his own kettle from the fire, the Indians showed no resentment.

Chippewa children seem to have had a carefree life. Boys had no duties except to acquire the skills of their fathers. They practiced with bows and arrows, learned to glide silently and swiftly through the forests, ran races, wrestled, swam, held sham battles with mud balls, and coasted down hill on sleds made of the ribs of animals and buffalo skins. They disciplined themselves to remain motionless for hours, to go stretches of time without food, and to bear pain and suffering without flinching. All a lad's training was for the purpose of making him a brave and able hunter and warrior.

An Indian girl was trained in the simple arts of her mother, so she would become a capable and useful squaw. She and her brother both tamed wild animals to be their pets - foxes, bears, wolves, raccoons, and fawns. Every Indian family had dogs, many of which were part wolf.

An Indian baby or papoose was comfortable in his cradle - a board lined with soft skins. A mother would carry the cradle on her back or hang it on a tree while she worked. At intervals she would take the papoose out of his cradle (tikinagan), so he could kick and stretch his muscles.

When a child was born, his father would invite his friends for a feast, if he happened to have food in the tepee. After the Indians acquired guns, it was customary for friends to fire a salute. The father would then give them a treat of either food or tobacco. The parents would designate someone to name their child. This person had two duties - to choose a name and to give a feast at which time he would announce the name. If he had no food for a feast, he would defer the ceremony - and the naming - until he could procure food.

Mr. Ely has left an interesting account of the games the Chippewas enjoyed. There was a ring game (pinjuebinige), in which the winner was the one who could more frequently throw an awl within three finger rings.

The mokisin game was played with four balls, one of which was indented or chewed, and four mokisins or mittens to cover the balls. "One party takes the four balls, placing one under each covering. The opposite party reaches for the bit ball. If he finds it in the first mitten he loses, if last he gains. If he strikes his hand down upon one of the covers he is not allowed to look father, if not he may look through all. If the party looking for the ball takes it last, he is allowed to have a second chance, and so on." Just a variation of the shell game!

A posikanon was the only article used in a game by that name. "It is composed of two sticks, three or four inches in length and one inch in diameter. A string twelve or fifteen inches long is attached at either end to the middle of the stick. This is tossed by a stick two or three feet in length; the stick thrust under the string and suspended in the air is suddenly tossed or thrown toward a certain point previously fixed upon between parties. Two points are fixed upon at some distance apart. One party uses every effort to throw or toss or carry on the stick the posikanon beyond that point. The others try to prevent this."

In the bowl game or pogessewog, the instruments were a bowl or pan, and nine small articles of different figures and sizes, "four of which are so constructed as to be made to stand alone, four are flat on one side and round on the opposite, one is of iron, sometimes round and at other times in the shape of a half moon - some made of copper, some of bone. The single one (of iron) is of the first importance; of second importance - the standing ones. These are placed indiscriminately in the platter.

"He who commences the game lifts the bowl and brings it down with sudden force upon the ground or floor. It depends then upon the position of articles in the bowl whether the striker gains or not. If one article stands erect, it gains 50. If it falls on a piece of round iron - 100, etc. The winner has the privilege of again first striking the platter."

With games, feasting, and dancing, the Indians seem to have had quite a social life along the shores of Lake Superior.

Although this region belonged to the United States at the close of the Revolutionary War, the War Department did not place an agency here until 1822. Among the agents who have left records of the Indians is Henry R. Schoolcraft, who wrote of his travels and experiences. It was his articles that inspired the poet Longfellow to write "Hiawatha".

By numerous treaties the Indians turned over their lands to the United States. The treaty of Prairie du Chien in 1825 was the first in which the Chippewas of northern Minnesota participated. The purpose of this council was to try to get the Indian tribes to keep peace among themselves, and to persuade them to agree on their boundaries, so that there would be some basis on which the United States could purchase their lands. At this conference were the Sioux, Chippewas, Sacs, Foxes, Ottawas, Winnebagoes, and Pottawatomies.

To ratify this treaty, on August 5, 1826, Governor Lewis Cass of Michigan and T.L. McKinney, commissioners appointed by the United States government, met with the Chippewas at Fond du Lac. Something new had been added - a clause that gave the United States the right to take any metals or minerals from this region.

In August of 1847, again at the Fond du Lac, J.A. Verplank and Henry M. Rice, representing the United States government, concluded a treaty by which all land westward and southwestward from the Head of the Lakes was ceded to the United States.

Although Minnesota became a territory in 1849, Duluth still belonged to the Indians. The last of the treaties was made in La Pointe, Wisconsin, near Bayfield, in 1854, when the remainder of the country along the north shore of the lake and the northern was ceded to the United States. About ten bands of Indians were present at this conference, along with their wives, children, dogs, and ponies, guests of the government. The United States paid the Lake Superior Chippewas about one million dollars for their lands. The Indians had learned a few things since the Manhatten Island deal.

Among other clauses in the treaty, the Indians were to receive $5000 a year for twenty years in money; $8000 in goods, household furniture, and cooking utensils; $3000 a year in agricultural implements, cattle, tools, and building material; and $3000 a year for moral and educational purposes. There were other provisions, such as 200 guns, 100 rifles, 500 beaver traps, $300 in ammunition, and $1000 in ready made clothing for the young men.

By one clause of the La Pointe treaty, Chief Buffalo of the Ontonagon band had his choice of four sections of land any place in the ceded territory, which he might direct to "some of his connections who have rendered his people important services". The Chief divided this land among his three sons and his son-in-law. Within a year the sons gave their land to the son-in-law, who later sold one-half of the tract to Frederick D. Prentice of New York.

Duluth was founded as more and more settlers moved in and built their homes. In 1883, Mr. Prentice instituted legal proceedings to oust residents from their property, claiming that he had the title to their land. There was confusion and uncertainty, and some men, fearful of losing their land, paid Prentice for it without going to court. In all, there were twenty claims. Not until 1894 was the affair settled, when the courts found that Mr. Prentice was barred by a twenty year limitation which had expired. The Spalding Hotel is built on the land that was a portion of Chief Buffalo's tract. The old Indian had good judgment in real estate, it would seem. However, the courts found that much of the land, according to description, lay at the bottom of Lake Superior. There was a suspicion that the original descriptions had been tampered with, but this irregularity was never proved.

The Treaty of La Pointe was ratified by the senate on January 10, 1855. At last, when the territory of Minnesota was half-way to statehood, it belonged to the United States.

CHAPTER III

Explorers and Traders

DULUTH'S heritage is French, the beginning of its history with white men being connected with New France, as Canada was called.

From Montreal came the French traders, garbed "in a motley array of hunting skirts, bright sashes, gay capots, and embroidered moccasins" (Kellogg). There were also the voyageurs, who traded by licenses issued by the French government, and the wandering, daring coureurs de bois, who traded without a license, outlaws who gave up their allegiance to their native country for the freedom of the forests. At one time, there were about one thousand of these men who had left New France for the west, where they lived with the Indians, took Indian wives, traded in furs, and explored the unknown streams.

Behind Duluth was New France and a government in which two parties with divergent policies struggled for supremacy. The governor, an imperialist, backed by merchants, army officers, and explorers, wanted to develop the west by means of French enterprise and to extend the empire. The intendant, appointed by the king to check undue pretensions of the governor, supported by the Jesuit missionaries, sought to keep the young men in the colonies to develop agriculture and industries. The missionaries feared the ruin of their young colonists in the reckless life of the forests. They had reason for their fears.

The white men came west not only to obtain furs, but also to enlarge the French empire and to search for passage to the great salt water and the Indies. They reached this region through Lake Superior, the Pigeon and St. Louis (then called the Fond du Lac) rivers in Minnesota, and the Brule river in Wisconsin.

To Etienne Brule goes the credit of discovering Lake Superior. The great Champlain in Montreal conceived and carried out a plan to have certain young men live with Indian tribes so they could become interpreters. He would make the arrangements with Indians who came to Montreal to trade. In 1610, Etienne Brule wintered among the Indians, and it is thought that during that time he must have reached the upper St. Lawrence, though probably not Lake Ontario. In 1612, Champlain had Brule join a band of Hurons that was returning west to their village. On this trip, he undoubtedly had sight of one or more of the Great Lakes. In 1623, Brule told of visiting a place farther west, where the Indians were mining copper. It is believed that this place was Isle Royale, in Lake Superior. In spite of his explorations, Brule cannot be highly respected. He was a dissolute and treacherous fellow, who deserted to the British and later turned to the Indians, acquiring their less attractive manners and customs. He became the first of the coureurs de bois. Brule was killed by one of the Hurons in a quarrel.

Champlain next sent out Nicolet, who may have paddled his canoe on Lake Superior. The Jesuit missionaries Jacques and Paymbault, at the Sault in 1641, could have explored the shining water. But this is only conjecture.

Radisson and Groseilliers are generally considered to be the first white men to enter and navigate extensively along the southern shore of Lake Superior. Radisson left records for proof. The dates are confusing, but the first expedition was about 1656 and the second about 1660. There is disagreement among historians as to whether or not these gentlemen reached the site of Duluth. Van Brunt contends that they made their headquarters at Chequamegon Bay, which might have been mistaken for the Head of the Lakes; Carey says that the white men traded with the Indians at Fond du Lac; Kellogg says the explorers held a great council on the site of Superior and then took the Sioux trail overland to the villages of the Sioux in eastern Minnesota; and Ford says they traveled the entire length of Lake Superior. Radisson left no maps with his records, so there are only interpretations, not proof, that the two white men came as far west as the Head of the Lakes. Duluthians like to give the credit for first arriving here to the man for whom the city is named.

Radisson's record, by the way, has an interesting history of its own. It is believed the manuscript was given to Sir George Carteret, vice chamberlain of King Charles II of England, for presentations to the king. It was found among the papers of Samuel Pepys, of diary fame, after his death. The record was not made public till 1885, nearly 200 years after the explorations were made, when copies of it were printed. Although Radisson was French, he wrote his record in English - and his exploits are written with little modesty. He gives interesting sidelights of his expeditions. For instance, in speaking of the reception by the Indians, he says, "We were Caesars, being nobody to contradict us."

Medart Chouart, Sieur des Groseilliers, was born near Meaux, France, in 1621, and came to Canada when he was twenty years old. He lived among the Hurons for about five years, serving as a lay helper in a Jesuit mission for the Indians. In 1646, he left the mission to trade in furs, and was evidently a successful businessman, as he bought an estate on the St. Lawrence. This estate was called

Groseilliers, meaning "gooseberry bushes", and from this he got his title of honor. In 1647, he married Helene, daughter of Abraham Martin, and important personage in French-Canadian history. She died in 1651, and two years later he married Marguerite, a half-sister of Radisson. Groseilliers had a mild and prudent disposition. He also had money, and probably financed the expeditions.

Pierre Esprit Radisson was more daring than the older man, and perhaps not so reliable. He was born at St. Malo, France, about 1635, and at the age of nineteen came to Montreal, where he lived with his parents. Within a year, he had been captured by the Iroquois while hunting (his companions were murdered); lived a prisoner in their village on the Mohawk in New York; escaped; reached New Amsterdam; sailed for Holland; went to France; and returned to his home in Montreal. He acquired experience and a good education even in the English language.

Radisson was scarcely twenty years old when he and Groseilliers started on their journeys. They left Montreal about 1656 with 150 men in their party, and returned one or two years later. They had navigated the summer waters in boats that were probably hollowed-out logs and the winter snows on snowshoes, called "racketts" They had seen the Great Lakes.

In love with the adventurous life - and the money to be obtained in fur trading - the two Frenchmen were ready for another expedition into the west, but they were refused a license. Angered by the unfairness of the governor, they came without permission of authorities. It is the destination of this trip about which there is controversy. The two men made friendships with the Indians, doing a good public relations job for France, and carried on a big trade in fur. Two years later they met with other Indians and traders at the Sault and returned to Montreal with 300 Indians and a fortune in furs. This is said to have been the first shipment of merchandise by way of Lake Superior. Radisson and

Groseilliers expected a welcome in Montreal for the great success of their trip. However, to punish them for trading without a license, the government confiscated the furs and imposed heavy fines on the adventurers.

Unable to get redress from France, the resentful Frenchmen turned over their talents and experience to the British, about 1665, and helped to form the English Hudson Bay Company. In 1668, they left the Thames with a British cargo. The two worked together under the English flag about sixteen years, but then Groseilliers refused to stay in a foreign service and returned to Montreal. Radisson, however, who had married the daughter of a director of the company, took his family to live in London, where he died at the age of seventy-four.

Beginning about 1671, the Chippewas and Sioux engaged in a warfare that closed the Lake Superior region to fur traders. Someone had to put a stop to this, if New France were to continue the lucrative trade. The man for the job was Daniel de Greysolon, Sieur du Luth, the first white man to lave records proving that he was on the site of the city which bears his name.

One can take his choice of the spelling of the gentleman's name. He himself spelled it du Luth; his father wrote du L'Hut; and the bronze tablet on his first house in Montreal reads Dulhut. His last name is found spelled Gresolon, Grisolon, Greysolon, and Gresolon. Only the spelling of Daniel is constant.

Du Luth was born at Saint-Germaine-en-Lays, France, a resort of the French court until the reign of Louis XIV, but he lived most of his French days in Lyons, with his mother's family. His birth date is generally given as 1654, although Kellogg gives it as 1635.

Daniel's father was one of the French gentry and his mother was a member of the Patron family of wealthy merchants. Of the lesser nobility, du Luth became one of the "Gendarme de la Garde du Roi", an honor which did not carry with it much in the pay envelope. Although he could have had a career in the French court, he seems to have preferred adventures and opportunities offered a young blade in New France, and in 1672, when he was eighteen (or thirty-seven, according to Kellogg), he arrived in Montreal. Two years later, evidently a convert to the Roman Catholic faith, he received his first communion at the Chapel of L'Hotel Dieu.

Du Luth returned to France in 1674 on family business and entered the royal service. He fought in several battles, including the battle of Seneff, where he was squire to the Marquis de Lassay, ensign of his regiment. A young priest, Father Louis Hennepin, was chaplain of the regiment. The same year, du Luth returned to Montreal, accompanied by his younger brother, Claude Greysolon, Sieur de La Tourette.

A retired officer familiar to life in the French court, du Luth was popular in the society of Montreal. He must have presented a dashing figure in his long black wig of curls and his satins, velvets, brocades, and laces. The boy knew how to dress.

Du Luth rented a modest house on Notre Dame Street at the corner of St. Sulpice (then St. Joseph) Street. On this house there is now a bronze tablet which reads: "1675, here lived Daniel de Gresolon, Sieur Dulhut, one of the explorers of the Upper Mississippi, after whom the city of Duluth was named."

From 1674 to 1678, du Luth engaged in trade, making a modest fortune. He bought five-sixths of an acre of land "fronting on St. Paul Street at the lower end of Jacques Cartier Square", where he built a rather pretentious residence overlooking the St. Lawrence. Here he lived with his brother and old friend, Jacques Bizard, a former officer of Frontenac's guard. His future seemed secure, quiet, and uneventful.

Then something happened. Some historians hint at a mystery which caused the young man to leave this pleasant life for the dangers of life among the Indians. In his history, Hugo, however, has an explanation. He says that du Luth was in love with a daughter of the Boucher family and built his new home for her. As the Bouchers became more socially and politically prominent, the girl disapproved of her suitor's being "in trade" and refused to marry him. Culkin says no basis can be found for this story, but "something like this must have happened". Du Luth sold his house to his uncle and took up his life "as a wanderer, a lonely man, an adventurer, discoverer, explorer, representative of a great country, and at all times a gentleman interested in promoting peace. (Culkin).

Du Luth was always a friend of Louis De Buade, Count de Frontenac, governor of New France, and was respected in his council. Some say Frontenac secretly countenanced his first expedition, but others think he was backed only by the great fur trading merchants and business houses of Montreal. Technically, he came as a coureur de bois, since he had no license for trading and no commission to explore. Moreover, he was planning to go into the Sioux country, although the king's subjects were forbidden to trade with the Indians in the west because of the dangers due to Chippewa-Sioux warfare and because of the depletion in the ranks of young men in New France. It is easy to believe that Frontenac approved of his activity, since the governor believed in French enterprise in the west.

In 1678, du Luth set out with a party of men including his brother, six or eight other Frenchmen, and three Huron slaves. The number varies according to historians, but it was a small group. His mission was to make peace among the Indians so that the French could safely trade in the west; to win their friendship for the French, so that they would trade with the French rather than with the English; and to extend the empire of France. Undoubtedly, he was also ambitious to find the Indies.

Du Luth and his men spent the winter at the Sault, where he gained the friendship of the Chippewas and showed them the benefits to be gained from peace with the Sioux and trade with the French. While at the Sault, du Luth wrote Frontenac of his plans and activities.

When the ice broke up that spring, du Luth probably skirted the south shore of Lake Superior till he reached Keewenaw Point and then crossed to the north shore for better protection from the prevailing winds. He would land at the base of Minnesota Point and cross Little Portage (where the canal is now) into Duluth Bay. Again, historians differ as to the route, but this is Hugo's conjecture backed up by Van Brunt and Culkin. He would be on Minnesota Point about June 28, 1679, since he was at the Sioux village of Mille Lacs on July 2, raising the French flag.

After making friendships with the Sioux, du Luth returned to "a rendezvous at the extreme end of Lake Superior", probably Fond du Lac, where he held a meeting of the Indians that resulted in peace between the Chippewa and the Sioux.

Du Luth spent that winter in the Lake Superior region. He visited Grand Portage, the first trading post in Minnesota, and set up little posts here and there which he manned with groups of coureurs de bois. He held meetings with the Indians, formed hunting parties that included both Chippewas and Sioux, and endeavored to build a closer relationship between the two tribes.

In June of 1680, du Luth started westward, probably in an attempt to find the ocean. He had met men who had salt which they had obtained "twenty days' journey west", and, knowing nothing of Great Salt Lake, his ambition must have been fired to discover the elusive route west to the Indies.

When he came to the Mississippi, du Luth heard that a priest and two other Frenchmen had been robbed and were being held captive by the Sioux, so with two companions, his Indian interpreter and a Sioux guide, he went in search of the men. After a chase of two days and two nights, he overtook the Sioux, a band of 1,100, at ten o'clock on the morning of July 25. He found that one of the captives was Father Louis Hennepin, whom he had last seen at the Battle of Seneff.

Du Luth was angry and, he sad, "I made no secret of my anger." He told the Indians that Hennepin was his brother, demanded his release, took the priest into his own canoe, and with the Indian party traveled to the Sioux villages at Mille Lacs. Here, after eight days, du Luth called a council, at which he returned two calumets the Indians had given him "telling them that I did not take calumets from people who after they had seen me and received my peace presents, and had been for a year always with Frenchmen, robbed them when they went to visit them."

The Indians tried to make excuses blaming each other, but du Luth demanded that Hennepin go with him. He realized the danger to all white men if the Indians were allowed to take liberties with the freedom of one, and he explained to Hennepin that it would be a blow to the French nation "to suffer an insult of this nature without manifesting resentment." He then abandoned his plan to find the great salt water in order to escort the priest to safety.

That winter, while at Mackinac Island, du Luth learned that he had been proscribed by the intendant Duchesnau, and as soon as spring came, he hurried back to Montreal to answer the charges.

La Salle, who was conducting explorations at the same time as du Luth, had a hand in this affair. He seems to have been jealous of du Luth, even accusing him of enticing away the men of his party. The probability is that La Salle was so unpopular with his own men that they deserted to du Luth. In a letter of August 22, 1682, La Salle dubbed du Luth "the King of the Outlaws", one of the charges of Duchesnau.

The serious charges brought against du Luth were that he was a leader of a lawless band of coureurs de bois; that he was trading illegally with the Indians; the he was trading with the English; and that he had a secret understanding with the Court de Frontenac.

When du Luth arrived in Montreal, Frontenac ordered him arrested and put in prison, but set him at liberty. It is said that while a prisoner, du Luth "had at all times a seat and cover at the governor's table".

That summer, 1682, du Luth went to France to plead his cause with the king. He was so successful that from the time he returned to Montreal, in the same year, till his retirement he was always officially in the service of New France, leading and participating in many expeditions among the Indians.

In ill health the last fifteen years of his life (he suffered from gout), du Luth retired at his own request in 1707. He returned to Montreal, where he rented a room in the house of Charles Delaunay, a master tanner. Only his valet, La Rouche, was with him till his death, February 25, 1710. According to his wish, he was buried in the graveyard of the Church of the Recollets, which stood at what is now the corner of Notre Dame and Helen streets in Montreal. He left legacies to his valet, Delaunay's family, and the Recollet priests. He was always more closely associated with the quiet Recollets than with the more powerful and aggressive Jesuit order.

Writers seem to agree that du Luth was a modest fellow, loyal and trustworthy. Professor Munro, in an article before the Massachusetts Historical Society, says, "In his brief memoir there is not a trace of egotism or bravado." Isura Andrus-Juneau, in "The Wisconsin Magazine of History", says, "There is no apparent desire for self-advancement or personal gain...When his governor attempted to dissuade him from undertaking a particularly dangerous mission, du Luth said, "I fear not death - only cowardice and dishonor!'"

From other writers, one gleans the same interpretations of the character of Sieur du Luth. He understood the Indians and was trusted and respected by them. He was a humanitarian - realizing that the traders were undermining the red men with liquor, he at no time would have whiskey traffic with the Indians. Du Luth also understood the coureurs de bois and could overlook their wildness in respect for their bravery and love of liberty. This man who was welcomed in wigwam and forest was equally at ease in the presence of the royal court. He was a man of dignity and courage, an able executive, a diplomat, and a skilled officer, who devoted his talents to the best interests of his country. Perhaps the best summation of his character was given by the Governor General, Marquis Phillippe de Rigaud Vandreuil, in announcing the death of du Luth to the king: "He was an honest man."

Louis XIV issued an ordinance May 21, 1696, revoking all fur trade licenses and prohibiting the French colonies from taking goods to the Indians. This action was taken partly for economic reasons, since the market was glutted with beaver skins, but it was also in line with the policy of the intendant and Jesuits to keep young Frenchmen at home. By the close of 1698, the posts were abandoned and the old method of trade was urged, whereby the Indians would come to New France with their furs each year. Neither the Indians nor the traders approved of this policy, and fourteen years later the French again issued licenses to fur traders.

The English Hudson Bay Company, organized in 1670, was the first fur company in the west, but by the time it was active the Indians had learned to like the French and continued to trade with them. When the British took over the government of Canada in 1756, the French traders were in the west, employed by the merchants of Montreal.

In 1783, Montreal merchants formed the Northwest Company and held its first conference in the Pigeon River area. An account of that business meeting is enlightening. It says that the French brought their cooks and bakers, much liquor and many delicacies from Montreal, and while the chiefs were banqueting in the council hall, "the merriment outside the tents was echoed by a mongrel legion of retainers - Canadian voyageurs, half-breed Indians, hunters and hangers-on, who feasted sumptuously without, on the crumbs that fell from their masters' tables, and made the welkin with the old French ditties, mingled with Indian yelps and yellings."

Jean Baptiste Cadotte is generally considered to have been the first trader regularly employed in the department of Fond du Lac for the Northwest Company. He took command of his post about 1792.

When the United States gained its independence from England, by the treaty of 1783 the English and French were ordered to leave this region, but transportation and communication were slow, the new government lacked power to enforce the treaty, and the traders were stubborn. Even as late as 1805, when Lieutenant Pike came to Minnesota he found many French and British traders in the field and the Northwest Company still carrying on a profitable business. John Jacob Astor, in 1809, established a post at Fond du Lac for his company, the American Fur Company, with William Morrison the first agent. But he failed, since the Indians continued trading with their old friends, the French and the English. As Culkin puts it: "The Indians loved the French, feared the English, and did not know the United States."

In 1812, Robert Dickson was acting as British superintendent of Indian affairs in this region, and Hugh

McGillis was stationed at Leech Lake and doing a brisk business in fur as a representative of the British nation.

It took the War of 1812 to make England respect the rights of the United States. The British were then forced to retire from United States territory, and Astor returned to his post at Fond du Lac. By 1818 he was sending outfits to cover the entire Lake Superior country.

The fur trade flourished for about two hundred years, bringing with it explorers, traders, and missionaries.

CHAPTER IV

Missionaries

ALONG with the fur traders into the west came the missionaries, or "black robes", as the Indians called them. Priests of the Order of Jesus, men of education and refinement, left the settlements of New France to suffer the hardships of the wilderness in order to bring Christianity to the Indians. They were seeking converts in the region when the English were establishing colonies on the eastern seaboard. Guthrie says, "They explored the country of the Great Lakes and the Mississippi River, seeking copper, the rich furs, and the souls of savages, for the conversion of the heathen was the avowed object of the early colonies founded by Champlain."

The priests left an account of their activities in the Jesuit Relations, published annually from 1632 to 1672.

As early as 1741, Jaques and Raymbault, Jesuit missionaries, were at the Sault and in 1660 came the first of the missionaries to this Lake Superior region. He was Father Rene Menard, traveling with Radisson and Groseilliers. Father Menard stayed at Chequamegon Bay, where he devoted himself to work among the Indians.

Before leaving Montreal, Father Menard said in a letter to another priest, "In three or four months you may remember me at the memento for the dead, on account of my old age, my weak constitution, and the hardships I lay under amongst these tribes. Nevertheless, I am in peace, for I have not been led to this mission by any temporal motive, but I think it was by the voice of God. I was to resist the grace of God by not coming. Eternal remorse would have tormented me had I not come when I had the opportunity."

During the first winter, the missionary lived in a cabin built of fir branches, "a small hermitage, not so much to shield us from the rigor of the season as to correct my imagination and persuade me I am sheltered."

The next summer, Father Menard, against the advice of others in his party, started a journey to the Hurons. These Indians had been driven north by the Sioux, but the good priest tried to follow them through the wilderness. All his companions deserted him except one man, and Menard became separated from him and was lost. No definite account was ever heard of him again.

The spirit and religious zeal of Father Menard is shown by what he said to his companions when they tried to dissuade him from making this journey: "I must go, if it costs me my life. I cannot suffer souls to perish on the ground of saving the bodily life of a miserable old man like myself. What, are we to serve God only when there is nothing to suffer and no risk of life?"

Father Menard was followed by Father Claude Allouez, who came to this area in 1665 and established the first mission at La Pointe on one of the Apostle Islands. He left a record that says he found hostile Sioux at the mouth of the St. Louis River.

Father Claude Dablon was appointed the first Superior of the Mission of the Lakes, and in company with Father Pere Marquette, he started for his station in 1668. His party landed in their canoe at Sault Ste. Marie and made there the first white settlement in Michigan.

In the Relation of 1669, Dablon wrote an oft-quoted description of Lake Superior: "The lake has almost the form of a bent bow more than 180 leagues long. The south side serves as a string and the arrow seems to be a great tongue of land projecting more than 80 leagues into the width of the lake, starting from the same south side about the middle. The north side is frightful by reason of a succession of rocks which form a prodigious mountain chain, which, beginning beyond Cape de Tourments below Quebec and continuing so far as this point over a distance more than 600 leagues in extent, finally comes and loses itself at the end of this lake."

Since the Jesuits would have no traffic with the coureurs de bois, it is probably from accounts of such missionaries as Allouez and Dablon that they drew a map of this region in 1670-71. This map, published in Paris in 1672, shows "Lac Tracy on Superieur," as the French called Lake Superior, with a river flowing into it at its western extremity. This river might well be the St. Louis. The map shows that the administrative headquarters of the Jesuit missions on Lake Superior was Chequamegon Bay, with La Pointe the center of their efforts. Here are shown "La Pointe du St. Esprit" and the "Mission du St. Esprit". Although Radisson's middle name was Esprit, it would be stretching the imagination to consider that the missionaries named their places in honor of him when one knows their attitude toward the coureurs de bois.

Father Hennepin is another of the missionaries whose name is familiar to the people of Minnesota.

Carey is the authority for this information: "About this time the Jesuit missionaries lost the fervid zeal of the good Menard. Some of them mixed with the preaching of the gospel to the Indians the desire to acquire the profit that there was to be made out of the trade in beaver skins. This departure from their calling and mission and the hostilities then existing between the Sioux and the Hurons and Ottawas of the lake region caused the active and zealous missionary effort of the Roman Catholic Church to come almost to an end in the Lake Superior region."

Those are the same hostilities which caused the fur trade to be interrupted for a time.

After the United States established its power here, Protestant missionaries took up work among the Indians. Robert Stewart, Presbyterian, was the principal agent, with his headquarters at the island of Mackinaw, where, in 1823, a large mission school was established for the education of Indian children.

The Reverend W.H. Boutwell preached the first sermon in English at the trading post in Fond du Lac, June 17, 1832. He was a native of Hillsboro, New Hampshire, and had been graduated from Andover Seminary and from Dartmouth in the class of 1831. He spent a year at Mackinaw in preparation for his mission work. It was here he first met Hester Crooks - but more about that later.

Boutwell's diary gives a description of the scene at Fond du Lac as his party (he was with the Schoolcraft expedition) beached their canoes. It reads: "The scene was such as I have never before witnessed and enough to fill one, unaccustomed to the like as myself, with wonder if not with fear. The yelling of Indians, the barking of dogs, and the crying of children added to the confusion." He was far away from the campus of Dartmouth.

From Boutwell's diary also comes an account of his day's services: "At ten o'clock I preached to about forty in English, the first sermon ever preached here; and at 4 p.m. I addressed, through Mr. Johnson, more than twice that number of French half-breeds and Indians, many of the latter of whom for the first time listened to the Word of Life. All listened with attention and interest.

"My interpreter sat on my right side, while a chief occupied a seat at my left. Around and below me on the floor sat his men, women, and children, in a state of almost nudity. Many of them had not more than a cloth about the loins and a blanket - all with their pipes and tobacco pouches, painted with all the variety of figures that can be imagined."

Lieutenant Allen, a member of the party, describes the trading post: "The buildings consist of a dwelling house, three or four stories high, a large house for the accommodation of clerks, and some other buildings for the Frenchmen. They are handsomely situated on the bank of the river, and directly in front of an island of about two miles circuit, of very rich soil, and a forest of large elms, where the Indians assembled in their lodges."

Boutwell's description reads: "The Fond du Lac trading house is situated at the base of mountains on a narrow piece of bottom 300 to 400 yards broad, in which the trader raises in his garden an abundance of potatoes."

The Reverend Boutwell, the following year, established a mission at Leech Lake.

Edmund Franklin Ely, one of Duluth's pioneers, left Albany July 5, 1833, assigned by the Board of Foreign Missions to a station at Sandy Lake, under the direction of Mr. Boutwell. His experiences are recorded in diaries that he wrote, which are part of the material at the St. Louis Historical Society. The diary for the period September 28, 1833 to December 7, 1835 is in a plain composition book, bilious green in color, with the multiplication table printed on the front cover and an advertisement of a bookstore in Buffalo on the back. There is no uniformity in the size or appearance of the books.

When Mr. Ely entered the Duluth harbor, August 22, 1833, his boat came through the Superior entry, since there was no Duluth canal. Minnesota Point was a narrow stretch of land extending out from the mainland. The harbor was unimproved, and the shore was unoccupied except for scattered Chippewa families. Until September 10, he stayed at Fond du Lac at "one of Mr. Aitkin's posts," where Mr. Cottee, the factor, resided. His reaction the first day was the same as Boutwell's the previous year, for he says, "The Indians were dancing in three or four of the lodges most of the afternoon and when we retired, the air was ringing with the sound of their drums, their songs, and their yells."

Mr. Ely spent some time at Sandy Lake as missionary and teacher, but in 1834 returned to Fond du Lac. A letter from S. Hall to David Greene, October 17, 1834, explains this move: "Because of the extreme scarcity of provisions throughout the interior of the Ojibway country, Aitkin advised Ely not to attempt to maintain school at Sandy Lake, so he came back to Fond du Lac. The trader who occupies that post, though a Catholic, was very desirous that he should remain there and open a school."

That last statement is odd in the light of Mr. Ely's account of his first Sunday: "This morning Mr. Cottee (the trader) read Catholic prayers, but I was ignorant of it. Why he did not invite me to be present I do not know. This evening I informed Mr. C. that I intended to sing with those of my scholars who had come in. He invited me to his home. When we entered, the room was filled. He said he first would say prayers. Accordingly the Catholic service was read, in which the Indians and children joined. They spent half an hour, or more, in singing Catholic hymns, and then told me there was an opportunity for my children to sing. We accordingly sang several hymns, one or two of which his congregation knew...I then asked him if I should join in prayer. To this he made no answer. I called on all to join me, and we knelt down. I concluded in Indian, in which one voice joined me."

The Indians must have been confused, wondering if they were Catholics or Presbyterians. Mr. Cottee continued his weekly Catholic services and Mr. Ely his Presbyterian ones. The Indians continued to dance and whoop and yell.

The Fond du Lac mission was a scene of excitement on September 10, 1834, when the first Christian wedding in these parts was solemnized there by Mr. Ely - the wedding of William Thurston Boutwell and Hester Crooks.

The couple had known each other when Boutwell was studying the Chippewa at Mackinaw, where Hester was at school. When he was at Leech Lake and she was a mission teacher at Yellow Lake, Wisconsin, they decided to marry, and they met at Fond du Lac, the half-way point, for the ceremony.

Hester Crooks' grandfather was a French voyageur and her grandmother a full-blooded Huron. Her father, Ramsey Crooks, born in Scotland, became a prominent fur trader in Minnesota, planned railroads, acquired wealth, and was among those who laid the foundations of the state. Her mother was a half-breed woman. Hester was born in a bark tepee on Drummond Island. She was a beautiful girl at the age of seventeen when she married Boutwell.

From an article by Culkin comes this account of the wedding, which appeared in the Duluth News-Tribune, October 20, 1918.

"The coureurs de bois decorated the long church that Ely had built the year before with boughs of sun-browned maple leaves and sumach, interspersed with green branches of balsam and spruce. The floor and approaches to this church on the hillside by the stream, they strewed with cedar boughs which were soft underfoot and gave out a pungent, refreshing odor. Flags were hung about, for they found old British and French flags which they put up here and there to keep company with the American flag General Cass had left years before.

"There was a home-made table split from cedar for the pastor, on which he could lay his book.

"Besides the French and half-breeds, there were a number of real Indians who came to the wedding, all garbed in their best, a motley mixture of civilized and savage costumes.   There were more than sixty persons present, counting the papooses.

"About the hour of ten in the morning, Hester and the missionary came from the trader's store. The groom led Hester by the hand.

"Her bridal attire was civilized and staid as a missionary, with many touches of color to prove her joy on her wedding day.   There was a trace of Indian, too, in her apparel, as her feet were encased in moccasins of whitest deerskin, covered with beads in all sorts of kaleidoscopic forms.

"They marched into the church and all the company followed, and then after a decent interval the Reverend E. F. Ely walked in and married them.

"After a simple ceremony they paraded to the table set out of doors with a wedding feast for all, where the wedding gifts were displayed.

"Bunches of wild blooms were placed about, which had been gathered by the lady missionary, the same bright spirit from New England, who had loaned her own gold ring for the wedding ceremony."

There were gifts for the couple - "from the trader, a sack of flour and shoes for both bride and groom, together with a cooking outfit and a roll of calico; from the French half-breeds, furs, really valuable beaver and otter and one big buckskin; from the Indian women, beadwork moccasins and other bright finery; and from the braves, plenty of fish and game for the feast."

It was a wonderful feast, with wild fruits and berries, maple sugar, wild rice, trout, whitefish, game, venison, bread from the trading post, and candies from New York.

After the feast, "there were tests of speed and strength on land and water" - with prizes.

There is a hint that some Indians who loved their old ways had a "dog feast" not far away and someone coaxed a jug from the trader. If this were true, Boutwell affected not to see the extra-curricular activity.

It was a real event - this first wedding at the Head of the Lakes.

The honeymoon trip was a journey to the mission at Leech Lake, where, Boutwell says, "We commenced housekeeping in a bark lodge. Then here I was, without a quart of corn or Indian rice to eat ourselves or give my man, as I was too late to purchase any of the mere pittance which was to be bought or sold. My nets, under God, were my sole dependence to feed myself, wife, and hired man. I had a half barrel of flour and ninety pounds of perch only before me for the winter."

Boutwell built a house for Hester that autumn, "a mud-walled house with a door, three deer-skin windows, a mud chimney, but neither chair, stool, nor bedstead. A box served for the former, and an Indian mat for the two latter."

So they lived happily ever after.

Ely was in La Pointe in 1835, where he made this entry in his diary: "Sabbath August 30th - This P.M. was married to Catherine Bissell, of the Mackinaw Missionary; ceremonies in church by Bro. Boutwell."

Catherine Goulais (Bissell) had been one of the mission teachers assigned to Fond du Lac earlier that year. She was partly Indian, and "a woman of refined manners, liberally educated, a kind and affectionate wife and mother, and a sociable and good neighbor", according to her friend Carey. She was probably a graduate of the mission boarding school at Mackinaw.

The Elys went back to Fond du Lac, accompanied by Peter Azhamigon, "a native of Fond du Lac, one-fourth white," who acted as interpreter and assistant.

Life at the mission was not easy, though Mrs. Ely, in her diary, writes mostly about little household affairs and her children. Here are some excerpts: "November 25, 1835 - This day I suppose I am eighteen years old...July 16, 1836 -

Mary Wright Ely, born Sabbath, May 29th. We think her on the whole a pretty good baby." According to her mother, Mary was the first white child of English speaking parents born at Fond du Lac.

Mr. Ely's diary tells of hardships and dangers. On returning from a trip he wrote: "May 1, 1839 - This week before I arrived home, Bezhikogninebi came in and asked Catherine for potatoes, which she refused. On going out B. locked the door upon her and hid the key in the entry. She forced back the bolt and went out to Sagakomin's lodge and asked Samuel for the key; after much talk he told her where it was. She sent word to him not to come into the house. He came, however, directly in and rebuked her for saying so much about the affair. She told him she did not want him here and he must go out. He replied he would go or stay as he pleased. Catherine said, `I shall tell Mr. Ely and your father.' He replied, `I am not afraid of them.' Some other conversation ensued. She told him to leave the house. He went out, and meeting our dog Rover, stabbed him in the side. He died immediately. Catherine, seeing his father afterwards, told him of it. He said he was very sorry, for he intended to have asked us for the dog. The old Bearskin had help himself to my canoe, paddle and gun, which he did not seem inclined to return."

It seems the Indians could be quite aggravating, according to this entry made on a trip to Pokegama: "May 22, 1839 - Routed my men by break of day and prepared for the voyage, but with mending moccasins and gumming canoes we are not off until sun a half hour higher...Came on slowly; my patience was somewhat tried with my men. They showed an inclination to linger with every Indian whom they met; had set their minds to camp at Kabamobi's village tonight, and finding they were drawing near too early, were not slow to imagine devices for staying - prospect of rain, leaky canoe, etc. When we arrived they sat inactive on the bank more than half an hour. I stick to the canoe, determined to show my opinion that way." The party did not sit at Kabamobi's village that night.

Mr. Ely and his family transferred to Pokegama, May, 1839, where they exchanged hardships for danger. The following year the mission was surrounded and attacked by one hundred Sioux warriors. Mr. Ely writes: "May 25th, 1840 - While I now write, the noise of battle rages without. Our settlement is attacked by a large body of Sioux. Nearly two hours since the terrible scene commenced."

The Chippewas within the mission finally drove off the Sioux.

Later, Mr. Ely was in mission work in La Pointe; in 1849 he went to St. Paul; and in 1854, leaving the missions, he came to Superior and then to Duluth.

Mr. Ely's successor at Fond du Lac was George Copway, a Chippewa, who was married to a white woman. He was assisted by James Simpson, and his wife, a sister of Mrs. Copway's, in establishing a Methodist mission school. The mission was continued until 1849, the last of the missionaries being Rev. J.W. Holt.

Another era had ended. Fond du Lac, which had been successfully an Indian village, a fur-trading post, and a mission school, would next become a village.

CHAPTER V

The Village of Duluth

DULUTHIANS lived in Superior, across the bay, when they came to settle this location. Although Minnesota was a territory in 1849, this area still belonged to the Indians, so white settlers could not take up land here until after the La Pointe treaty of 1854. Superior, with no such restrictions, had a head start toward becoming the metropolis at the Head of the Lakes.

In 1853, when ground was broken for the building of the Soo canal and copper was being mined in the interior of Wisconsin, men envisioned a rosy future for this area and cheerfully endured the hardships of pioneering so that they might realize their dreams of a building a city - while cashing in on their adventures.

Superior was quite a place. It had the only entry to the harbor, a landing of sorts, a weekly newspaper, a barroom, shanties, and any numbers of tents. It even had a hotel, a log building opened in June, 1854, although not quite completed. One guest said that he "climbed a ladder to the second story of the hotel, not yet enclosed, made a bed of shavings on the floor, and fought mosquitoes all night." Those mosquitoes must have been life-sized. Even Mrs. Nettleton's hens complained about them vociferously.

Residents of Superior - all fifty of them - would look across the bay to see only hills of rock, forests, and Indian tepees. There seemed little reason to believe that future "cliff dwellers" would build homes on those forbidding hills.

One industry seems to have been organized on the Point. According to Pauline Day, the fishing industry was started about 1836, when 300 barrels of white fish and trout were sold at $11 a barrel. She says that "there was a fish-farm on Minnesota Point, near the lighthouse. Bradshaw Brothers and Bly of Superior operated the plant."

George R. Stuntz is credited with being the founder of both Superior and Duluth. A brief biography of the man says that he was the son of a Hessian soldier who had deserted from the army, remained in America, married, and came west. In July, 1852, Stuntz, a surveyor, came to Superior to run the land lines and subdivide certain townships. The following year, "I built a residence on Minnesota Point under treaty license before the territory was sold to the government." The building was located at the end of the Point, about where the old lighthouse was later built. "At the time there were only missionaries or licensed traders in the tract, as it belonged to the original Indian territory."

August Zachau, another pioneer, mentions the Stuntz settlement when telling about his arrival. "We got into what is now Superior Bay just before dark on November 8, 1853, and landed on Minnesota Point and there found Benjamin Cadotte and Joe Londerer, two half-breeds, building three log houses for George R. Stuntz. The whole Point was dotted with big Indian tepees."

Mrs. George E. Nettleton, in her reminiscences, says, "I think it was the winter of 1852-53, while we were in Crow Wing, Mrs. Nettleton left there and came to Duluth, where he put up his trading post. I remained in Crow Wing. He took some goods from his store there and I think he brought two men with him. He had two or three to bring the goods. Then he had a horse and a birch bark that he rode in. It was built in the shape of a shoe, and he was fastened in so that it might roll over as often as it pleased and he couldn't fall out. The horse drew him, and he came through with his goods, the men to pack them, and provisions. He built the first agency here, cutting trees and building his shanty that he had for shelter near the base of Minnesota Point in Duluth. He left a man in charge of it until he bought it from the Government, which was in September."

According to others, the Stuntz building was the only one on the Point in the winter of 1852-53. Van Brunt points out that Mrs. Nettleton says "I think." He suggests that Nettleton built his shanty in the summer of 1853 when his wife was back home in Ohio, and that she was thinking of the date when he got his license to trade in the winter of 1853-54.

Carey, who was on the spot about the same time, says that William Nettleton and his brother George came to Superior the St. Paul colony in 1853-54. "They took part in settling Superior in 1855, and with Col. J.B. Culver, were carrying on a large grocery, provision, and general supply store there."

A year or two difference in the arrival of the first settlers had little effect on the community that was to become Duluth. It is said that during the winter of 1854-55 not a single white person was living on the North Shore between Minnesota Point and French River. Stuntz even closed his trading post that winter.

However, men were thinking of staking claims here. R.B. McLean, at Superior with a mining company, had advance information from an Indian that the Treaty of La Pointe would be signed. With a few other men (Clark, Zachau, Palmer, Bothwick, and Anthony) and "with not a word spoken above a whisper," he stealthily slipped out of

Superior at ten o'clock on a Saturday night and sailed across to Minnesota Point to take up a claim. The next morning, the men decided they must build a cabin in order to hold possession of land. They cut logs and put up a 14 by 16-foot cabin, six logs high. Anthony, Bothwick and Palmer, the best ax-men, who had done most of the morning's work, refused to do more work without more food. There was no more food. McLean says this was the first labor strike at the Head of the Lakes. The party went back to Superior "and voted to call it a pleasant Sunday outing and say nothing about it."

Other men were interested in townsites on the Minnesota side of the bay. The first of these ventures was in the winter of 1853, when W.G. Le Duc, Henry M. Rice, Governor Ramsey, H.H. Sibley, John S. Watrous, and J.B. Culver proposed a townsite on Minnesota Point, but nothing came of it.

The following year, Mr. Ely, who had given up his mission work and was living in Superior, wrote in his diary that he had been assigned some lots in Endaion (Endion). Van Brunt says there must have been a mistake in copying the date, thinking it unlikely that any of the townsites were platted that early. Ely was interested in Oneota, which Alfred Merritt says was located immediately after the Treaty of La Pointe.

It was during the winter of 1854-55 that Orrin Rice and his brother-in-law, Zack Brown, built the first house on the Duluth side of the bay. This was on Rice's Point, now called Garfield Avenue.

In 1854, John I. Post built a cabin on the site of the present market on Second Avenue East between Second and Third Streets. He named this location Portland. About the same time, Sam McQuade, Colonel W.W. Kingsbury, and Robert Johnson built a house farther east on the lake shore, and called their location Endion, an Indian word meaning "welcome."

Some of these men were jumping the gun, as the treaty was not ratified until January 1855.

Even before the treaty, back in 1852, people here were thinking about a railroad from the lake to St. Paul. W.G. Le Duc that year introduced the first charter in the territorial legislature, and Rice, delegate from Minnesota, presented it so effectively that a land grant of ten sections to the mile was voted. However, between the passage and enrollment of the bill in 1854 there was a bit of scandal with charges that the bill had been changed, so the grant was repealed.

Then the Minnesota and Northwestern, charted by the territorial legislature in 1854, claimed the land for a projected line from Lake Superior to St. Paul and down to the Iowa line. This matter was juggled in the courts for three years, and by that time land grants were unpopular and a depression was not conducive to building railroads through the wilderness.

In 1854, through the efforts of Henry M. Rice, Minnesota's delegate in Congress, Congress appropriated money for constructing a road to be built "from the Falls of the St. Croix to Fond du Lac" and for establishing a mail route. This was good news for the Duluth area. However, Superior, remembering that in years past there had been a trading post called Fond du Lac on the Wisconsin side of the river, decided Congress must mean Superior would be the terminus for the road, so "they organized a force of choppers and set them to work in cutting out a winter road on the proposed line from Superior to what was then Chase's Camp on the St. Croix River. This road was then blazoned on maps as the `Military Road from Point Douglas to Superior'." The North Shore townsites were still without a road.

After the La Pointe treaty was ratified by Congress in 1855, and with the completion of the million dollar Soo canal, an epidemic of townsite platting broke out along the

North Shore, although there was as yet no land office with which to register property. Fond du Lac was the only place having a name as a town, but it probably was not yet platted; so although it had had residents for nearly two hundred years, it was no better off than the upstarts. Some there were who believed it had a great future. In the Minnesota Yearbook for 1851, William G. Le Duc had prophesied, "Fond du Lac is destined to be a place of great importance, its situation making it the lake port of Minnesota."

Other townsites projected were Oneota, the largest settlement, situated by the bay where the Missabe ore docks are now located; Portland, a section from Portland Square, on Fourth Street between Ninth and Tenth Avenues East, extending to the lake shore; Endion, now the East End of Duluth; Clifton, north of Duluth; Middleton, on Minnesota Point; Montezuma. Further down the shore; Buchanan, beyond what is now Lakewood; Rice's Point, on Garfield Avenue; and Duluth, on Minnesota Point. Individuals were also making preemptive claims, building their shanties, which they sometimes had to defend from other preemptors with force and firearms.

Like any raw, new country, this region made up a few of its laws as it went along. There were elections, for instance.

Carey says: "Before Duluth was platted or had occasion for a name, on the first Tuesday in October, 1855, there was held the first election in St. Louis County for a delegate to represent the territory in Congress. Running for election were Henry M. Rice, Democrat, and William R. Marshall, Republican. This is said to have been the beginning of the Republican Party in Minnesota. The election was held in George E. Nettleton's trading post, a shanty on the mainland near the base of Minnesota Point, about 150 feet east of the present First Avenue East." The voters, like Carey himself, lived in Superior and came over by boat. "Had we taken the land route, the density of the forest, the crossing of streams, and the climbing of rocky ridges would have compelled us, even if we reached the polling place in time to vote, the camp overnight before our return...On arriving in Nettleton's claim shanty, we found a cosmopolitan congregation made up principally of Yankees, Buckeyes, Kentuckians, Wolverines, Badgers, not to forget Canucks, French, Irish, Dutch, Scandinavians, with a fair representation of Chippewas minus blankets, but bedecked in coat and pants as evidence of their qualification to vote."

This election seems to have been a sociable affair, with liquid refreshments and much discussion. The latter, strangely enough, did not center so much on the election or the candidates as upon the merits of the various townsites. "Notwithstanding the hilarious effect of the contents of the jug and the entire absence of a sheriff, constable, or other officer of the law, the day passed off without any disturbance or breach of the peace. My recollection is that 105 votes were polled, 96 for H.M. Rice and 9 for William R. Marshall."

Carey's account of the first election is corroborated, but McLean has left another record: "The first election in St. Louis County was held in early September, 1855. The election was held in Orrin Rice's house on Rice's Point. I went over to that election with R.B. Carlton, Kingsbury, and all the other boys living at Endion. The only candidate voted for was W.W. Kingsbury, as delegate to Congress.

Kingsbury was sent to the Territorial Legislature in 1856, and if the above is authentic, must have been sent to the Territorial House of Representatives at the first election, but this has not been proved.

Kingsbury, by the way, was a resident of Wisconsin when he went to the Minnesota legislature, "but that was a small matter in those days." It is interesting to note that the gentlemen living in Wisconsin held such an interest in Minnesota as well as their own state that they voted impartially in both states.   One writer said that the Minnesota settlers thought Wisconsin people paid them a nice compliment in coming over to vote in elections.

A boom was on in 1855, and the Indians must have looked upon all the activity with wonderment.   Robert E. Jefferson, the first to locate a claim on the site of the village of Duluth, built a frame structure, a hotel which he called the Jefferson House about 500 feet north of the present ship canal on what is now Lake Avenue.   This is generally believed to be the first frame structure in Duluth, although some claim that Fred Ryder built the first frame house a mile up the North Shore.   Stuntz carried on a commission business, and his dock on the Point was the first and only landing place for steamboats and sailing vessels bringing passengers and freight to Superior.   The Territorial Legislature that year granted him exclusive right for fifteen years to have a ferry from the Point to Superior.   Wheeler, Ely, and their associates built a steam sawmill at Oneota. Col. Culver built a store down on Lake Avenue, the first general store here.   Culver and Nettleton located a sawmill on Lake Avenue.

A railway survey, probably begun the year before, was being conducted, but there were still only three ways of getting into or out of this part of the country.   Hiram Hayes of Superior explains: "One route was up the Mississippi and St. Croix - trek fifty miles through the woods; another way by the Mississippi, Sandy Lake, and the St. Louis River; a third was by the Great Lakes. Other paths there were none, except as the crow flies.   The rivers were navigated by batteaus, rowing, poling, trecking, wading, or carrying; we grounded in shallows and tipped over in the rapids."

A side wheel steamer, the *Baltimore,* was a familiar sight on the lake.   It took six days for this steamer to make the trop from the new Soo lock to the Stuntz dock.   A glance over the past shows that in 1731, La Ronde, the French Commandant at Chequamegon, had built above the falls at

49

the Soo, at his own expense, a 40 ton vessel, which was the largest vessel on Lake Superior for many years.   It disappeared soon after 1763, when the English took over Canada. In 1772, Alexander Henry's sloop of 70 tons was built above the falls. In 1812, the British had four vessels on the lake, one stout enough to carry six guns. The Americans captured three of these, and the other was hidden safely at Isle Royale. A half dozen little sloops were used by the Hudson Bay Company and the Northwest Fur Company, but by 1830 these had disappeared and "there were no boats on the lake with a sail bigger than a blanket." Modern navigation on the lake began in 1835, with the *John Jacob Astor*, a 113-ton schooner. About 1840, vessels were being built on the lower lakes and hauled on rollers over the Sault Ste. Marie portage. The first of these, the *Algonquin*, was a two-mast schooner, 54 feet long, and capable of carrying 60 tons, used by the Hudson Bay Company. For several years it carried the entire commerce of the lake. The *Astor* was wrecked at Copper Harbor in 1844.   In 1845, came the *Independence*, a steamboat of 280 tons with a speed of four miles an hour.   From the time the first Soo lock was completed in 1855, there were more and larger vessels on Lake Superior.

A lighthouse was erected at the end of Minnesota Point to guide ships through the Superior entry.   R.H. Barrett of Superior, the first lighthouse keeper, took care of the oil lamps, and blew the foghorn - literally blew it, because he used such a horn as cooks use in a lumber camp to call men to dinner. Although the lighthouse is nearly obliterated, the ruins of its base still stand to mark the "zero point", the beginning of all original lake surveys made by Lieutenant Bayfield.

The mails came through - sometimes. Carey says, "Settlers were wholly dependent on Superior, and the service there was few and far between. In 1855, a monthly mail service was allowed by the government, from Taylor's

Falls to Superior, a distance of about 125 miles. The mail route was through a forest wilderness, on a blind trail. The mail was carried by packing it in regular Indian fashion, on the backs of the carriers. I remember that in the fall of 1855 one of the carriers on the route got lost in the woods and wandered for a number of days exhausted and almost famished before he reached an outlet to civilization." In summer, the mail was brought by steamboats.

It took men of vision and courage to found Duluth. Mrs. George Nettleton says of her husband, "I thought he had a pretty long head to see there was going to be a city sometime where there was then nothing - just a pile of rocks. When he first spoke of starting Duluth, and said that he thought here would be a city the proprietors of Superior just laughed at him. They said, `The idea of thinking you can ever have a city on that piles of rocks'!"

Mrs. Nettleton has given some delightful personal sidelights on early life at the Head of the Lakes.

"Mrs. Orrin Rice came from St. Paul, and she was a beautiful woman. When the Rices had been there in Duluth about four weeks they came down to visit us, and Mrs. Rice said, `Ladies, I didn't bring any work, for it has been so long since I have seen the face of a white woman I just want to sit and look at you all the while.' The Rices lived on the Point, close to the river, and just had a little log shanty. There wasn't any of us that had anything more than that, however...We had a nice company and enjoyed all the pleasures of the new country, which were a good many, after all; we all knew each other and liked each other."

Mrs. Nettleton could tell some bear stories, too: "Bears were common visitors in those early days. They had not been hunted much and were not afraid of the settlers. One day the little daughter of Thomas Clark slipped into the printing office (in Superior) and timidly inquired: `Please sir, will you come over to our house and kill a bear?' The office force turned out and went post haste to the house of

Mr. Clark, where, sure enough, one of the largest specimens of black bears was leisurely enjoying the liberties of the ample yard which surround the dwelling. A lady present exclaimed as one of the men was ready to fire at the bruin: `Oh, wait until I make a sketch of him!' The rifle lowered, bruin good-naturedly keeping still until a rude sketch was made. He was then dispatched by two rifle bullets and a blow from an ax. He was an exceedingly large animal and his skin was given as a trophy to Mr. Clark's little daughter. The carcass, which was fat and tender, made many a toothsome feast for the neighbors.

"While speaking of bears, it may be well to remark that one of them caused greater fright to Mrs. Ashton than even the Indians. While the men were absent with some surveyors one afternoon, Mrs. Ashton thought to take a nap. As evening drew on, she arose to prepare the evening meal. Her attention was attracted by what sounded like snoring. She was greatly frightened, having supposed the house to be entirely deserted except by herself and baby. On looking around, however, she discovered the cause of the disturbance in the shape of a large black bear, which had pushed open the door, eaten a pan of dried applesauce, and then crawled under the table to sleep. Of course Mrs. Ashton fled. The noise of her hasty exit aroused the good-natured animal, who arose, scratched his neck leisurely, and after calmly looking around, made for the woods. Numerous as were these animals, there is no record that they ever did greater harm than stealing the settlers' hams, butter, eggs, and small groceries."

Then there were the Indians. "Of course, the country was alive with Indians during the early days. Mrs. Ashton had never seen Indians before her arrival and was wholly unacquainted with their ways. One day, while she was at home alone making her toilet, several stalwart Chippewas entered the cabin as noiselessly as cats, for Indians never rapped at a door or otherwise announced their coming. Her long, beautiful hair hung below her waist. Attracted by it, they walked up to her, stretched the bright, curly tresses the length of their arms and, looking significantly at each other, began a most unintelligible but earnest and clattering jargon. Mrs. Ashton, believed she was about to be scalped, uttered a scream, which brought the neighbors to the rescue. She did not know it, but the fact was the Chippewas were very friendly; being unable to speak English, however, they were admiring her long, beautiful hair, so unlike their own, in their own style and language. Nevertheless, Mrs. Ashton was as badly frightened as though they had in truth been intending to scalp her."

Mrs. W.S. Woodbridge, who came to Duluth only a few years later, tells some of her experiences: "The first year or two, there was no mirror at the Head of the Lakes. Those who were fortunate enough to have a new tin boiler, or new tin dishes, could get along very well. One of the early settlers has told me that he has frequently seen the women combing and arranging their hair by the reflection in the wash boiler or dishpan...I used to watch the Indians, who were a common sight, especially in the winter, when they would come into town with their dog teams, the sledges laden down with skins which they exchanged for provisions. There were usually three or four dogs driven tandem with a simple harness consisting of a collar and strap around the body of each...The Indians did not know the use of a door bell, neither did they stand on ceremony, but if they found the door of a house unlocked, they walked in without knocking."

That was the Head of the Lakes in the '50's.

Superior was farther advanced than Duluth. The residents even had a church service early in 1855, the first by an ordained minister other than a missionary to the Indians. The Reverend John M. Barnett preached to about twenty people in the unfinished hotel "in what was intended for the barroom, but was still a work and barber shop, with workbench, shavings, and a washbowl still in plain view." Later, he held services in the Buckman building or in the Minter building. He used the second floor of the latter for church purposes, while the first floor was "occupied by a saloon and the third by a gambling room, so the preacher could often heard the jingle of glasses below and the noise of the card tables above."

Although the Duluth side of the bay did not boast a resident preacher, there were no such distractions when the Reverend Joseph G. Wilson came over from Superior to Oneota late that year. He held religious services in the homes, and had among his congregation the Merritts and the Wheelers.

The Ely family had not yet moved over from Superior, and of the Merritts, only the father, Lewis Merritt, and his son, Napoleon, were here. They had arrived July 3, 1855, on the side-wheeler *North Star* to erect a sawmill on Conner's Point. Mr. Merritt took squatter's rights on a piece of land which became part of Oneota, now West Duluth.

The winter of 1855-56 was a bad one. The boat that was to have been the last of the season, bringing the winter's provisions, failed to arrive, so the settlers faced near-famine as well as intense cold. Flour was sixty dollars a barrel, and potatoes and butter were non-existent. Some families had little to eat but cornmeal. Dough cake and salt pork were a routine dinner menu.

On May 9, 1856, the steamer *Manhattan* arrived in port. The editor of the Superior Chronicle wrote: "As it steamed through Superior entry and reached the pier, the whole populace, wild with excitement and joy, was there to receive her...Bells were rung, anvils were fired, and every possible manifestation of joy was indulged...The gloom of the morning was forgotten; men, women, and children ran about the streets, shouting their glad hurrahs, and having feasted and been feasted to their hearts' content, the western sun went down that evening upon truly the happiest little community to be found anywhere within the limits of civilization."

With the new lease on life that food and the *Manhattan* brought, things began to hum again in 1856. R.B. McLean, who traveled the North Shore as the first mail carrier, has told of some of the men and families who were developing this region: "In May, Richard Relf, a civil engineer, surveyed and platted the village of Duluth; in June, J.B. Bell finished building the house the Sunday picnickers of '54 had started and gave it the name of Bellville; in July, Fred Ryder, one of the preemptors around Duluth, built and occupied the first frame house built in the village of Duluth. Some time in November R.E. Jefferson, Quince Allen, C.E. Martin, and J.B. Ellis were building houses in the village. C.E. Martin and others platted the town of Endion at about the same time, or it might have been in December."

Mrs. Lewis Merritt came to Oneota in 1856 with five of her seven sons. Napoleon was already here, and Lucien remained in Austinberg, Ashtabula County, Ohio, to attend school. The family arrived October 28 on the propellor *Manhattan,* of which Captain Lyman Spaulding was master, and "Big Mouth Charley" second mate. F.E. Ely also moved his family to Oneota from Superior. He and H.W. Wheeler, with some St. Paul and some eastern men, had bought squatter's right from Bacon and McCracken to start the town. Henry C. Ford of Philadelphia established a sawmill a mile above Oneota. His preemption claim of 80 acres was called Milford.

Oneota was a thriving community of twenty inhabitants, three dwellings, two huts, a dock, a sawmill, the Oneota Lumber Company, and the first post office. Mr. Ely was postmaster, but his work scarcely constituted a full time job, since the first quarterly account current, September 30, amounted to only $2.46.

The townsite of Oneota conducted the first public school on the North Shore of Lake Superior in 1856, with Jerome Merritt the teacher of twelve pupils - four Merritt boys, five children of the Ely family, two Wheelers, and Christian Hoffenbecker. The following year, a frame schoolhouse was built at 42nd Avenue West, the first building for school use erected in northeastern Minnesota.

Both Mr. Peet and Mr. Barnett came across the bay regularly in '56 to hold religious services in the homes.

Some controversy arises about whether the village of Duluth was platted in 1855 or 1856. The foundation was laid in '55 however, when George E. and William Nettleton, J.B. Culver, and Orrin Rice (all living in Superior), and Robert E. Jefferson (Minnesota Point), formed a partnership and made a survey of the site on the Point. George R. Stuntz and John D. Ray may have joined the group.

With a perfectly good townsite on the Point, the proprietors wanted a splendid name for it. Stories about the occasion of bestowing the name do not agree, although they are told by reliable people who claim to have been present at the christening.

Perhaps the most colorful story is told by Mrs. Nettleton: "One day we had a picnic party of Superior people over on Minnesota Point. Among them were Mrs. Post, Orator Hall and his wife, my husband and the Rev. Mr. Wilson, a Presbyterian clergyman from somewhere near Boston, I think, and a number of others. During the picnic various names for the new town started on Minnesota Point were proposed, and Mr. Wilson at last proposed "Duluth". He named the city in honor of the first navigator and explorer who ever came here. Since that time it has always been known as `Duluth'!"

The Duluth *Minnesotian* in 1869 printed a letter by Mrs. J.L. Smith, which reads in part: "The city...is named Duluth, and received that name from Rev. J.G. Wilson, of Pittsburgh, Pennsylvania, one summer day in 1856. The

Nettleton brothers had leased lands upon its site where they foresaw a great city must arise someday. This city must have a name; and it is no trifle to name a city, or a baby, or a boat, or a pet canary. That name will live, and it will influence destiny...A day was appropriated by the brothers when the boats would be in readiness to convey their friends across Superior Bay for a picnic on the Point, and every guest must bring a name for the city.

"Arrived; a grassy hillock was selected for spreading the cloth, on which were placed the toothsome contents of many a napkin-covered basket; and the champagne was set out in readiness for the great decision. Many an appellation was suggested, discussed, and sentenced to death: `too short'; `too hard'; `too commonplace'; `too fanciful'; until at last the wit and genius of the party arose, and from a slip of paper read: `Duluth'. Then followed a short history of the man, Daniel C. Greysolon Du Luth. The name was received with acclamation; there was a popping of corks, and congratulations of the hero of the happy thought. And there, standing in the glow of the setting sun we drank to the future city, soon to be acknowledged `Queen of the West', and the naming was over. Among those present at the naming were George E. Nettleton and wife, Julia, Rev. John M. Barnett, William Nettleton, Judge R. Carey, Orator K. Hall and wife, Laura, Mary C. Post, Thompson Ritchie, and Rev. James G. Wilson."

Judge Carey, with whom Mr. Wilson was living, says there is nothing to that story: "There was no public celebration or demonstration on Minnesota Point or anywhere else in hone of adopting the name." He says that Mr. Wilson of Logansport, Indiana, told him that the proprietors had promised him a deed to two lots for a good name for the town. Looking through the books in George Nettleton's home, he came across an English translation of the Jesuits, in which was an account of du Luth. At a meeting of the proprietors at the home of George Nettleton,

Mr. Wilson submitted several names, and after the group had discussed the merits of each name, they selected `Duluth'. Then Mr. Wilson wrote an article on the life of Daniel de Greysolon, Sieur du Luth, which was published in the Superior *Chronicle.*

So that's that. The name was suggested by Mr. Wilson of Boston, Pittsburgh, or Logansport. The time might have been in the winter or in June or July. The year was undoubtedly 1856.

Up the North Shore, just this side of Knife River, there was a dent in the wilderness which W.G. Cowell hopefully named Buchanan, in honor of the President of the United States. It had a hotel, dock, boarding house, and several saloons. In the summer of 1857, the United States Land Office was established there. Preemption claims and townsites could be legally registered with Samuel Clark, register, and John Whipple, receiver. A steamer *Seneca* provided transportation from Superior to Buchanan. Although the land office was supposed to open September 26, the plats, record books, and instructions were not on hand, so the opening was delayed. The equipment got lost somewhere between Taylor's Falls and Superior on the overland route and did not arrive till the latter part of November. The land office started in business, December 1, with a bang. Among the first entries were those of William and George E. Nettleton, the town of Portland, the Buffalo heirs, J.B. Culver, Harriet E. Luce, John E. Watrous, and the town of Duluth.

While a man was living on and proving up his claim, he was entitled to cut timber on his land to maintain himself. But soon it was discovered that all timber on a claim would be cut before the claim was proved, and then the claimee would leave for other land. Sawmills were going full blast - all lumber coming from public lands. Clark didn't seem anything to do except get rid of the land as quickly as possible before all the timber was stolen.

The townsites which later were incorporated in Duluth, registered at the Land Office were, besides Duluth and Minnesota Point: Portland - proprietors James D. Day, Clinton Markell, Daniel Shaw, N.B. Robbins, John I. Post, Joseph Gregory, and Albert McAdams; Oneota - council Lewis H. Merritt, William E. Wright, F.A. Buckingham, J.R. Carey, and Dwight Abbott; and Fond du Lac - trustees Ruben B. Carlton, Alexander Paul, D. George Morrison, J.B. Culver, and Francis Roussain.

Those were the days when every town was going to be a "city of destiny", and truly big projects were planned. The Minnesota Point Ship Canal Company was organized by those hardy pioneers, George E. Nettleton, James D. Day, and Edmund F. Ely. They got authorization to "cut a ship canal through Minnesota Point, 300 feet wide." But a panic put an end to that.

Dreams of a railroad were becoming brighter, when a territorial charter was granted in 1857 to the Lake Superior and Nebraska railroad, with its southern terminus in Omaha. Although this project also faded away, the plans became the basis of the Lake Superior and Mississippi which materialized later.

Sidney Luce arrived in Duluth in 1857, with no intention of staying, but "I had an offer of three dollars a day to work on a house so I concluded to wait awhile and go to work." The "awhile" extended to twelve years.

"Not being well-versed in western wildcat ways," says Mr. Luce, "I was soon induced to build a warehouse." This house, built on the lake shore down from the where the Hotel Duluth is now located, was thirty feet by forty feet and three stories high with a garret above. "The foundation was partly made by an excavation of rock on the bank of the lake and party by crib work in the lake, the foundation being almost seven feet above water level...The third floor was about on the level of the bank in front. Loose boards were used for a temporary third floor, and packing boxes used in the shipment of household goods were found to provide lumber for partitions and cupboards. The stovepipe led out a window, and there were no doors. This floor constituted our apartments for first housekeeping."

The warehouse became the most important building in the entire county. It was used at various times for the Duluth post office, United States Land Office (moved from Buchanan in 1859), and offices for the register of deeds, county auditor, and county treasurer. Organization of a new office or moving of an old one meant another cubby hoe set up in Luce's warehouse. Practically all meetings for the county, township, or schools were also held there.

J.B. Culver was the first postmaster when Duluth was given a postoffice in 1857. He had "a soapbox office in Horace Saxton's house near the canal". When Luce became postmaster, he moved the office to his warehouse. Thus the Duluth postoffice was really located in Portland, but that was too small a matter to quibble about.

In an article for the Duluth Historical and Scientific Association, Mr. Luce gives a census of Duluth when he arrived: Mr. and Mrs. J.B. Culver and children, and a sister of Mrs. Culver (who afterwards married William Eplen) living at the base of Rice's Point; William Nettleton on his preemption claim at the base of Minnesota Point; Frederick Ryan, wife, and two sons and one daughter, a farmer having a preemption claim a mile or more north of the town; E.H. Rice and wife, who kept the hotel on the Point (the Jefferson House); H.S. Burk, a carpenter and joiner; Charles Chester "and reputed wife"; J.J. Brown and Indian wife. Living a sort of Indian life, afterwards sheriff; Samuel Badger and Indian wife, sister of Brown's wife (Badger was a Philadelphia lawyer "who, before his coming to Duluth, was married to a highly accomplished lady of that city); William Ord, head sawyer for Culver; John Dunphy and family, "one of the few making good improvements on his claim"; R.C. and Adam Borthwick, laborers; Waterman Green, wife and children, a carpenter and joiner in Portland, "one of the preemptors who wholly complied with the law"; Harry Fargo, cabinet maker, later murdered by the Indians in a logging camp in Wisconsin; Samuel Franck, employed at the Culver sawmill; Robert E. Jefferson; John B. and Antoine Le Duc, occupying a blockhouse on land afterwards excavated for the canal; Amos Woodbury and wife, laborer; I.T. Whitmore, joiner; B.F. Whitmore, surveyor; R.H. Barrett, register of deeds, and family; W.B. Robbins and Austin Smith, looking after the interests in Portland.

Another handful of settlers was camping out at Oneota and Fond du Lac. That was Duluth in 1857.

"We were all rich in anticipation, and were all going to be perfectly happy," says Mrs. Nettleton.

Then came the panic of 1857.

About three-fourths of the families in both Duluth and Superior had hurried away by the time the last boat left. John Bardon, of Superior, writes: "The lake steamers were overcrowded, carrying people away, and the Military Road to St. Paul had more southbound pedestrians than Coxey's army ever numbered." Some of those who were ready to give Duluth back to the Indians had no money to pay for transportation, having invested everything in land. Many found help from Captain Ben Sweet of the steamer *North Star*, who "took out" over seven hundred passengers, with only their notes in payment for passage. He afterwards said that all but one redeemed the notes.

Those who remained in the villages concerned themselves with the business of keeping alive. They trapped fur for trading, as the original white men in this region had done. After the first year, they raised a few potatoes. And they ate fish. "The Ancient and Honorable Order of Fisheaters" included every inhabitant of the Twin Ports. In that unorganized organization were the aristocrats of Duluth - those who stayed because of their faith in

Duluth - and those who didn't have money enough to get out.

With near-famine came disease, and an epidemic of scarlet fever in 1859-60 further decimated the community.

Money was not merely scarce - it was practically non-existent. Not a store was kept open in Duluth, so the few stores in Superior were the shopping center of this community for the next ten years. Orrin C. Rice offered to trade two corner lots in what is now the business section of Duluth for one pair of boots. He had no takers. In 1910, those lots sold for $18,000 each.

The Reverend James Peet, in his diary of June 25, 1859, writes: "My boots are out at the sides, heel, and toe, so I can run my hand in at the leg and out through the foot. In this condition I wear them to preach in, and expect to until I can get better, and I have no money to buy another pair with."

When Judge Carey moved to Duluth from Oneota in 1865, he took the Jefferson house, but he said, "All the houses then in Duluth were unoccupied, and had been for three years, so I had a perfect freedom of selection. The name `Duluth' was all that was left to the town on the Point, and even that, including the postoffice, had been appropriated by Portland." Only two other houses were occupied, one by Dorus Martin and one by Z.J. Brown.

The following year, Carey became one of the capitalists of the town. He says that after his "eight years' experience in navigating the land and water of St. Louis county, logging in the lumber woods, working in the sawmill, farming, officiating and enjoying all the emoluments and honors of probate judge, United States commissioner and poundmaster all at the same time," he still could not make enough out of all his offices to feed his big Newfoundland dog Duff. Therefore, he bid for and was appointed carrier for the weekly mail service between Duluth and Fond du Lac for the salary of $200 a year. He used his boat for summer trips and Duff for winter travel. "There was no road, nor even a good trail between Duluth, Oneota, and Fond du Lac except the St. Louis River in summer and the ice on it in winter." Carey had to make the trip by land for the first time, and got lost in the forest after crossing Bardon's Peak. He says of that incident: "Duluth today may claim the undivided distinction as the only city in the United States where a person that claimed to be an experienced woodsman got lost in traveling on the regular route between two of its parts." For fifteen years, mail within the present city was carried on a trail by packer and dog train.

In 1858, Minnesota became a state, with Henry H. Sibley the first governor. Of the first state election held in Duluth, Sidney Luce wrote: "Election laws were construed to meet the emergencies of the candidates for office. Neighboring towns were well supplied with a migratory population ready to respond to calls for assistance. An old coat and hat served the purpose of habilitating the Indian, rendering him a fully-fledged voter."

The first United States senators were Henry M. Rice and General James Shields; W.W. Kingsbury became United States congressman for the North Shore district; Col. R.B. Carlton was elected state senator, and John S. Watrous was voted state representative for the St. Louis County and North Shore District.

An election for county officers was held in Duluth in he fall of 1858, and most accounts of it agree. William Epler describes it: "A number of foreign squatters, Huns, Russians, etc., not being familiar with American methods, got the idea that the election meant no good for the claim-holders, and that it should be stopped. A dozen of them got together, and arming themselves with stones and clubs, rushed the polling place, a small house standing on the lake shore, about two blocks below the portage. J.B. Culver, Sidney Luce, and Mr. Green were judges. Another young man, I think it was R.E. Jefferson, and I were clerks. The first we knew of the trouble, a huge stone came through the window, followed by a chorus of wild yells from the outside. Mr. Luce snatched up the ballot box and Mr. Culver the poll books, and darted out of the back door into the brush. Mr. Green, who was cornered, was indiscreet enough to show fight. I have forgotten what became of Mr. Jefferson. I was a mere boy. The mob, perhaps thinking I was an onlooker, paid no attention to me, but gave all their attention to Mr. Green. Just here I exhibited my indiscretion by encouraging Green in his unequal fight. A big Hun, about seven feet tall, took my by the collar, swinging a club over my head meantime, and commanded me to be quiet. I cheerfully obeyed. No one got hurt."

In spite of poverty, famine and sickness, the community, far from dying, thought of the future for its children. The county commissioners, April 5, 1858, divided the county into four townships - Fond du Lac, Oneota, Duluth, and Carp River - and organized school districts. District No. 1 was Fond du Lac and vicinity; No. 2 - the part of the county which is now New Duluth; No. 3 - the neighborhood of Spirit Lake; No. 4 - Oneota and vicinity; No. 5 - Duluth and Portland; and No. 6 - the lower half of Minnesota Point. On February 12, 1861, the school funds apportioned were $75.40 for the Oneota district and $37.70 for Duluth.

Life went on in a subdued sort of way. In 1859, four of the unemployed thought it might be a good idea to build a brewery, since one of their number was a brewer. So at Brewery Creek on Washington Avenue, a brewery was built by H.S. Burke, Gilbert Falconer, Harry Fargo, and J.G. Bush.

Turning to county matters - Carey says that from 1855 to 1862: "any location of the county seat of St. Louis County was a desperate question. There was no law locating it, nor any existing record that it had ever been located by the board of county commissioners, that body having been empowered to do so by law." Much of the county business was transacted at the home of Mr. Culver, sometimes called the "capital of St. Louis County", at other homes, and at Luce's warehouse, - in fact, at any convenient place. After 1862, Duluth seems to have been conceded the county seat.

The first court in Duluth was held on August 1, 1859, in a little unfinished room, but "in the absence of the honorable judge, S.J. McMillan, the court was adjourned by the clerk." Badger, the Philadelphia lawyer, was appointed district attorney. The journal of the District Court of St. Louis County, by the way, also contained records of the organization of the Masonic Lodge, sitting of court in other counties, and records of issuance of certificates of marriage.

The settlers hung on to their land - some of them. In 1860, personal property in St. Louis County was valued at $9,620 and in 1864 at $2,179. The federal census of 1860 showed 406 residents in the county, including half-breeds, and 80 residents in Duluth. That year Wheeler ran for the state legislature and received every vote cast in the county, a total of twelve votes.

In 1860, General Sherman with other military officers visited Superior, arriving over the old Military Road. He probably found no tougher traveling on his march to the sea, for this Military Road seems to have been called a road by courtesy only. Ashton, telling of a trip over it says: "The roads were very muddy, which made the traveling bad, and the wagon got stranded several times. The passengers had to do considerable walking."

Luke A. Marvin probably best describes a trip on the Military Road, as he came over it in 1861 from St. Paul. "We were a week making the 150 miles or so, and it was a terrible trip. The whole distance lay through a dense forest, and through this forest the trees had been felled on a space wide enough for a road on which teams could pass each other. Stumps stuck up all over the road. In many places it was very marshy, and trees had been cut down to make corduroy. There were no springs to the coach, and we would go bumping over stumps, in momentary danger of upsetting at times; at others our wheels would be past the hubs in mud, out of which it would take the utmost power of the horses to pull us. At intervals along the road there were relay horses, and places where we would generally pass the nights. All the accommodations were of the roughest and most primitive kind. After reaching Superior, we were ferried across the river to Duluth, which contained ten or twelve families huddled about the base of Minnesota Point."

Lewis Merritt made the round trip from Duluth to St. Paul in four weeks, when he moved Ely and his family there in 1862. The following year, Alfred took 30 days for the trip, when he drove a yoke of oxen from Superior to St. Paul.

A regular stage coach service was established over this road, with Concord coaches (so named because they were built in Concord, New Hampshire). "The bed of the coach rested on thorough braces (no springs), with a front booth for carrying mail and express, and a hind booth for carrying trunks and heavy baggage. On both sides, near the top of the coach, running along the whole bed of the coach, were rings to which ropes could be attached, so that small articles could be tied on top. This carryall of transportation was hauled by four or six horses. These horses were all trained the same as fire horses, and knew their respective places. There were fourteen relays of horses between Superior and St. Paul...When first started it took six days to make the trip, but it was finally reduced to three days."

The Civil War, starting in 1861, further ravaged the struggling little communities that later became Duluth.

Minnesota was the first state in the union to offer assistance to President Lincoln in this war. Alexander Ramsey, governor of the state, was in Washington D.C. on

April 13, 1861, when Fort Sumter surrendered, and was one of the few to know of the event that night. Early the next morning, he went to the War Department, where "I tendered one thousand men to defend the Government...Thus Minnesota became the first to cheer the President by offers of assistance in the crisis which had arrived."

St. Louis County had a total of forty-six men subject to draft in 1862. Sixteen men volunteered and five received bounties of public money voted by the county commissioners. No draft was demanded of Duluth until the later years of the war, and then it was found that the village had practically fulfilled the quota of men required.

According to Van Brunt, a list of those soldiers who were then residents of St. Louis County or who later lived here gives the names of 581 soldiers of Civil War service; among them are 58 who served in Minnesota military units. Duluth was not large enough to organize an even company, so the men left individually, paying their own expenses to various places to enlist. Leonidas J. Merritt walked all the way from Duluth to Ft. Snelling to enlist.

Robert E. Jefferson, a victim of depression, had no money to go by either lake or stage to St. Paul, so with his wife and baby daughter he took the journey by way of the grand portage of Fond du Lac, up the St. Louis and Savannah rivers, down Prairie and Tamarac rivers, into Sandy Lake, and then down the Mississippi to his old home in St. Paul - a route some 200 years old, well known to the explorers of this region, but tortuous for a woman and child to undertake. He enlisted and died in the service within a year. His wife died soon afterwards.

Robert's brother Ernest, who had come to Duluth in 1859, joined the army before he was 21 years old, and lost a leg at the battle of Gettysburg. Thomas H. Presnell, later printer's devil on the *Minnesotian,* was one of the few survivors of this bloody battle.

Duluth men enlisted in various states. Colonel J.B. Culver helped to organize the Thirteenth Michigan volunteer infantry. Freemen Keene enlisted with the First Michigan battery in Detroit. John G. Rakowski enlisted in Washington D.C. with the Eighth New York volunteer infantry, and after three months' service re-enlisted in the Eighth Ohio Volunteer infantry. Julius Gogarn was in a Michigan regiment. Of those known to have enlisted in the home state, Robert P. Miller was in the Fourth Minnesota; William Bailey in the Fifth Minnesota; and Alonzo Wilson in Brackett's cavalry battalion in Minnesota. Other Duluthians known to have been in service include F.A. Buckingham, U.S. Ayers, Andrew Reefer, Samuel McQuade, Cal Shurbrooke, Dorus Martin, George Shurbrooke (killed at Vicksburg), and John Falk (killed in the Battle of the Wilderness). There is no proof that this list is complete.

Van Brunt tells the story of Dorus Martin, a man well over sixty, who borrowed twenty-five dollars to get to St. Paul to enlist. He was rejected because of his gray hair, so he dyed his hair, went to Wisconsin, and enlisted, as a man of forty years, in a Wisconsin regiment. Back home from the way, Martin was so proud of having been a soldier that he wanted to die in his uniform, and as he was "getting along in years", he would frequently dress in his blues. "One morning in 1867, he was found motionless, seated in his chair near the open door of his cottage, in full uniform even to his hat. He was dead. But the sturdy old patriot, quadroon though he was supposed to be, was reverently given full military honors and buried in Franklin Square, Minnesota Point. Later, his body was removed to the Soldiers' Rest in Forest Hill Cemetery, his grave being number 7 of tier 1."

Minnesota's record in the Civil War is an illustrious one. Two regiments marched with Sherman to the sea. The second Minnesota was at Chickamauga; the Third, at Fitzhugh's Wood; the Fourth, at Vicksburg; the Fifth saved the day at Corinth; and the First turned the tide at Gettysburg. Of the 262 Minnesota men in that battle, only 47 were uninjured. Official reports show that Minnesota regiments were engaged in all the sixteen major battles of the war.

With the white men away at war, leaving their homes unprotected, the Sioux Indians went on a rampage around New Ulm in August, 1862, terrifying those residents that they failed to scalp. People in the Duluth-Superior region became uneasy, fearing the Chippewas might get the urge to do a bit of scalping. The St. Louis County board of commissioners protected the citizens of Duluth from and Indian uprising - in a mild way. The board passed a resolution that R.B. Carlton "be appointed to employ (if to him it seem necessary or desirable) a suitable person to keep watch over the actions of the Indians near us, and on any appearance of trouble to give the alarm to our citizens."

Superiorites were taking no chances. They inveigled a company of soldiers from their state government and built a stockade near the bay front. They also offered Duluth protection in the stockade, if trouble arose.

The war over, General Sherman again visited the Head of the Lakes. It is said that Dorus Martin, resplendent in his uniform, "constituted in himself the army, to receive the inspecting general."

Superior's welcome to Sherman is recorded by Ashton: "The boys built bonfires in honor of him. There was an old cannon that was left here by the Regulars during the Indian scare of 1862. The boys loaded it up and attempted to fire it when they heard the rattle of the coach coming up Second Street, but it refused to go off, so they removed the charge and reloaded it, and attempted to fire it again. This time it exploded, just as the coach drove up to the hotel, scattering fragments of cannon in all directions. Fortunately, no one was hurt, but it broke several windows in the Avery House." The General must have thought he was back in the war.

Following the Civil War, Duluth veterans organized the J.B. Culver Post of the national Grand Army of the Republic.

The panic was over, the war was won, young men returning home - and Jay Cooke came to town.

CHAPTER VI

The City of Duluth

DULUTH used to be called "Jay Cooke's town," because of the financial backing that gentlemen gave the village.

Jay Cooke was an Eastern financier, head of one of the greatest banking houses in the country. The main offices of the firm of Jay Cooke and Company were in Philadelphia, but there were also branch houses in New York and London, as well as the First National Bank of Washington D.C. The statue of "the man and his dog," as the children describe it, at Ninth Avenue East and Superior Street, is a memorial to Jay Cooke's association with Duluth.

The panic and the Civil War had almost wiped Duluth out of existence when Cooke came to the Head of the Lakes in the summer of 1866. He and his wife, arriving by steamer, stayed at the old Superior Hotel, there being no place for guests in Duluth. George M. Smith, a teen-ager, rowed him across the bay and conducted his tour. They left the hotel at five o'clock in the morning, Mr. Cooke resplendent in dress, even to a light-colored silk hat.

Landing on Minnesota Point, Cooke was interested in the wigwams, and, like most Easterners, he wanted to see the Indians. George, speaking Chippewa, woke up the

the Indians. George, speaking Chippewa, woke up the village, and assembled the Indians before the financier. At 6 a.m., "Mr. Cooke stepped upon a large stump, and, taking off his silk hat and holding it in his hand, made a little speech to the Indians. He told them that he was the man who had negotiated the sale of the United States Government bonds during the Civil War; that he was going to build a railroad from the Mississippi River to the head of Lake Superior; that he was going to build a railroad from Lake Superior to the Pacific Ocean; and many other things of interest."

The Indians were extravagant in their enthusiasm for the "Great White Father," especially when he gave each adult a bright new 25-cent piece, each of the younger children a new dime, and each little one and papoose a five-cent piece. Smith demurred about the financier's generosity, however, when he gave an Indian a quarter for a whitefish which anyone could buy for a nickel, the lad was afraid the Indians might get ideas about high finance.

George then took Mr. Cooke to the home of Saxon. "As it was not yet seven o'clock, the family had not made its appearance. Wishing to arouse Mr. Saxton, I opened the door that led to the stairway to the second floor, and gave the familiar Chippewa Indian war-whoop." The announcement that Jay Cooke of Philadelphia was there "seemed to shake the very foundations of the house." Mr. Cooke spent the day discussing the terminus of the Lake Superior and Mississippi Railroad, then under construction from St. Paul to the head of Lake Superior. In conference with Cooke were Saxton, J.D. Ray, Luke Marvin, Sidney Luce, W.R. Nettleton, C. Markell, J.R. Carey, Col. J.B. Culver, and a few others. They held this historic meeting at the United States Land Office, on the lake shore between First and Second avenues east.

With a railroad, Duluth would be ready to forge ahead. Many railroad projects had been started, but had

Superior with the Mississippi River, the state was willing to make huge grants and inducements to a railroad company to get it. The Lake Superior and Mississippi River railroad had been incorporated by the legislature in 1861, but the war had deterred the building of it. Woodbridge and Pardee say jocularly of the charter "It was a friendly sort of charter...If the engineer saw anything he wanted, he was to take it." Besides the land grants from the state, there was a congressional grant in 1865. Then Duluth, fearing that Superior might become the terminus of the road, came into the picture, and in 1866 St. Louis County was authorized by the state legislature to vote bonds for the road, "not more than $40,000 for each five miles nor more than $150,000 in all." But the road was not assured until Jay Cooke took a hand in it.

A rumor of finding gold in the country around Lake Vermilion brought thousands of men through Duluth the year after the Civil War ended. The rumor of gold in "them thar hills" determined men to trudge through the wilderness, carrying on their backs packs of supplies and provisions. With nothing but an Indian trail between Duluth and Lake Vermilion, George Stuntz was put in charge of building a road. In a little over two months after the clearing was begun, the road was ready to travel. A memorial plaque at the intersection of Washington Avenue and First Street marks the beginning of the Vermilion Trail.

The gold rush soon died out. Few men could see that another ore lay there that could make them a fortune. Back in 1863, North Albert Posey, a blacksmith, had brought specimens of iron ore to George Stuntz. In 1866, during the epidemic of gold fever, Professor Henry H. Eames, geologist from Pennsylvania, published his report of explorations showing the presence of iron ore in the Vermilion Range. Although this discovery failed to excite men interested in gold, Lewis Merritt, accompanying a group to the gold fields in 1866, had another viewpoint when Posey showed him a chunk of iron ore. Alfred Merritt says, "Father told us boys that some day there would be great mines there, worth more than all the gold of California."

The Harbor was being improved at this time by the Federal Government, which was building piers at the Superior entry, still the only entry to the harbor. In 1867, a sub-contract was awarded to Vose Palmer, J.B. Culver, William Nettleton, J.D. Ray, and Sidney Luce, to furnish 1000 to 2000 cords of stone and a quantity of brush for this project. The following year, Alfred Merritt as pilot and Martin Wheeler as engineer brought the first tug to the Head of the Lakes, the *Agate*. They used the tug to tow scows carrying stone to the piers.

Duluth had dreams of greatness. At a Fourth of July picnic on the Point in 1868, Dr. Thomas Foster, who came here to publish a newspaper, made an historic speech in which he called Duluth "the Zenith City of the Unsalted Seas." It is this phrase, frequently quoted, that is responsible for the name Zenith being used on many Duluth products.

Dr. Foster, in this panegyric, spoke imaginatively upon the future of Duluth: "...it would not be amiss to dwell mentally for a while upon the future of this region, which is even now looming up in the near distance, promising to pierce and lighten up these forests with roadways and farm homesteads, to mine these rocks into material wealth to whiten yon huge sea with clouds of canvas, or fret it with volumes of propelling steam, to cover the shores of these broad calm bays with mast-studded wharves and monster grain warehouses, and to erect within the sound of the surge of Superior's waves a great city, which shall be the abode of commerce and manufactures, and refinement and civilization...the dawn comes; the daylight is really breaking in the east, in the west, in the south; and soon the sun of our progress, keeping pace with the steam railroad car, will shed its effulgence upon these pine and birch-clad and rock-bound shores."

Those were extravagant words, but Dr. Foster's prophecy began to come true the following year, when the great influx came to Duluth. Although in January of 1869, there were only fourteen families living at the base of Minnesota Point, by July 4, there was a population of 3500, and more were pouring in by boat, by stagecoach, and by foot. All sorts and conditions of men came - construction workers for the railroad, businessmen, and lumbermen from Maine.

On June 16 alone, 200 Swedish immigrants arrived, with all the townsfolk down at the dock to greet them. Since quarters were not ready for them the single men were taken to boarding shanties, and Duluth homes took in the thirteen families with true pioneer hospitality. The Immigrant House was built on Fifth Avenue West below Michigan Street to house future boatloads of men. Sometimes there were 700 men there in one day. Luke A. Marvin gives a vivid description of the ingress: "In the latter part of 1869, and in 1870, the people just came flooding in; in a few months there were two or three thousand people added to the population. There was no place to put them. There was not a hotel in the place, and every family had taken in as many as it could accommodate, and yet there were thousands to be provided for. They lived in tents; they put up the rudest kinds of shacks for a temporary shelter, until they could erect houses. As fast as the sides and room of a building were completed, and before the doors or windows could be supplied, the place would be rented out for lodgings. The owner would take a piece of chalk and mark off on the floor space sufficient for a man to lie down, number the space, and rent it out. Tenants had to provide their own bedding and blankets. They would buy a piece of ticking, sew it into a bag, and go out and fill it with straw, shavings, sawdust, leaves, anything that would answer the purpose of a bed, and then buy their blankets. They would do their own cooking over fires in the open air, or, if they were fortunate, they would get some of the inhabitants to give them table-board."

The men who came to Duluth that year called themselves the sixty-niners. One of these, Henry Truelson, landing May 8, gives this description of Superior Street: "...only a country road that had been cut through. The hillside forest ran right down to the street or road, and when a settler wished to erect a cabin, he was compelled to clear away the forest. The street was up and down, like a billowy sea, and later-day grades were made by filling in the hollows."

Another sixty-niner, Fred Smith, who arrived at Christmas, gives this picture of Duluth: "Superior Street was a continuous succession of hills and gullies, connected its entire length by a four foot plank sidewalk, with the plants laid endways, bridging the ravines and tunneling the hills. To walk it was hazardous in the daytime and almost sure death after dark. To find a place for crossing the street was a question of great deliberation and caution, and to actually cross was an act of recklessness, forfeiting your life insurance...The haphazard, scraggly and repellent settlement, a mixed combination of Indian trading post, seaport, railroad construction camp, and gambling resort, altogether wild, rough, uncouth and frontier-like, bore not the remotest resemblance, physically or otherwise, to the city it is now. Now did it seem within the range of the wildest imagination that a city could ever be built there. In only one particular did it then forecast its future; it was long, all long and not wide; extending from the old Bay View House, then completed, on Fourth Avenue West, in a broken interval of buildings to Decker 's brewery back on the creek at about Eighth Avenue East."

James J. Egan, another sixty-niner, suggested that since 1857, "Stuntz, Nettleton, Ray, Saxton, Carey, Luce, and Marvin had kept vigil over the lifeless corpse of Duluth.

The lifeless corpse, touched by the wand of Jay Cooke, now sprang full-armed from the tomb."

Duluth may not have been an attractive place, but things were happening that year. Portland became a part of Duluth in order that streets might be platted with uniformity. Alfred Merritt and Henry S. Ely built the first sailing vessel constructed at the Head of the Lakes, a 49 gross ton schooner-rigged vessel the *Shasta*. General George B. Sargent, an agent of Jay Cooke's, started a banking house. A ladies' seminary was operating. The Spalding brothers built a store where the hotel now stands, a fine location for shooting ducks on the marshes of Michigan Street. R.S. Munger erected a steam sawmill on the lake shore. The initial meeting of the Palestine Lodge of the Masonic order was held. The Bay View House was completed on the corner of Fourth Avenue West, "a long narrow three-story frame building, the front part propped up on stilts and the rear burrowing into the ground up the hill." Camille Poirer had a shoe business, and Jackson and Rickey operated a barber shop.

The Northern Pacific railway company built a freight wharf on the west side of Rice's Point known as De Costa's dock, and work was begun on the Citizen's Dock, which extended 600 feet into the lake just east of the present canal. Another project under construction was a timber-crib breakwater near the foot of Fourth Avenue East, parallel to Minnesota Point, to provide an outside harbor for Duluth. The Lake Superior and Mississippi railroad company built the breakwater to 400 feet, and the Federal Government extended it to 1030 feet in length.

Duluth had a subscription library maintained by private groups in 1869 - a reading room on the second floor of a building at 106 West Superior Street. The following year, Philadelphians interested in the culture of Duluth collected $350 to purchase new books for the library.

And Duluth had its first newspaper, the weekly *Minnesotian*, published by Dr. Thomas Foster, the first issue dated April 24, 1869. It was a four-page paper, five columns wide, devoted chiefly to advertising, clippings, and editorials. There was little local news, and no telegraphic news, since there were no telegraph lines in Duluth. At the top of the front page was the state seal of Minnesota. One of the characteristics of the paper was the vituperative editorials Foster wrote in his feud with R.C. Mitchell, editor of the Superior *Tribune.*

Copies of the *Minnesotian,* which are on file at the St. Louis County Historical Society, make interesting reading. Here are items from the file of 1869:

"Newcomers should comprehend that Duluth is at present a small place and that hotel and boarding house accommodation is extremely limited; however, lumber is cheap and shanties can be built. Everyone should bring blankets and come prepared to rough it at first."

"School trustees, in order to accommodate the recent influx of children, will raise the present building and fit up a basement for the purpose of opening a primary school in connection with the present one. Now 65 scholars are in attendance."

"We are requested to make inquiry concerning the whereabouts of the town plow, which seems to have disappeared from Duluth. As it is needed for improvement purposes, its early return is desirable."

In the November 14 issue: "The last regular train over the Dakota Division of the Northern Pacific Railroad this season is expected to arrive at Fargo tonight. The division will be closed till spring." There evidently was a season for trains as well as for boats.

The editor of the *Minnesotian* complained about the condition in which the mail arrived. He said, "Our papers have reached us damp enough to give us a touch of rheumatism every time we handled them. The St. Paul papers seem to have had a lively tussle on the road, grinding each other to pieces and coming through more like pulp than paper. Our letters are moist, pamphlets ruined, and magazines spoiled."

The 1869 schedule for mails follows:

"Eastern Mail - Arrives from St. Paul every Monday morning and every Monday, Wednesday and Friday evening. Departs every Monday departs every Monday, Wednesday, and Friday evening.

"Duluth and Houghton Mail - Arrives on the steamers *Keewenaw, Meteor, St. Paul,* and *Northern Light,* semi-weekly. These boats generally depart on Sundays and Fridays. Mail departs on same boats.

"North Shore Mail - Arrives and departs to Beaver Bay once every three weeks.

"Vermilion Lake Mail - Arrives on the first and third Wednesdays of each month; depart on the second and fourth Thursdays of each month.

"Oneota Mail - Arrives and departs every Saturday."

On October 1869, telegraph lines for the Northwestern Telegraph Company were first stretched along Superior Street. B.H. Squires of New York arrived to take charge as operator. On May 7, 1881, this company was leased to Western Union for 99 years.

At 7 p.m., Thursday, November 11, the first paid through dispatch was sent to Chicago via St. Paul by Charles B. Newcomb, vice president and managing director of the Elevator Company. The line was formally opened the following day when this dispatch was received from St. Paul: "To Duluth City - St. Paul City, head of Great River, sends greeting to Duluth, sister of the Lakes and Gateway to the Seas. The Mayor and other citizens." At 2 p.m. the answer was sent: "To St. Paul City - The Great Lakes answers the Great River; the electric tie in words is well; the iron tie in deeds is better. The metropolis of Minnesota hails the Capital. Horace Saxton, J.B. Culver, H.B. Luce, J.J. Egan, committee on telegraph celebration."

Also on November 12, this dispatch was sent out: "To the Mayor of Chicago - Telegraph completed. Duluth, the infant, sends greetings to Chicago, the Giant City of the Lakes. George B. Sargent and other citizens." The answer came back immediately: "Hail, sister of Lake Superior. May the energy of your people make your future a realization of the promise of the present. J.B. Rice, Mayor of Chicago."

The activity of 1869 was only a prelude to 1870. That was the year "when no plan was too exaggerated, no dream of the future too fantastic for Duluthians to try to bring it to completion. "

Duluth was made a city, with an aldermanic form of government, by an act of the state legislature on March 6, 1870. At the first city election, April 4, Colonel J.B. Culver was elected mayor.

In his inaugural address, Culver said, in part, "Duluth commences her existence under the most favorable and auspicious circumstances. Nature has placed her at the head of navigation upon our great chain of water communication with the Atlantic, and railroads are about to unite her with the Northwest and the Pacific Ocean. She stands admitted by all as destined to be one of the great cities of the West."

George C. Stone was elected the first city treasurer; Orlando Luce, city comptroller; and Henry Silby, city justice. There is a rumor that again an extra pair of trousers "large enough to fit the portliest redskin or to draw in at the waist for the leanest" was provided by politicians. It would seem these pants were standard equipment at the polling place.

Among the officers appointed by the mayor and council was the city attorney, James J. Egan. He says, "The great lawyers of the place - because there were only two - were Edward F. Parker and myself. We had no law business or books, and when the waves dashed high on

Minnesota Point, the half-breeds and newcomers gambled as to who was the best lawyer. One day it would be Parker, and the next day Egan." Evidently the city attorney was appointed on a day when the odds favored Egan.

E.A. Silberstein, who came to Duluth in 1870, gives this picture of the new city: "Superior Street was a mere trail cut through the woods, so rough that sledges and wagons, which constituted traffic, had to wind their way carefully around tree stumps and boulders...Wolves, bears, and deer living in the surrounding woods used to come to the edge of town to peer curiously at the usurping humans, and at night the cries of wild animals could be heard...The Indians here were all of the Chippewa tribe, living in what is now the State Teachers' College district. These local members of the tribe had a camp there, where they carried on their main occupation of making maple sugar, which they boiled in huge cauldrons into solid cakes. They sold these cakes of pure sugar to the settlers."

A full-fledged city had to have a fire department. This was a strictly volunteer affair, with each volunteer paying a two dollar initial fee for the honor of belonging to the organization. This entitled him to wear a red flannel shirt, blue trousers, and a fireman's hat (bought at his own expense) at the annual fireman's ball. E.M. Bloomer was elected foreman for the department. Fire-fighting equipment consisted of a Silsby engine and hook-and-ladder outfit, for which the city incurred a liability of $10,000. The department owned no horses to draw the apparatus, so evolved this plan: when the firebell rang, all teams would dash for the firehall; the team arriving first would draw the outfit, and its driver would be paid five dollars. The history of the equipment is brief. At the first call for duty, a fire on the Point, the men stoked the steam engine - and engine and firehall caught on fire and were destroyed completely.

The police department had an inauspicious beginning. One Robert Bruce was appointed Chief of Police on April 21. In June he disappeared along with the pay for the construction crew of the breakwater. Major J.L. Smith succeeded him. Police duties were not heavy, so the chief was also poundmaster and lamplight on moonless nights.

The city water department was not yet organized. Camille Poirer took over the water supply system single-handed. Concerning this venture, he said, "I had a large hogshead put on a cart, got a man to take charge, and started the first water delivery in Duluth. It went very well, but my servant proved unfaithful; he ran away with about $400 of my money, so I sold my outfit to the Collins brothers, who did a good business for many years." Water was taken from Lake Superior and used without the benefit of filtration or chlorine.

The city, proud of its new status, began to make improvements financed through the sale of bonds, with a fine disregard of city indebtedness. It issued $50,000 in bonds to the Lake Superior and Mississippi railroad to assure its terminus in Duluth; built a warehouse and a passenger depot at Fifth Avenue West - a one-story building; graded Lake Avenue; and made financial inducements to new industries to come to Duluth.

Elevator A, begun in 1869, was completed in 1870, erected by the Union Improvement and Elevator Company in the outer harbor at the foot of Fourth Avenue East. It had a capacity of 350,000 bushels, and was quite a far-sighted project, since the Dakotas had not yet started their great wheat farms. Munger and Markell built Elevator No. 1 in 1872 at the foot of Second Avenue East, with a capacity of 200,000 bushels.

The first passenger train arrived in Duluth on August 1, 1870, on the brand new Lake Superior and Mississippi. The town turned out to greet the train when it got in at 11:35 p.m. It had made the run of 154 miles from

St. Paul in sixteen hours and twenty minutes, a little less than ten miles an hour. With speedy transportation like that, Duluth could go places! This road was later reorganized as the St. Paul and Duluth and is now the Northern Pacific.

Another railroad project came up - the Northern Pacific. President Lincoln had signed the bill creating the Northern Pacific Railroad Company July 21, 1864, "to build a railroad and telegraph line from Lake Superior to the Puget Sound on the Pacific coast, by the northern route." Jay Cooke became interested in this venture. The road was to connect with the Lake Superior and Mississippi at Kokomo, near where Carlton now stands, and come to Duluth over its tracks. The actual breaking of ground took place at Kokomo on the Dalles of the St. Louis, February 15, 1870. This called for a celebration there, in which about seventy-five civic-minded Duluthians and Superiorites joined.

In describing the event, Hiram Hayes of Superior said, "Speeches were made around the fire - a bonfire heaped with crackling limbs and burning with alacrity. The deep snow melted and ran in torrents of water; the snow liquefied, as did the crowd. The earth thawed incidentally, and so did all present, for the occasion was one of hilarity and rejoicing for the start that was made."

The event was not without trouble. The first hitch came with the prayer which was to open the celebration. The Presbyterians contended vociferously that their minister, the Rev. Mr. Suter, should give this prayer, since the Presbyterians organized the first church in Duluth. Episcopalians claimed the honor, on the grounds that they had erected the first church building. When the host and mast of ceremonies, General Spaulding, asked the Episcopalian clergyman, the Rev. Mr. Gallagher, to give the invocation, the Presbyterians acted as if they felt the whole Northern Pacific enterprise would be damned. A religious war was averted, however, when Spaulding invited Suter to give the benediction. The only one who objected to that was R.C. Mitchell, editor of the Superior *Tribune*, who said there were too many prayers.

Another incident occurred after Hiram Hayes, representing the city of Superior took a spade and filled a wheelbarrow with the thawed-out earth. Since no one in the Duluth delegation had been appointed to represent the city and therefore have the honor of wheeling and dumping the first load of dirt, it was decided to give that honor to the man who had lived here the longest. Practically everyone in the delegation claimed to be the oldest inhabitant and was ready to back up his claim with fists if necessary. General Spaulding stopped this feud by selecting Colonel Culver for the honor.

In 1870, Duluth had two newspapers to compete with the *Minnesotian*. The fist daily was the *Morning Call*, a cocky little paper, size 6 by 7 1/4 inches, which had a brief life of about a year. The first issue came out Tuesday, November 28. Its editor, Seth Wilbur Payne, expressed his views and none too greatly.

R.C. Mitchell, after making derogatory remarks about Duluth while he was editor of the Superior *Tribune*, moved here to publish the Duluth *Tribune*. In an editorial he explained his move, saying he "preferred to carry on business in a growing, prosperous, and flourishing city rather than in a dead one." Having thus incurred the wrath of Superiorites, he had to move his equipment across the bay by night in order to get it out of town safely. In 1872, he changed his paper to a daily, but the following year again published it as a weekly.

The tenor of editor Payne's sentiments is given in this editorial: "Have not the extravagances created by the flush time of the war been brought down with increased taxes to the realities of peace? Before the war, the well-to-do farmer was content to ride to church in his every day lumber wagon with the new box on. The steady team looked substantial and comfortable in their plow harness. Now the well-to-do farmer must have his carriage and a silver-topped team."

Advertisements showed that laborers were being paid 50 cents a day. Wood was $2.00 and $3.00 a cord; eggs, 15 cents a dozen; butter, 25 cents a pound; and meat, 12 to 18 cents a pound. "Living is high," says Payne, "but it will come down."

One issue of the *Morning Call* states: "On April 17, navigation will be resumed. In a little time passenger trains will be running out 150 miles over the Northern Pacific road. Two weeks more and we can go down to the docks and depot and look good times square in the face."

The eagerness with which people in this isolated city waited for the first boat in the spring, before the railroad came, is shown in the Episcopal Church records of 1870. On a Sunday morning in spring, the service proceeded in due order until nearly the close of the morning prayer, when the steamer *Keewenaw*, the first boat of the year, blew her whistle. Almost instantly the church was emptied of everything except Mr. Gallagher, the minister. That evening, after the service, Mr. Gallagher announced: "Services will be held next Sunday at half past ten, Providence permitting - and if the whistle of the *Keewenaw* doesn't blow."

With the interest of Jay Cooke, St. Paul's Episcopal church was the first church building in Duluth, across the street from the present Masonic Temple. It was finished in time for Christmas, 1869, although the walls still smelled of fresh paint. "A good audience attended the service, and a spirit of peace on earth, good will toward men prevailed."

Both peace and good will were wanting that Christmas at Ruelard's saloon, where the Swedes battled the French and Irish. The death toll was two.

The first Catholic church was erected in 1870, on the site of the present Cathedral. It was a small frame building, painted white, which could be seen against the hill for miles out on the lake. The Reverend Father Keller was the pastor. Miss Brigid Meigher, who lived in Superior, was the organist. Every Sunday, an Indian brought her and her melodeon across the bay. Miss Meigher and W.P. Farrell were the first couple to be married in the little church, taking their vows even before the building was completed. In this church, in 1890, was installed the first bishop of Duluth, the Most Reverend James McGolrick. Mrs. Camille Poirer has left a record of the first Easter service, in 1871: "A few precious house plants were loaned, and fires were kept up all night so they wouldn't freeze. Indians brought pine and fir boughs and worked out some decorative designs similar to those seen in their beadwork."

Father Chebul, the missionary priest who founded the parish, had been sent to this district by Bishop Baraga. He had a large territory to cover - Duluth, Superior, Bayfield, La Pointe, and the Indian settlements along the shores of Lake Superior. He would carry his food and vestments in a pack and travel by foot, canoe, or snowshoe.

The Baptist Church Society, and the Presbyterians, Methodists, Lutherans, and Congregationalists were organized and building their churches by 1871.

The *Minnesotian* of June 26, 1869 says: "A Masonic hall, being, of course, one of the indispensable institutions of a place of our destiny, Mr. William Nettleton has commenced the erection of a good-sized building on the corner of Superior Street at East Second Avenue, the second story of which is designed for this special purpose. The building will be a substantial two-story frame, 22 x 50 feet, the lower story to be let for a store.

Palestine Masonic Lodge was granted a charter January 11, 1870. The first recorded meeting was held at the home of Mayhew on Minnesota Point. Among those present were William H. Newton, George R. Stuntz, Ruben R. Carlton, J.B. Culver, J.D. Ray and Frank Ely.

Ionic chapter of the Masonic lodge was founded in the old Hayes Block (owned by former President Hayes) at 30-32 East Superior Street in 1889. According to William D. Underhill, "the mule cars went by the door and in going to a Masonic funeral, they rode the car to Twelfth Avenue East, which was the end of the line, and then formed a procession through the woods to the cemetery, which was located about Tenth to Fourteenth Avenue East about Fourth Street.

The Young Men's Christian Association was founded in 1870, with its quarters in either the Pioneer building or the Graves building. The latter two-story frame structure was the place where the Congregationalists and the Methodists held their organization meetings, and where the Duluth Street Railway Company was formed. The Y seems to have passed away in the depression of 1873, but was reorganized in 1882.

The Bethel had its beginning in 1870, when the Western Seamen's Friend Society of Cleveland sent Robert Smith here to work among the sailors. According to Gilbert Fawcett in his radio series *Historic Site Ahead*, "In those days, most of the shipping that came into Duluth harbor was unloaded in slips adjacent to Lake Avenue, a district made up of saloons, gambling dens, and flop houses. Here, on shore leave, congregated the seamen, swarming the gin mills, gaming tables, and other places of amusement, in riotous release from the monotony of life aboard ship. Here, too, gathered those who garnered a livelihood by preying on the reckless sailors, and rash, indeed, were those who ventured into this lawless terrain." These were the men for whom Bob Smith worked.

Along with the development of religious institutions, schools were being reorganized. The Board of Education of the Independent School District of Duluth was incorporated in 1870. Orlando Luce was president; R.S. Munger, treasurer; J.R. Carey, clerk; Luke Marvin, elected April 19, but resigned, and J.H. White chosen to fill his place, April 30; Ansel Smith; J.D. Ensign; the Rev. George Suter, who resigned and was replaced by I.C. Spalding; and the Rev. Mason Gallagher, who resigned and was replaced by W.S. Woodbridge. The first superintendent of schools was R.D. Haynes, Esq., elected the same year. The board records called all superintendents Esquire until the salary dropped below $1,000 a year. After that they were plain Mr. The high branches, to a limited extent, were included in the schedule. In 1873, plans were contemplated, but not carried out, for a high school building. However a high school course was scheduled.

Records of the Board of 1870 give these rules governing teachers: "Resolved by the Board of Education that all teachers are required to see that fires are built in their respective schoolhouses at 8 o'clock in the morning, and the teachers are also required to have their schoolhouses neatly swept every evening after the dismissal of school." Later, the board allowed "the several lady teachers five dollars a month to build the fires."

Fred W. Smith gives this account of school life: "A few rods back (from the post office), and facing the angular direction, the incident to all Portland buildings, stood the only schoolhouse. Here, under the severe teachings of Merritt and Hussey, we youngsters received our first insight into the principles of higher education and lower corporal infliction. Many a time, at the request of the master, have I gone into the adjacent brush and, with care and assiduity, prepared a pliant birch, wondering the while for whom it was intended, only to find upon my return that I was the appointed one. Low, rough and unpainted, with a porch ten feet high and a six-foot ceiling, with its giant box-stove and wooden walls, it was then a fit representative of the educational opportunities in Duluth...School life was a strenuous one in those days and learning came hard, from whichever end we got it, but the lessons were remembered, yes, and some of them felt, for long afterwards."

With business, industry, and commerce going full blast and churches and schools established, the progressive gentlemen of the city organized a Chamber of Commerce on August 5, 1870. The officers were: Henry A. Gould, president; C.B. Newcomb, first vice-president; John Mercer, second vice-president; C.M. Cushman, secretary and treasurer. Directors were R.S. Munger, J.C. Hunter, John W. Pendleton, George C. Stone, William Branch, Charles H. Graves, Edgar Nash, and Luther Mendenhall. A board of arbitrators consisted of A.N. Seip, W.W. Hawkes, and E. Ingallis; and a board of appeals included J.B. Culver, W.W. Spalding, A.S. Cushman, J.D. Ensign, and W.W. Billson. It would seem to be the kind of organization in which each member had an office. It died in 1873.

Although the railway company and the Philadelphia financiers thought the breakwater extending into the lake would be sufficient to make a safe harbor for vessels, the residents of Duluth, on familiar terms with northeasters, were not satisfied. They wanted the harbor in the bay and a canal cut through Minnesota Point to that harbor, a pet project since 1857. Since the city charter granted the council power to construct such a canal, and since the council had no hesitation in issuing bonds to finance improvements, in the fall of 1870 the work was begun.

Superior was aghast. Such a canal would curtail their commerce, since not all ships would then have to use the Superior entry. The work must be stopped - they said. They appealed to the government on the grounds that the new canal would change the channel of the St. Louis River, fill up the natural entry, and ruin the improvements being made on that entry by the Federal government. They wanted an injunction to stop construction work on the canal.

Dredging could not be carried on during the winter, but early the following spring, while matters were being studied by the government, work was recommenced, with J.H. Upham in charge. Finally, a tiny stream of water connected the lake and bay, and the next morning a current of the river had forced the opening so wide that Captain George W. Sherwood ran his steam yacht *Fero* from the lake to the bay. When the injunction arrived, the canal was 50 feet wide, with eight feet of water.

According to the *Morning Call* of April 30, 1871: "An event occurred yesterday of greater importance to Duluth that would have been the commencement of the Northern Pacific docks. We refer to the opening of the canal across Minnesota Point."

In the same paper, May 2, is this item: "A telegram was received yesterday from St. Paul which stated that George Stuntz is on his way to Duluth with an injunction on the canal. A few hours too late. The canal is open and the water is fast doing the work of the dredge."

Tradition has a version of that story dear to the hearts of Duluthians, and there were people living that day who have vouched for its truth.

The story goes that the dredge was working against time on Saturday morning, when it struck frozen gravel. Then came the telegram that Congress had granted Superior the injunction to stop the work, and that the papers would arrive Monday morning. Stunned for only a moment, citizens passed the word around, and every man, woman, and child in Duluth "who could handle a spade or shovel, or beg, borrow, or steal a bucket or a bushel basket, flocked down to the Point and dug, scratched, and burrowed at the canal till it was finished." (Bridges) While the papers were on their way, all day Saturday and Saturday night, and all day Sunday and Sunday night they worked, while women kept fires going and provided food and coffee for the workers. On Sunday, Superior residents rowed over, astounded at the audacity of the Duluthians, to watch the work and heckle the workers. Then, just at dawn on

Monday morning, Captain Sherwood ran his tiny steam yacht *Frank C. Fero* from the lake into the bay, its whistle tied down, screaming defiantly, while the crowds on shore shouted jubilantly. As the little yacht turned to retrace its course, the army engineer arrived - too late.

That's the story Duluthians like.

The citizens of Superior were so worked up over Duluth's defiance of the government, and threats were so ominously and generously exchanged, that an enterprising business man ran an advertisement in the papers for several days announcing a sale of muskets in Superior to help the good people of that city enforce the injunction of Duluth. Since these muskets were advertised as being left over from the Civil War, this was probably the first authorized sale of war surplus goods.

Superior and the army engineers thought a dike into the bay might help save the Superior entry, so Duluth, already $50,000 in debt, blithely issued bonds for another $100,000. The dike was built from Rice's Point, but was destroyed by the force of the current about the time Superior decided it should be removed. Federal appropriations finally removed the last 75 feet, so that vessels could proceed between Duluth and Superior.

The Duluth canal made one important change in the harbor. Before it was cut through, the bay was dotted with floating islands. Enterprising gentlemen plotted these islands and sold lots. But with the canal, the river currents changed, moved the islands about, and finally sent them out through the canal. It must have been a shock to see your city lot, the location of your future home, floating down the lake.

In 1872, the canal was completed with the help of the Northern Pacific. It was 250 feet wide with a depth of 16 feet. Piers consisted of rock-filled, timber cribs 24 feet wide with an aggregate length of 2470 feet. That year, Congress made the first appropriation from which federal money could be spent on the Duluth Ship Canal - $50,000. In 1873, the Federal Government assumed control of the harbors of Duluth and Superior.

In a storm of 1872, the breakwater was torn out, but the canal remained. Legal proceedings concerning it continued bitterly for six or seven years, but the government finally abandoned its litigation.

The 1870 Report of the Lighthouse Board has the following to say about the need for a light at Duluth, Minnesota: "This is the terminus of the railroad from St. Paul, Minn. to the head of Lake Superior. The place is becoming rapidly built up; wharves, elevators for grain, and piers are being built; and although there is a lighthouse at Minnesota Point, at the mouth of the St. Louis River, Superior City, yet it only serves as a general guide for that side of the Head of the Lake. A light having been asked for to guide to that side of the lake, an estimate of $10,000 has been submitted in the annual estimates of this year. The numerous petitioners for this light, upon six different petitions, represent that while the harbor of Duluth is easy of access and safe during the day, or when land marks are visible, it being without beacons, is difficult and dangerous at night when the weather is thick; that vessels are now arriving and departing daily, and with the prospect of greatly increased trade to follow the completion of the Lake Superior and Mississippi Railroad, which will be ready for through traffic in a few weeks; that the Northern Pacific Railroad Company is about forwarding the iron and other materials for building its line to Red River (over 200 miles) to this port, which will make the trade this season exceedingly large. An immense future commerce is also assured by the building of the above named two roads to this port, the most westerly point to which the Great Lakes can be navigated; that the nearest harbor of refuge on the south shore of the lake is at Bayfield, 75 miles distant, while the nearest safe harbor on the north shore is still more distant. Sudden storms at this end of the lake, therefore, render the harbor at Duluth one of peculiar and exceeding importance to the commerce of the lakes. We therefore pray your honorable board to take such measures as will lead to the early establishment of such lights and guards as may be necessary for the protection of the large shipping interests from all the lake ports now centering there."

On the recommendation of the Board, therefore, Congress appropriated $10,000 on March 2, 1871 "for the erection of a beacon light and dwelling for the keeper of Lake Superior, at the terminus of the Northern Pacific Railroad, Minnesota." The money was expended, $5,490.90 in 1872 and $4,509.10 in 1873.

The 1871 report states: "The act of Congress appropriating for this lighthouse provides that it shall be located at the terminus of the Northern Pacific Railway. Consequently, the Chief Engineer of that road was written to, informing him of the provisions of the appropriation and asking him to designate a site for the lighthouse; also, in case the proposed site were not the property of the United States to take the requisite steps to ascertain the owner, and, if practicable, initiate negotiations for the purchase of the site. After some delay, he replied that he had referred the communication to the road, but no further answer has been received.

Later a reply was received from J. Gregory Smith, President of the Northern Pacific Railroad, 120 Broadway, New York, who apparently had suggested a site for the beacon at the outer end of the southern pier.

On November 6, 1871, the Board of Directors of Lake Superior and Mississippi Railroad Company adopted a resolution: "Resolved: By the Board of Directors of the Lake Superior and Mississippi Railroad Company that Lot 229 on Lake Avenue, Upper Duluth, St. Louis County, Minn., be conveyed in fee simple to the United States for the purpose of erecting thereon a domicile for the use of the Officer or

Persons to have charge of the Lighthouse or Beacon about to be erected on or near Minnesota Point, and for such other public purposes as the U.S. may see proper to use the said premises, and that for the purpose of so vesting the title to said Lot in the United States, that the President of this Company be and he is hereby authorized to execute a deed for said Lot to the United States on behalf of the company and under its corporate seal, with covenants of warranty as to the title in the usual form, and to acknowledge and deliver the same as the act and deed of this corporation." The company on November 10, 1871, for a consideration of $100, deeded "that part and parcel of land situated in the county of St. Louis in the State of Minnesota, and known as Lot 229, Lake Avenue, Upper Duluth, in the City of Duluth in said country, according to the recorded plat thereof on file in the office of the Register of Deeds of said County." On the same day the deed was approved by C.K. Davis, U.S. District Attorney, and then forwarded by the Railroad Company to the Attorney General of the United States at Washington along with a copy of the charter of the railroad and abstract of title and copies of deeds, etc. On December 18, 1871, the Attorney General returned the deeds with his opinion that they were valid.

In the 1872 report of the Board it is noted that a contract for the erection of the station "has been made and the work is now in progress."

In 1873 the Board reported "after much delay the keeper's dwelling and as much of the elevated walk as can be built at present were completed during the month of May. Owing to the damage sustained by the pier in a storm, last fall, it is not in fit condition to receive the beacon, and work has been suspended until the repairs to the pier are completed, when the contractor will be required to finish the beacon. Meanwhile a temporary light is exhibited from the outer end of the north pier of the canal."

In 1874 it was reported: "This station after a great delay on the part of the contractors was finally completed during the month of January, 1874, and lighted for the first time on the night of June 2, 1874."

Business continued to develop in the next two years. The wholesale district was composed of William R. Stone's wholesale grocery, the first wholesale business in Duluth. The Duluth Blast Furnace was erected (some think on city bonds) on Rice's Point, controlled by the newly organized Duluth Iron and Steel Company. The Lake Navigation Company of Minnesota, comprised of Duluthians, organized the first Duluth steamship line to build the steamers *Metropolis* and *Manistee*. Munger and Gray put up a sawmill at Fifth Avenue West. The city erected a wire suspension bridge for foot travel across the canal. A franchise was given the Duluth Street Railway Company for a streetcar system to be installed in 1874. Two more banks were started: the First National Bank of Duluth with J.C. Culver president and the Duluth Savings Bank organized by John C. Hunter. Robert D'Unger established the *Daily Herald,* which he published for one year.

Detailed commercial statistics for the harbor date back to 1871. The 92,820 gross tons consisted of grain and flour and receipts of coal and miscellaneous merchandise, chiefly handled over docks in the outer harbor. That year in the Duluth harbor, 545 vessels arrived and departed. The following year, 556 steamers and 182 sailing vessels arrived and departed.

Duluth, in 1871, had six hotels "ready for summer guests", according to the newspaper. The tourist industry was evidently thriving. The hotels advertising in the paper were Bay View, the Lincoln, the Second Avenue Motel, the Globe, the Minnesota House, and the Clark House.

The Clark House, located on the present site of Wahl's Store, was "the place to go", the center of social events until it burned in 1881. Built under the direction of

General Sargent, it was "a homely and angular structure that constituted the main hostelry and political headquarters." It had a frontage of 150 feet, and a back wing of 110 feet long and was three stories high. A long, pillared veranda, reached by many steps, spread along its entire front. There was a huge dining room, lobby, and parlors large enough for any public event. In the lobby stood a great stove which is said to have taken four-foot cordwood for fuel. Egan said: "The Clark House was a great figure in those days. All the bloods boarded there; parties were held, the ladies young and old of the city assembled, and the gentlemen in swallow-tailed coats, and kids welcomed them to the lancers and the waltz. Across the hall Colonel Hull and Mr. Scott, the proprietors, presided, both of whose names, for good fellowship and kindness, should ever be treasured I the hearts of the old citizens."

The *Morning Call* tells of one of those parties at the Clark House: "Great care was exercised to admit none by those of undoubted respectability." The hotel was the popular place for "dances, banquets, and performances of the Dramatic Association, transactions of the Debating Society, and meeting of the Musical Association."

Duluth's social life centered around the Clark House and Ashtabula Heights, the "exclusive" residential sections.

Duluthians did not slight entertainments and amusements in their leisure time. There was at least one regatta, March 14, 1871, "with aboriginal birch bark canoes in the outer harbor and hundreds of people cheering from the dock." "Mrs. Jarley's Wax Works" was presented to raise funds for the Congregational church. At the Dramatic Temple, a one-story building on the site of the present Norshor theatre, plays were given. A skating rink was located at the corner of First Street and Third Avenue West. The United Irishmen held their banquets, and the Knights of Pythias organized. There was always fishing or hunting on the marches of Lake Avenue, or, in winter months, skating, tobogganing, and snowshoeing.

On May 5, 1871, according to a local paper, the first private carriage in Duluth was on the street; but Indian wigwams still dotted Minnesota Point and the hillside.

Duluth, with its Indian tepees, squatter's shacks, and muddy streets, was on its way to being one of the largest cities on the continent. The inhabitants admitted the fact, in such terms as "Duluth is a wonder - wealth and dauntless enterprise have built a metropolis whose towers reach the sky. Her stupendous growth and grand development have marked her as the coming leader of the western continent."

It was the Honorable J. Proctor Knott of Kentucky who unwittingly gave Duluth its greatest national publicity. The scene was the House of Representatives in Washington - the time, 1871. It happened this way. The projectors of the Bayfield and St. Croix railroad were asking the Federal Government for aid for their road from Hudson, Wisconsin, to Bayfield and Superior. Mr. Knott was a trifle confused about the affair, thinking the terminus was to be in Duluth, whereas Duluth was opposing the land grant. In speaking against the measure, Knott made one of the greatest satirical speeches in the records of Congress, and through his ridicule of Duluth brought this city a little fame.

Among the gems of his irony are: "Who will have the hardihood to rise in his seat on this floor and assert that, excepting the pine bushes, the entire region would not produce vegetation enough in ten years to fatten a grasshopper?

"...I was utterly at a loss to determine where the terminus of this great and indispensable road should be, until I accidentally overheard some gentlemen, the other day, mention the name Duluth. Duluth! The word fell upon my ear with peculiar and indescribable charm, like a gentle murmur of a low fountain stealing forth in the midst of roses, or the soft sweet accents of an angel's whisper in the bright, joyous dream of sleeping innocence. Duluth! Twas a name for which my soul had panted for years, as a hart panteth for the water-brooks."

The entire speech goes along in that vein, as Knott discusses the climate - "a terrestrial paradise fanned by the balmy zephyrs of an eternal spring, clothed with the gorgeous sheen of ever-blooming flowers, and vocal with the silver melody of nature's choicest songsters"; commercial resources - "inexhaustible mines of gold, immeasurable veins of silver, impenetrable depths of boundless forests, vast coal mines, wide extended plains of richest pasturage...the fortunate combination of the buffaloes and the pigeons satisfies me that Duluth s destined to be the beef market of the world."

This speech, with its rich satire and hyperbole, had such publicity value for Duluth that a wire went out to Knott offering him two choice lots in the city. Duluthians see no reason why the city could not live up to Knott's advance notices.

Then, in 1873, came the failure of Jay Cooke and Company - and all was lost.

CHAPTER VII

Village and City Again

When Jay Cooke and Company failed, September 18, 1873, business was paralyzed and widespread panic followed throughout the nation. To Duluth, the failure meant disaster, as the city was leaning heavily upon the backing of the man who was financing the construction of the Northern Pacific Railroad.

"The first receipt of the news in Duluth was scarcely credited, but the next day came full confirmation with details of more disastrous effects and more direful forebodings. From the giddy height of a veritable boom Duluth fell into a very slough of despondency. Real estate values went down, down, down…Then followed for several years a period of business stagnation and general depression which seemed to grow only more severe as time passed. Banks failed, goods of all kinds were sold at sheriff's sale, and vacant houses and business blocks added to the general air of desolation."

Mitchell, editor of the *Tribune*, said "there was an utter state of demoralization, especially in Duluth, which had sprung up like magic and whose business chiefly depended upon its being the supply point for the Northern

Pacific Railroad. I am safe in saying that inside of sixty days more than half of the men engaged in trade in Duluth went out of business, many of them going bankrupt and others selling out for what they could get, and ...left the place."

The dark days were back. Again people rushed out before navigation closed down for the winter. Again vacant houses and office buildings stood staring out of blank windows. Again city lots could not be traded for the small necessities of life. Again Duluth's aristocracy got up early in the morning to catch fish for the day's meals. "Jay Cooke's town" was on its own and those who were fearful left the stricken city. Population dwindled from 5,000 to 1,300.

Those who remained were living in a city head over heels in debt, with no credit whatsoever. The city council petitioned Congress to grant $250,000 and petitioned the state legislature for exceptions from the levy of state tax. The citizens held mass meetings at which they discussed repudiation of bonds in angry terms, and "the editor of the *Minnesotian* struck the editor of the *Tribune* in the face."

With no organized charity in the city, Robert Smith and other men interested in his work with the seamen, extended their services to help the families in distress. They incorporated a Duluth branch of the Bethel Society, with the incorporators, Luke Marvin, R.S. Munger, J.C. Hunter, Ludwig Hegardt, B.S. Russell, Luther Mendenhall, H.F. Johns, Sextus Hoffman, and W.W. Billson. Mission services were held in the open air at the corner of First Avenue West and Superior Street.

City affairs remained in a chaotic condition until 1876, when John Drew, the mayor, with the aid of the state legislature, effected a plan by which the city died. By a new charter, a village was organized of "the settled part of Duluth", the first and second wards, "under a promise to pay off its indebtedness at fifty cents on a dollar, through the judge of the District Court." The village would include land north of the canal to the alley between Third and

Fourth streets, between Mesaba Avenue and Third Avenue East. As indebtedness was paid off, more of the former city could be included in the village, but until that time these sections had no organized government. The legality of the procedure was approved by a test case in the United States Court.

The city of Duluth died at the age of seven, on March 12, 1877, when the last meeting of the city council was held. The empty safe and the fire apparatus was turned over to the village, and $51,000 worth of canceled bonds and coupons was burned. On March 14, the trustees met: Andreas M. Miller, president; W.L. McLennan and Albert N. Seip, trustees; W.W. Davis, recorder; Luther Mendenhall, treasurer; and E.P. Martin, justice. They made a radical reassessment of the district and issued village bonds for actual expenses.

When the village had its first election, January 8, 1878, John Drew was elected president; Frank Eaton, recorder; J.D. Howard, J.P. Johnson, and Edward Main, trustees.

From a city that had always depended on outsiders to do things for it, the village now began to rely on itself. The council went in strong for economy. By lighting the street lamps only on moonless nights, the cost for a year was $6.78 a lamp. The village marshall could be seen every moonless night carrying his ladder and oil can along the streets. A later measure was not too popular with the citizenry: not allowing individuals to borrow the fire ladders when they wanted to do a bit of painting or the fire engines to pump out cellars or excavations.

Wheat helped in the reconstruction. Many men, not only from Duluth but also from the East, had left the cities stagnating in the panic, and gone westward to develop vase wheat fields in Dakota and along the Red River Valley in Minnesota. Western Canada and Manitoba were also producing vast quantities of wheat. One writer says: "In

1878, the quiet of this wilderness was broken by the woodman's ax; the broad plain had become dotted with towns and cities and countless homes. These were to pay tribute to Duluth for all time to come; they were the substantial witness that the city at the Head of the Lakes had a mission to perform in the commercial world that should draw to her a wealth of mind and money that would make her what she is destined to become - the Metropolis of the Northwest." By 1878 the elevator capacity of elevator "A" was doubled, and in 1880 the construction of elevator "B" was begun. During the years of the village, C, D, E, F, and G were built. Within ten years, the number of bushels of wheat stored grew from 460,595 bushels to 22,425,730 bushels, and it was estimated at least ten million bushels were turned away because of lack of storage facilities.

As the grain poured in, lumbering was also a big business. After winters spent in the forests, the "lumberjacks" came into the village, and the trees they had felled went to the sawmills and then down the Great Lakes.

Duluth had the prospect of a new railroad to give it another ray of hope for future prosperity. In 1878, the Duluth and Winnipeg was given a land grant from the state, and Duluth looked hopefully to the north. However, this project did not materialize until the company was taken over by the Great Northern in 1896, and then it was made a Superior road.

Another newspaper, the *Lake Superior News*, made its appearance July 4, 1878. The publishers were Woodbridge and Delplain. Mitchell bought out the *Minnesotian-Herald* that year.

In 1878, the population of Duluth was 2,200. By 1879, the village was pulling out of the depression, and was daring to look into the future. It was steadily retiring bonds. One of the first municipal actions was the re-establishment of a public library, former efforts having been struck down by the panic.

That was also the year when the American Exchange Bank, the oldest in Duluth, emerged out of the former Duluth Savings Bank, with capital at $25,000. And the first class was graduated from a Duluth high school - two proud alumnae, Gertrude Olmstead and Addie Wilkenson. One of the diplomas is at the St. Louis Historical Society.

Improvements were continuing to be made on the piers. In 1880, a fog bell "struck by machinery" was erected at the lighthouse station, and a request was made for a beacon light "at the inner end of the south harbor pier, to form, with the present pier head light, a range for entering the harbor." An appropriation of $2,000 was recommended then and again in 1881. In 1883 a new walk was built, the old one repaired and the fog-bell house moved to a more suitable position. In 1885 "the damage done to 120 feet of elevated walk by a schooner, on October 4, 1884, was repaired and the walk on the inner end of the pier straightened." A fog whistle, installed in October, 1886, was a 10 inch whistle operated by steam. A fixed red 4th order light replaced the 5th order light which had flashed red and white. On September 1, 1889, a new inner range light on the pier was installed at a cost of $2,264.58. It was a 4th order light flashing red at intervals of six seconds, the arc visible 360 degrees. Sixteen days later, its foundations were damaged by the steamer *India* and were repaired at the cost to the owners of the steamer.

By 1881, enough bonds had been redeemed so that the boundaries of the village were extended to included Rice's Point to the west and four more blocks east. A new village arose across the canal, the village of Park Point. It is odd that this location, the original townsite of Duluth, was not included when the city went back to village status. The first meeting of the board of trustees of Park Point, at the shop of R.E. Jefferson, was held April 9, 1881. The board was composed of: R.H. Palmer, president; Henry Kitchli, James S. Pierce and F.T. Gowin, trustees; Z.D. Scott, treasurer; J.M.W. Thompson, recorder; and D.E. Holston, justice of the peace. One of the village ordinances prohibited the same of intoxicating liquor to the Indians.

Municipal improvements were being made. Grading was begun on Michigan Street; a survey was made for a sewer on Superior Street; a plank road with sidewalks and bridges was built on Rice's Point; and streetcars started running. Crowds gathered along Superior Street one bright day in 1881 and excitedly screamed and applauded as the first streetcar clattered down the track. There were two or three little "bob-tailed" cars drawn by patient mules on the single track which ran from Eighth Avenue West to Third Avenue East. The following year, the track was extended to run from Garfield Avenue to Eighth Avenue East.

One matter which was a cause of much argument in the village council was a bill for $445 for fighting smallpox on Rice's Point. Some members of the council contended that the disease had been brought in from outside the city, so the state should pay the bill, but the council finally became generous and ordered it paid.

The Duluth Board of Trade dates back to 1881, its incorporators being George Spencer, Clinton Markell, A.J. Sawyer, Owen Farguson, W.T. Hooker, W.W. Davis, R.S. Munger, Charles H. Graves, and Walter Van Brunt.

A new Chamber of Commerce was also organized to replace the one which had gone out of existence in 1873. The officers were: J.B. Culver, president; Charles H. Graves, vice president; and George W. Kimberly, secretary.

A 30-year franchise granted the Duluth Gas and Water Company in 1882 started trouble for years to come, but the villagers felt very metropolitan with gas lamps.

The Duluth Telephone Company was organized in 1881, with H.C. Kendall, president; Charles H. Graves, secretary; and Walter Van Brunt, treasurer and manager. Van Brunt had become interested in the new invention in 1877, and that year installed the first telephones in the city -

two instruments connected on a line between the First National Bank building and a grain elevator located on Third Avenue East. The first telephone directory was issued in 1882 in the form of a card 9 1/4 by 2 3/4 inches, which listed the 30 subscribers and warned the public: "These instruments are private property." All persons not subscribers to the company were prohibited from using the telephones.

Electricity for lighting and power in Duluth was first supplied in 1882, when a steam driven electric generator was placed in operation in the engine room of the Scott and Holston sawmill on Lake Avenue South. The first electricity was made available only for arc lighting of streets; later arc lights were installed in stores. About 1885, incandescent lamps were used for lighting buildings. Electricity in those days was available only in the evening, usually from dusk until 11 o'clock. Respectable people were probably supposed to be in bed by that hour. With the invention of the electric iron, electricity was supplied on Thursday mornings. Those were the times when housewives worked on a schedule, with wash day on Monday and ironing day on Tuesday, and with no soap operas to interrupt the laundry work.

Citizens were shy about issuing bonds, so voted down a new city hall and courthouse. A veneer brick building, "a remarkable shack," was constructed for the courthouse at Sixth Avenue East, where the public market now stands. For 20 years, whenever more room was needed, a "wart" was added to this building. The city council continued to rent quarters for itself and the police court over a saloon on Superior Street.

W.M. West was superintendent of schools from 1880 to 1884. He added a new rule for the teachers: "Visiting each other's rooms except on business of the schools is forbidden." As a janitor, "He shall in particular make and regulate the fires, keep the water buckets filled with good water, sweep, dust, and when necessary scrub the rooms and halls and wash the windows." There were rules for pupils, too: "No pupil shall not anywhere around the school premises carry firearms, sling shots, or other dangerous weapons or instruments." Pupils in high school were regarded as on trial the first term, and at the close of any month of that term could be reduced to the grammar grades.

By 1881, school enrollment was 748, and cases of corporal punishment numbered 184. The city had six schools: Portland, erected in 1859; the high school, West Third Street School, and Minnesota Point, all built in 1871; the first Adams, 1880; and Washington, 1881, built on the present site of Central. In addition, the board rented the Smith building and the German church school.

In those days, the purpose of the high school was to prepare students for college, as these schools were beginning to take the place of academies. The course of study in the Duluth high school in 1883 included: first year - physical geography, physiology, algebra, Latin grammar and reader, English history, and the study of words; second year - natural philosophy, geometry, Caesar and German; third year - chemistry, geology, ancient history, modern history, Cicero, rhetoric, and bookkeeping; fourth year - political economy, civil government, astronomy, English literature, Virgil, study of American authors, and study of English authors. The school year was divided into three terms.

In 1883, there were 23 teachers ("1 male, 22 female") and 1182 students, 39 of these in the high school. The following year, to accommodate the influx of pupils, Jefferson, Jackson, Madison, and Monroe schools were built, and new boundaries were adopted.

For the school year 1884-85, William H. Stultz was superintendent. Of the appointment, George W. Kimberly, clerk, said, "From a large number of applicants, which might with a little stretch of imagination be supposed to include all males in the business of teaching in the United States and the Dominion of Canada, Mr. Stultz appeared to be the one...most suited to our wants."

Duluthians were reckless about school expenses. Probably the reason for the avalanche of applications for the superintendency was the attractive salary - $1,500 a year. The tax levy had risen from $7,500 in 1881 to $31,000 in 1883. Robert E Denfeld, a graduate of Amherst with a master's degree, became superintendent in 1885, a position he held for 30 years, and began developing a modern school system. A supervisor of drawing and a music director were appointed that year. In January of 1886, the present Adams school building, the oldest in use today, was first occupied, and a high school was built, the building now used for administration.

The first parochial school, the forerunner of Cathedral, was held in a remodeled carriage shop in First Street and Second Avenue East in 1881. It had 150 pupils and three teachers, Sisters of the Order of St. Benedict. In 1884, classes were held in the vacant public school building on the site of the present administration building, and from 1885-1904 in the St. Thomas school erected on Second Avenue West and Fourth Street. St. Mary, Star of the Sea, (now discontinued) was built at Fourth Avenue East on Fourth Street in 1884, and St. Clement at 21st Avenue West and Third Street in 1887.

St. Luke's Hospital was founded during a typhoid epidemic. The Rev. J.A. Cummings of the Episcopal Church called a meeting on St. Luke's day in 1882, and the first hospital plans were formulated and the old blacksmith's shop selected as the site, "at 12 Third Avenue East." C.H. Graves paid the first $25 rental. Mr. Cummings said, "Three or four chairs and three beds, with bedding, was all I could gather together at the time, and a stove was donated by the British Government from the emigrant station. No sooner had the furniture been installed than an old man, a charity patient, sought care at the hospital and Dr. McCormack attended him. A nurse was needed and Mrs. Jessie Gowin of Park Point, was named superintendent of the institution and remained for four years...I placed an advertisement in the papers that the hospital was open, and in one week we had twelve patients. At the end of the month, there were 29 being care for in a little shack."

The St. Louis Hotel was a "magnificent structure", built by the owner of the Clark House, which had burned down in 1880.

The YMCA, which seems to have gone out of existence during the panic of 1873, was reorganized in 1882. There were 24 charter members. Officers were James Seville, president; W.G. Peck, vice president; George W. Kimberly, secretary; and Robert C. Ray, treasurer.

The Y leased a building at 10 East Superior Street from the Free Reading Room and Library Association. Along with the lease, the Y agreed to assume the $1000 debt of the Library Association and the expense of maintenance, including insurance, to the amount of $3000. They also painted the building.

Activities of the Y included religious meetings, lectures, social games and gymnasium classes. In 1883, James Seville and W.S. Woodbridge were delegates to the International Convention at Milwaukee. In 1884, at the celebration of the anniversary, Cyrus Northrop, President of the University of Minnesota, gave the address. In 1885, Daniel Cole of Boston was employed as physical director.

The Chamber of Commerce reorganized in 1883. "The organization was accomplished with great éclat and took a leading part in all discussions, from the establishment of a park system to the settlement of European tariff disputes."

The *Duluth Herald* was started by Mille Bunnell that year.

The swaying footbridge across the canal was a fearful thing in the best of weather and impossible for use in a northeaster, so in 1883 a ferry service was started, with Charles Winters in charge of the rowboat. The ferry ran from 6 a.m. to 10 p.m. on weekdays and till 11 p.m. on Saturdays and Sundays. Rates were five cents a trip; one dollar a month for families; and 25 to 50 cents a month for groceries. In the winter, planks were laid across the ice. The next year the village of Park Point asked for a bridge across the canal, but Congress decreed that the canal must be unobstructed.

Exhibiting their faith in the future of the village, Munger and Markell built the Grand Opera House at the corner of Fourth Avenue West. The Public Library had a room in the building. The Village council showed its appreciation of this enterprise by granting the owners exemption from all taxes and licenses for one year. The theatre was destroyed by fire in 1889.

The progressive village council established the Board of Health in 1884. This action is said to have met with the disapproval of "several old timers who were deprived of their almost immemorial privilege of keeping pigpens underneath their neighbors' windows." The council also renumbered the streets and put up signs at the corners designating the names of streets and avenues.

Other indications that Duluth was developing into a city again were: the first uniforms for policemen in 1882; organization of the Kitchi Gammi Club in 1883; in 1885, organization of the Boat Club with H.W. Pearson the first president; construction of St. Luke's Hospital at Second Avenue East and Fourth Street; and organization of the Duluth Produce Exchange. The village was redeeming old city bonds at seventy-five cents on the dollar.

A group of young men of military age organized Duluth's National Guard in 1884 - Company K, Second Minnesota Infantry. They had their headquarters in

Hunger's Hall. The first reference to the Duluth unit is found in the biennial report of the Adjutant General of Minnesota for 1885: "not yet one year old, and for the opportunities it has had it has made decided progress and bids fair to make the best company in the regiment." The company was described as "composed mostly of Americans, some Germans, and Swedes; arms in good conditions; records not in good shape, but will be attended to; discipline good; military courtesy fair." The following year, the Inspector General reported: "This company has made more progress than any other company in the Regiment and is by far the best drilled." The following year, however, he reported: "Company not in as good condition as expected, and has undoubtedly retrograded since last year when it was considered the `crack' company in the Second Regiment."

The first company commander was Captain E.A. Barns, who resigned on January 2, 1886, and was succeeded by Captain Henri De Witt.

Company K attended its first summer encampment at the Fair Grounds in Faribault for one week in June 1885. "The supplies were purchased by a non-commissioned officer under the supervision of the company commander, the men paying for the supplies out of their pay, $1.50 a day." Two officers and 33 men, out of the total company strength of three officers and 49 men, attended the encampment.

The first record of K Company serving in an emergency is found in an account of a riot of several hundred workers employed on the public sewers of Duluth. The city police "were driven into an open sewer and forced to fight for their lives." Captain De Witt, hastening double time to the scene with 44 men of the company, "dispersed the mob at the point of the bayonet and rescued the police and the laborers without firing a shot."

Meanwhile, there was activity of the Vermilion Range. Charlemagne Tower, a Philadelphia capitalist, had become interested in iron ore deposits there in 1875. He sent geologist Professor A.H. Chester of Hamilton College to the range (Stuntz accompanied him), and the report was so favorable that Tower organized the Minnesota Iron Company and began to mine ore. To transport ore to the lake, the company built a railroad, the Duluth and Iron Range, from the mines to Two Harbors. In July 1884, the first shipment of iron in this region was carried over the road to be sent down the lakes on the steamers *Heckla* and *Ironton*. Before the season was over, 62,000 tons had been shipped.

The following year, a connecting link of the Duluth and Iron Range was built from Two Harbors to Duluth. Another railroad entered the city that year, the Chicago, St. Paul, Minneapolis, and Omaha, the first railroad train over a bridge across the St. Louis River. Crowds welcomed the first passenger train on this line when it arrived over the Northern Pacific tracks, July 6, 1885. The next year, the "Omaha" had its own tracks and depot. Other railroad news - sleeping cars were operated from Duluth to Minneapolis and Chicago.

By 1886, Duluth had recovered from the depression of '73. Its population was approximately 35,000. The commerce in the Duluth-Superior harbors totaled 1,903,565 tons valued at $37,195,660. One new commodity was lumber, first carried in 1881. Arrivals and departures of ships, of which about 25 percent were powered by wind and sail, numbered 2,337. Steel ships over 300 feet in length were just making their appearance.

The Duluth District of the United States Engineers established an office and a vessel yard in Duluth, September 21, 1886. The office consisted of two rooms in the Fargusson Building (now the Northland). The office was later moved to the Providence Building. Captain James B. Quinn was appointed the first district engineer with a staff of five civilian employees. John H. Darling was the principal civilian engineer until his retirement in 1913.

Improvements were being made in the harbor. The channel bottoms had not always been kept free from shoals, so vessels had a bit of difficulty navigating the harbor. An early account says that very early one morning in 1884 the citizens of Duluth were aroused by such a loud and prolonged whistling of a vessel that they rushed down the docks to learn the trouble. They angry captain told them "I just wanted to show you folks the kind of harbor you have." The natural entrance was a winding channel over a shifting sand bar which had an available depth varying from nine to eleven feet. The water in the bays was eight to nine feet in depth. In 1886, the controlling depth was established at 16 feet.

One of the unsolved mysteries of Lake Superior occurred in the eighties, when the *Manistee* disappeared. The *Manistee,* a cargo and passenger ship, had seen much hard service on the lakes since she first entered the Duluth harbor in the early seventies. On a Friday morning in mid-November, the sturdy craft left Duluth bound for Cleveland, in the face of a rising northeaster. After battling the waves for hours, the ship put in at Bayfield, where it was stormbound for six days. Then, learning that other ships had weathered the storm safely, the captain ordered his boat out, "though the waves were perpendicular walls and the wind a swirling gale." Twice, he attempted to leave the harbor and had to return to port, and each time some of the more fearful passengers left the ship to proceed by train. At midnight, the *Manistee* again left port with 23 persons, including the crew, aboard. "The storm was a roaring hurricane, and the waves were as high as mountains, but the craft sailed boldly away." - never to be heard of again. It is thought the *Manistee* went down somewhere below the Apostle Islands.

Land for the Duluth Life Saving Station was donated by the City of Duluth to the Life Saving Service on June 19, 1886, for a consideration of $1.00. The plot, known as Franklyn Square, was on Minnesota Point. On July 29, 1890, the City of Duluth gave a warranty deed, but this was not recorded until 1894.

The first mention of this station is in the "Annual Report of the Life Saving Service For the Fiscal Year Ending June 30, 1894" under "Establishment of Stations," which says regarding stations built: "Two others have been built, and now are receiving their equipment, one at Duluth, Minnesota, and one at Portsmouth, North Carolina." The 1895 Annual Report states "The new stations at Duluth, Minnesota, and Portsmouth, North Carolina, which are mentioned in the last annual report are receiving their equipments, have been manned and put in operation xxx." The station was listed in that report for the first time unde the Tenth Life Saving District.

Vessels had been stranded in the locality in 1885 and 1888 and two were recorded as stranded during 1895. One of these to who aid the new life saving station crew came was the schooner *Sam Flint*, of Port Huron, Michigan, which became disabled one mile north by east of the new station. The vessel was skippered by a Captain Stevens and was 499 tons burdened. It was proceeding to Duluth from Tonawanda, N.Y., with a cargo of copper ore valued at $10,000. The vessel itself was valued at $12,000. It was salvaged by the life saving crew and a tug. All nine persons on board were saved. The loss was estimated at $100.

In 1886, a great activity was experienced in real estate transactions. The village had a carrier mail system with four carriers, Henry Clow, Irvin Moore, Tom Nolan, and John Frizzel. One carrier served Superior Street residences and business houses from Seventh Avenue East to Second Avenue East, making these trips daily. The first flourmill was erected R.S. Munger and ran night and day to produce 250 barrels of flour a day. A regular fire department was established. The Point of Rocks was cut through and West Superior Street was graded. Telegraph wires were strung on Superior and Michigan streets by the North American Telegraph Company. And the Chamber of Commerce was reorganized again, this time filing articles of incorporation.

The village had made such tremendous strides that in 1887 it became a city again, with a charter permitting it to extend its boundaries to the former city limits. The village mayor, John B. Sutphin, was reelected mayor of the city; Fred J. Voss was treasurer; E.P. Martin, municipal judge; and Alfred Jacques, special municipal judge. The city was divided into six wards. The mayor and aldermen each received an annual salary of $300. The first meeting place of the council under the new chapter took place March 22, 1887. The last of the old bonds were retired in April.

Now that Duluth was a city again, it was scarcely dignified to hold council meetings over a saloon. It needed a city hall commensurate with its new status, so it immediately bought a site at Second Avenue East and Superior Street, and started construction on the building now occupied by an electrical shop.

Since the condition of Superior Street was so bad that "horses were mired right in the business section of the city," the council ordered the street paved with cedar blocks. Other city improvements included the construction of the first fire-hall, at First Avenue East and Third Street, and the establishment of a fire-alarm system. The new organized Board of Public Works surveyed "a driveway along the face of the hill," designated as the Terrace Drive, but now known as Boulevard Drive, a part of the Skyline Parkway.

In its first year as a reborn city, Duluth turned over the title to the ship canal to the Federal Government, and the harbor became known as the Duluth-Superior harbor.

This was the year in which the Duluth Clearing House was established, as well as two new banks - the First National and the St. Louis County State Bank.

With the coming of "lumberjacks", railroad men, miners, and other homeless men, the work of the Bethel was extended, and a building for the mission was erected on Lake Avenue. Dr. C.C. Salter had given up his pastorate of the Pilgrim Congregational Church in 1886, to become Chaplain of the organization.

Railroads popped up again in 1888. The *Duluth Daily News* announced the coming of the Duluth, South Shore, and Atlantic as "Duluth's declaration of commercial independence" since Duluthians could travel east without going to the Twin Cities or Chicago. The line followed the South Shore to the Sault, where it connected with the Canadian Pacific. The paper also announced the reorganization of the St. Paul and Manitoba by building the Eastern Minnesota road, bringing the Manitoba system directly into Duluth; the beginning of construction on the Duluth and Winnipeg; and the Red River Valley line from Winnipeg to the boundary, connecting with the Northern Pacific. Work was again started on the Northern Pacific, but there was no celebration such as there had been at Kokomo in 1870. Duluth worked out plans for the entrance of any road into the city, under a charter "which insures unobstructed access to the center of the city to all roads."

The *Daily Tribune* of February 8, 1888, says: "Captain Quinn of the United States Engineers' Office has received a bill covering the construction of a bridge across the canal entrance. The bridge is to be constructed to provide for passage of railway trains, wagons, street cars, vehicles, and foot passengers." New items relative to the bridge appeared frequently for the next sixteen years.

The city council and the Chamber of Commerce working together established the park system, laying out Cascade Park of 41 acres; Chester Park, 69 acres; and Lincoln

Park, "following the banks of Miller's Creek at the West End". Portland Square at Tenth Avenue East and Fourth Street was already a park. The following year, 1889, a Board of Park Commissioners was created by the state legislature. Officers included Hon. W.K. Rogers, president; J.H. Upham, vice president; F.W. Paine, secretary and treasurer; and R.S. Munger and Mayor, ex-officio. A special election was held in which the vote was practically unanimous for a $300,000 bond to finance work on the park and the Terrace Drive. This was the first election in Duluth using the Australian system of balloting. An article in the *News* on the latter project states: "There is only one other drive in the world worthy of comparison with it - the Corniche Drive along the Mediterranean.

In 1888, the city council gave a franchise to the Duluth Electric Light Company to install lights on Superior Street.

The Sisters of St. Benedict established St. Mary's Hospital at Twentieth Avenue West, when another epidemic of typhoid fever brought a need for more hospital service. The building is now used for St. Anne's Home.

A new village sprang up in 1888 when the West Duluth Land Company started West Duluth. This was an industrial section "on the level", with the Duluth Steel Company and the Minnesota Car Company starting in business immediately. When the village was incorporated, it included the townsite of Oneota.

Only one blot seems to have stained the city's claim to being a modern metropolis. It had pirates - the Pirates of Park Point. The Point was sparsely inhabited in those days. There were few houses and not a sign of a road - only sand dunes and scrub pines. The pirates, about six young fellows, built themselves a cave near the present site of Oatka, a strategic spot with open water on either side. Although they lacked the standard equipment of pirates - dashing mustaches, bloody cutlasses, gay headgear, and

116

"pieces of eight" - they conducted themselves in legendary style, plundering vessels, sawmills, and warehouses. But R.A. Gray could not appreciate the romance of pirate life when the fellows tried to steal his lumber. "The pirates had a large sailboat and managed to escape in the darkness, but Mr. Gray found their lair and captured the gang after a fierce battle and landed them in the penitentiary." Exit, the Pirate of Park Point.

The riot of 1889 caused gunfire to be heard in the city streets. Strikers of a local contracting company, refused a raise in wages, demanded that workers on a job for the city also strike. These men refused to quit work and the strikers refused to cease picketing, so the foreman called the police, who disbanded the picket line. The following day, the strikers, "reinforced by a crowd of ruffians from this city and Superior, armed with guns and revolvers and rocks", came again, and again the police were called. This time, an all-out fight ensued. "Every officer of the force took part in the riot, and every officer was either shot or sustained bruises during the strike." Company K was called out, and after a short time the trouble came to an end. The policemen received medals for their efforts, and the labor organizers established the Federated Trades Council of Duluth under a charter of the American Federation of Labor. The officials of the new organization were: E. Applehagen, president; D.S. Blanchard, vice president; J.H. Baker, treasurer; Edward M. Grace, secretary; Robert Chichester, sergeant-at-arms; and M. Shanahan, M.E. Terry, and Archie McLean, trustees.

In the last year of the decade, Oneota joined with the city. The village of Park Point refused to become a part of Duluth until it could have a bridge across the canal. New Duluth was platted for a village, with the principal street named Commonwealth Avenue. A syndicate, composed of Norton, Webber, Stewart, Hudson, Jacques, Lovett, and Brown, was capitalized for a million dollars. The men could envision an industrial section on this flat location with five miles of waterfront. Morgan Park and Riverside were included in New Duluth.

The Grand Opera House burned that year, but the Masonic Temple Association immediately erected the six-story building on the east side of Second Avenue East for their temple and the Temple Opera House. It also housed the library. The grand opening of the theatre was held on October 21-22, with Miss Coghlen appearing in "Jocelyn". The *Daily News* gives a description of the ornate splendor of the interior of the theatre: "The foyer is richly dressed. The windows are curtained in gorgeous vallours in old gold. Two of its fine doors are covered in vallours in sold Spanish red portieres and valances, and the other three are in Spanish red and old gold valances, all hung on brass poles."

The *News* boasted: "Duluth's fame as a summer resort has spread like a wildfire within the past two years. Duluth has hotel accommodations second to none." The new built Spalding Hotel, with its huge lobby and high-ceilinged rooms, was opened July 11, "with appropriate ceremonies."

Duluth seems to have taken up culture. The Cecelian Society was organized, and the Mozart Association was formed "for encouragement of musical culture." The Saturday Club (a women's organization), the Chatauqua Circle, and several debating societies were established "for those in literary tastes." An additional levy of one-half mill was placed on taxable property for construction of a public library to replace the one destroyed in the Grand Opera House fire.

Social life was not eschewed. The Kitchi Gammi was the principal social club, occupying extensive quarters in a building on Second Avenue West and Second Street. The Boat Club, organized in 1885, had a clubhouse and boathouse on the Northern Pacific slip; it owned a complete equipment of shells and was laying the foundations for later national and international fame. Northland Country Club was incorporated and purchased 100 acres for golf, archery, tennis, and trap shooting.

The Eastern Minnesota railroad ran its first trains between Duluth and St. Paul on June 16, 1889. "The opening of the new route was signalized by the announcement of an entirely new schedule of freight rates, independent of Chicago lines."

The Manitoba road established the Northern Steamship Line with six ships - the *Northern Light, Northern Wave, Northern King, Northern Queen, North Wind, and North Star.* All alike, these steel ships attained a speed of seventeen miles an hour and carried a cargo of 2,700 tons, or about 90,000 bushels of wheat. The American Steel Barge Company of Duluth continued to build the whaleback type of steel freight boats which Captain Alexander McDougall had invented the previous year, when he built the famous `101'. In 1899, the `102' and `103' were completed and the `104' was nearly finished. This revolutionary type of freighter was ridiculed by sailors, who called it "pig" for its resemblance to that animal. But the whalebacks, which had a carrying capacity of 3000 tons, proved their efficiency as lake boats. Lake freighters that year took East 120,000,000 bushels of grain and 7,000,000 tons of ore. Need was seen for enlarging St. Mary's Canal, and a delegation from the Chamber of Commerce attended a two-day convention at the Sault to push the project.

Fishing was becoming a big industry. A. Booth and Sons bought out Cooley, La Vacque, and Company, which operated the *Siskiwit,* a boat built by Captain McDougall. The Booth organization employed about 120 fishermen along the North Shore. The fishing steamers made the round trip from Duluth to Port Arthur, a distance of 400 miles, in three days, including the numerous stops along the shore. It is recorded that in one year, 1886, the catch was about 1,900,000 pounds of herring, siscowet, lake trout, and white fish.

Within the city, construction was begun on the Fourth Street carline. The longest incline in the world was started in West Duluth, 7,300 feet long with a rise of 600 feet. It connected West Duluth with Bay View Heights. First Avenue West (for six blocks neared the heart of the city) and Michigan Street were paved with cedar blocks. Many public buildings were erected, including the Manhattan, Palladio, churches, and schools, as well as 451 new homes. Land was condemned for a new Union depot. A patrol wagon was purchased. And discussions continued on the feasibility of a tunnel or a bridge under or over the canal.

In ten years, the total banking capital of Duluth had increased from $50,000 to $2,625,179. Population had grown from 3,000 to 33,000.

The *Daily News* proclaimed: "In all the marvels of city building, the world has seen nothing that equaled the record that Duluth has made...It is today the fifth maritime port of the United States; it handles more coal than any other lake city, Chicago alone excepted; it leads all in its wheat and flour traffic; it is the ninth city in the Union in the extent of its lumber business; and as a financial center it ranks with those cities of four times its population...Duluth is emphatically a city of big things."

Others agreed with the *News*. An article by Frank Wilkeson in the *New York Times* said in part: "These Duluth men seized every opportunity to develop their town and the region which is tributary to it. If an iron vein was discovered, they thrust their hands deeply in their pockets and developed the mine and began to ship ore. If they needed more ships and better ships, they boldly incurred indebtedness and built them. Time came when their hotel accommodation was not sufficient. They built and furnished the Spalding Hotel at a cost of $500,000. They needed steel and iron works. They built them."

Joaquin Miller echoed the sentiment in an article about Duluth which appeared in the *New York Independent*:

"They are going to build a city here as big as Chicago. And when they have got a city built in Duluth as big as Chicago, they will begin right off, the very next day, and build a city a great deal bigger than Chicago...Do not quite despise this wandering scribe when he says that Duluth is to be the greatest city this side of the Rocky Mountains."

Such articles also appeared in 1889 in the *London Financial Times,* November 22; *New York Observer,* January 24; *New York Evening Post,* April; *Harper's Weekly,* August 17; *and Cosmopolitan,* February.

Duluth entered the nineties, a city with a checkered past, a prosperous past, and a glowing future.

CHAPTER VIII

The Nineties

Iron is the keynote of the nineties, and to Duluth, iron is inevitably associated with the Merritt brothers, whose story Paul de Kruif tells in his book `Seven Iron Men'.

It will be remembered that the Merritts were a pioneer family who settled in Oneota. They remained here during the vicissitudes of the village and city, leaders in the development of Duluth. The seven sons helped in the struggle for existence, lumbering, working in the saw mill, farming, fishing, sailing, and building boats - doing any work that came their way. Remembering their father's prophecy, they also cocked an eye for iron ore as the ranged the countryside.

In 1887, Cassius was head explorer when M.B. Harrison and W.K. Rogers ran a survey for a railway line from Duluth to Winnipeg. In running the exploring line, he discovered a boulder of iron ore on the Mesaba Range, near the present site of Mountain Iron. He brought a sample of the ore, "the first chunk of pure ore taken off the Mesaba," to Duluth, where it was found to assay 65 percent iron.

Alfred and Cassius reported to State Auditor Braden that they believed the land held in trust by the state for schools was of great value. The auditor appointed the two men and George C. Stone to decide what price should be paid as royalty on land leased by the state. This committee, in spite of pressure to place the royalty as low as ten cents a ton, unanimously recommended 25 cents a ton, and the agreement was made.

In his unpublished autobiography, Alfred Merritt says, "the year 1889 the first work was done on what is now the Mountain Iron Mine. I took a crew of six men in by the way of Tower on March 17. Started from Tower with three dog trains, and we were the dogs. We went in by way of Pike River, and then to Rice Lake, then to Mountain Iron. We dug test pits and finally drilled...We found that we were too far north for the ore and on going south found the ore on Section 3 and 4, directly south of our first work, the summer of 1890."

With K.D. and A.S. Chase, Donald Grant, and others, the Merritts acquired titles to many of the best iron ore locations by lease from the state. Mining organizations, each capitalized for millions, were formed to develop the mines - companies in which the Merritts held the controlling interest. These were combined in Consolidated Iron Mines Company.

The discovery of the ore fields led to a stampede of men to Duluth, similar to the influx of thirty-four years before, when the gold rush was on. Woodbridge and Pardee say: "The hotels were crowded day and night with speculators, and men made paper fortunes in a few hours or minutes. In the first flush of the craze nothing was too wild or impractical to attract the greedy investors. Even the most conservative men were caught by the craze and invested their savings in all kinds of schemes. The woods were full of prospectors for the previous metal...There was no holding Duluth, thinking in millions, dealing in futures, depending on prospects, building on expectations.

Through the swamps and forests went the prospectors, carrying on their backs equipment and supplies. Test pitting was carried on with bucket and windlass. Men marveled that mining could be done merely by stripping the surface and scooping out ore.

A railroad was necessary to carry the iron ore to Lake Superior. Neither the Northern Pacific nor the St. Paul and Duluth could be interested in the project. The officials could not see any future in carrying ore. The Duluth and Winnipeg, however, would make a traffic connection at Stony Brook if the mines would build a railroad from Mountain Iron to that point, a distance of 48 miles. So the Merritts organized a railroad company, the Duluth, Missabe, and Northern, with Alfred president and Leonidas vice president. Needing more financial backing, they enlisted the Rockefeller interests to advance money. The road was first used in 1892 and completed to Duluth in 1893. The panic of '93, with its commercial disasters, combined with delays in getting money from the east, made it impossible for the mining companies to pay back money when demanded. Consequently, the Rockefeller interests got control of the entire enterprise - mines and railroad. Later, Carnegie took over most of the Minnesota mines for the United States Steel Corporation, and his associate, Henry W. Oliver, became head of the Oliver Iron Mining Company.

In regard to the Rockefeller deal, Alfred Merritt writes: "Our loyalty to Duluth was the main reason for our building into Duluth. It proved to be a poor move for us, because in order to get the money, we got mixed up with John D. Rockfeller and his gang, and in the end we lost all our interest in the road and mines. I myself owned one-tenth of the Duluth Missabe and Northern Railroad, besides 120 one thousand-dollar bonds of the railroad and also all my interest in the mines. It was all stolen. My interest in the Lake Superior Consolidated Iron Mines Company, which controlled the railroad and the different mining companies, was turned into the United States Steel Company when it was formed at $7,500,000. The dividends on my share of the railroad stock along has been over $800,000 several different years. The courts said that it was a fraud. I say it was a plain steal.

"Naturally, one will ask, how did he do it. It was simply a case of our having confidence in him. We were working away in the interests of the company, getting traffic contracts, fully trusting him. We woke up too late."

Certain themes run through the annals of Duluth in the nineties: trouble with the Gas and Water Company; a bridge over the canal; a bridge to Superior; the Point of Rocks; and a deep-sea waterway.

An entire book could be written on the negotiations between the city council and the Gas and Water Company, with a chorus of complaints and epithets by the citizens of Duluth. The whole history seems to be one of broken water mains, damage by floods when mains burst, insufficient force to fight fires, analyses of the water and blame on the company for typhoid epidemics. In the majority of the meeting of the council, the Gas and Water Company popped up. This continued from 1882 till 1898, when the council, after an election in which the voters expressed their wishes, completed negotiations to buy out the company. Since then the Water and Light Department has been owned by the city.

It took even longer to procure a bridge over the canal. Council records and newspapers give accounts of many plans for a draw-bridge, lift-bridge, or roller bridge, or for a wood and steel tunnel, but all walk talk until the next century. However, the village of Park Point remained hopeful, and joined the city in 1890. A free rowboat ferry operated twenty-four hours a day for the new part of the city. In 1895 a steam ferry was put on the job.

125

Park Point had a street railway in 1890, unlike any other in the country. Stretching across the narrow strip of land for three and a half miles, it furnished the only means of transportation for the residents of the Point, since there was no road or street. On the single track the small cars, pulled by horses, carried all freight and passengers. Because of the sandy soil, planks were placed between the tracks so that the horses could have a footing. The cars made five or six trips a day in the summer, and suspended service in the winter, when supplies were brought in over the ice. In 1899, the streetcar was electrified.

The bridge to Superior was a subject for controversy entered into by residents on both sides of the St. Louis River. In 1890, a bill was introduced in Congress for a bridge between Superior and Duluth "to provide for the passage of railway trains, and at the option of the corporation by which it may be built, it may be used for the passage of wagons and vehicles of all kinds, for the transit of animals and for foot passengers for such reasonable rates of toll as may be approved from time to time by the Secretary of War." The following year the Senate passed a bill authorizing the construction of the bridge. There followed bickerings and mass meetings in Duluth and in Superior. Arguments centered around the kind of bridge and the place where it should be built. In 1893, a committee of men from both cities worked together on the problems and it was agreed that a combination bridge be erected between Rice's Point and Connor's Point.

The inter-state bridge was completed and dedicated July 13, 1897. City bands played and about 4000 people attended the formal dedication, of which Colonel Charles H. Graves was chairman. The *New Tribune* called the affair a "steel wedding of fortunes of Duluth and Superior."

Dedicatory speeches show the type of oratory rampant in those days. Mayor Starkweather of Superior declaimed: "The marriage of Helen of Troy was not more pregnant with gorgeous possibilities than the one we now celebrate. Amid all the pomp and circumstance let the ceremony that shall join our two cities be complete...To my right, the bride, decked in the glittering garlands of young cityhood, with her eight systems of railroads, her steel plant, her shipyard, her 36 miles of paved streets, her magnificent system of sewerage, her unsurpassed elevator capacity, her immense flour mills, her docks and other industries, together with her unconquered and unconquerable spirit of progress and proficiency proclaim that from her munificent endowment shall come homes to harbor the prairies' prolific progeny. Aye, see the queen of destiny as she rides the sea of this busy, restless century of ours. See the church spires, piercing the cerulean blue of God's overhanging heavens; sing hosannas to Christianity triumphant.

"The left the groom, who from his castle in the clouds comes to meet the bride upon the sea's highway - Duluth! Duluth! peerless in his advancement, born in the lap of fame, and baptized in the scroll of futurity during the reign of Proctor Knott the first."

Starkweather regretted the toll on the bridge. "But the cities can buy this huge structure. We can and should own it."

The speech concluded: "I declare these two cities joined together by this imperishable bond of steel, and let no man, for selfish purpose, attempt to keep them asunder."

Excerpts from the speech of Mayor Truelson of Duluth show that he, too, had a way with words: "This day shall be recorded in the pages of history, and coming generations shall speak of this day of union between the two great cities at the Head of the Lakes...When the bride locates new industries, the groom shall come and rejoice with her, when the groom adds to the future greatness of his city, the dear girl will be happy with him."

Speaking of the toll, Truelson said: "Love should be free, free as the air we breathe, and our happiness will not be complete until this bridge is made free to every man, woman, and child, and when that is accomplished our union will be complete...Let us purchase this bridge just as soon as we can."

The controversy over the Point of Rocks was - and is - a local thing. The *Duluth Herald* of April 7, 1892 says: "The Board of Public Works has decided that the overhanging rocks at the Point of Rocks on Superior Street and Twelfth Avenue West are dangerous, and that part of the cliff will be cut away." A portion of the rocks had already been cut through in 1887. Since then, parts have been whacked away at intervals, as a loose rock would fall and frighten people. At one time, the city bought a rock crusher and went to work in earnest, gouging out rock for a year. At other times, a plan comes up for cutting the whole thing away in order to build another street. There are some residents of Duluth who believe the Point of Rocks divides the interests and sentiments of those living on either side, so that Duluth is a divided city. They advocate the removal of the rocks in order that Duluth may act as a whole. Others call the rock a tourist attraction; and many say the removal would be too expensive. Council proceedings still refer to the removal of the Point of Rocks - and the rocks still stand.

The Great Lakes-St. Lawrence tide water project did not seem far distant in 1892, when President Harrison's message to Congress advocated the deep waterway. The *Duluth Herald* of October 8 of that year contained an editorial on "a strong movement to establish deep-water communication between the lakes and the Atlantic Ocean." This is the waterway first projected by George Washington. In 1792, after he had obtained the passage of an act of incorporation by New York State for constructing a waterway between the Hudson River and Lake Erie, he said "The people of the entire interior, from the Pacific Coast to the Allegheny Mountains, are interested in securing a deep-waterway to the sea which will permit the passage of ocean-going vessels." The proposed waterway would consist of 33 miles of canals between Lake Ontario and the sea, the channel at Montreal. It would bring ocean vessels to Duluth, providing world markets for the interior. Through the years, the St. Lawrence waterway has been a dream of Duluth and the surrounding territory.

Great strides were made in city improvements in the nineties in opening up new streets and avenues, paving, installing a system of sewerage, and extending streetcar lines. The viaduct was built over Lake Avenue and the swamps were reclaimed to make more room for the wholesale district. Streets were lighted with 183 arc lights. A new jail adjacent to the city hall was completed to replace the one built in 1882, and prisoners were removed there for Christmas. Building was going on at a great rate and manufacturing and business houses were starting up in the city.

Lakeside, West Duluth, Fond du Lac, and New Duluth were annexed in this decade, giving the city a length of approximately thirty miles.

In 1890, the streetcars were first electrified, and by the following year all streetcars in the city except the ones on Park Point were run by electricity. The *Tribune* of November 4, 1890 says: "A trial trip was made last night over the streetcar line from the car barn at Eleventh Avenue West to Eighth Avenue East. A rate of twelve miles per hour was attained. The company expects to have at least three cars on the Superior Street line by the end of this week." A rate of speed of six miles per hour was determined upon for the new cars.

The name of London Avenue was changed to London Road. Here was some property bought by a London Syndicate which invested $1,000,000 in Duluth property in 1889. Boston and Philadelphia capitalists also bought real estate. Even today, a person purchasing property in Duluth frequently has to get in touch with agents of some titled person in Long or of men in the East.

The Duluth Public Library was formally organized in 1890, with a reading room and a circulation department of about 2,000 volumes. By 1895, 18,000 volumes were in circulation. Quarters were rented in the Masonic Temple building.

In 1891, the St. Paul and Duluth and the Northern Pacific railroads completed construction of the $400,000 union depot still in use today. The old building had been used since the first train arrived in Duluth 21 years earlier. The Hardy School on Woodland Avenue was finished. The cornerstone of Central high school was laid, June 8, "before the assembled school children of the city and a large gathering of citizens. The noted orator, Ignatius Donnelly, gave the principal address. Superintendent Denfeld, in preliminary remarks, pointed out that by the end of the year Duluth will have nineteen schools costing more than a million dollars."

An incline railway was completed that year, running from Superior Street to Eighth Street at Seventh Avenue West. The line, built at a cost of $250,000, was 3,000 feet long and contained 1,300 tons of rolled steel plates and beams. The fact that the streets had already been graded caused a problem in construction which was overcome by sinking the tracks between great plate girders five feet high. Engineering also overcame the problem that in warm weather the steel expanded so that the structure was thirty inches longer than in cold weather. It took 16 minutes to make the ascent of 500 feet. The cars had a floor space of 16 by 40 feet. Running on cables, one car would ascend while the other descended the hill, stopping at a station on each street. The fronts of the cars were glassed in, so a ride on the incline afforded a splendid panoramic view of the city and harbor. Although built for the convenience of residents on the hills, the incline was especially popular with tourists, who would invariably take a trip on it for the scenic beauty it unfolded to them. The line was in use until 1939, when the use of busses for city transportation made it unnecessary.

The Lyceum Building, with its life-sized stone lions on either side of the high, wide steps of the imposing entrance (the lions are now at the zoo), was built in 1891 - "the best opera house west of Chicago." It was one of the few theatres with a stage large enough for the complete production of the chariot race scene in "Ben Hur". Duluth was a "show town". Broadway plays went on the road in those days, and included Duluth in their itinerary. Show bills for 1892 advertise at the Temple and the Lyceum Mr. and Mrs. Sidney Drew and Julia Marlowe as well as Primrose and West, Lew Dockstader's Minstrels and Mrs. General Tom Thumb and her Lilliputians.

Another place of entertainment and recreation was the Duluth Pavilion, built next to the power house at the top of the incline. It was opened, July 2, 1892 by the manager, H.M. Barnett. The Pavilion was a two-story building, 100 by 300 feet, overlooking the city. On the first floor were a promenade, refreshment hall, and kitchen. A hall seating 2,500 people occupied the second floor. There were open balconies and an observation platform facing the lake. The city band played there every afternoon and evening; Professor Baldwin made his balloon ascensions; the Cherry Sisters gave a concert; Robert Mantell, matinee idol, appeared in drama; and other artists were on the boards. The Pavilion burned in 1901, when the power house caught on fire. In the holocaust, an incline car, its steel cables melted by the intense heat, dashed headlong from the top of the incline to Superior Street.

In 1892, according to the *Daily News*, Duluth was a city of 50,000, with 41 churches, 34 public, private, and parochial schools, and 100 saloons.

The *Tribune* was sold to the *News* and became the *News-Tribune*. In 1892, the Salvation Army was organized under the command of Staff Captain Howells. In 1893 Superior was connected by telephone cable across the bay, and in 1899 a long distance wire connected Cloquet, Carlton, and Duluth. By 1897 there were 1,155 telephone customers.

Issues of the *Herald* that year devoted much space to the completion of the Duluth, Missabe, and Northern railroad. In planning a celebration of the road, an editorial declared, "It (the railroad) will be of immense value to us, for it is controlled by Duluth capital and will be run in the interests of Duluth as far as any railroad can be run in the interests of any one city." On October 6, the railroad was opened by officials, who took their guests over it. At Mountain Iron, the party inspected the 40 various test pits before the return trip. Eleven days later, ten cars loaded with ore were shipped over the track to an ore dock at Allouez. One car of 20 tons came to the Union depot so that Duluth could gaze upon the ore and dream of the future it would bring them. The following year, the first Missabe dock was erected at Thirty-fourth Avenue West, and the railway was built into Duluth.

The *Duluth Press* was a newcomer in the journalistic field, one of three newspapers in the country conducted by women. It was published by Cody and Wetmore. Cody was "Buffalo Bill's" wife and Wetmore his sister, who lived in the Cody home in West Duluth.

The Hartman Electric Company bought out the old Duluth Electric Power and Light Company in 1892. Says the *Daily News:* "The magnitude of the electric light business is perhaps not understood by many. The two companies now have in operation 465 arc lights and about 12,000 incandescents. Wires went under ground that year on Superior Street, with a subway built for electric, telephone, and telegraph wires. By 1895, electric power was available at all hours of the day and night.

The Duluth Street Railway Company, on September 17, 1892, set in motion at their new Eleventh Avenue East power house, the largest drive wheel in the United States, according to a local paper, which declared, "This is a new era for Duluth in rapid transit. The power house serves as a model for other and larger cities."

Everything in Duluth was big in the nineties - even the storms. The blizzard of '92 was one to be remembered. On the 9th of March, the morning broke bright and clear, but almost immediately the sky was overcast, the cold became intense, and a thick curtain of snow fell swirled by a wind that became a gale. People who had arrived at their work had to remain there. To go out of doors was almost certain death, since there was practically no visibility, and one immediately lost all sense of direction. The storm lasted three days. The city was nearly buried in snowdrifts from eight to ten feet high packed so hard that they could bear the weight of a heavy person. Houses were snowed in so that people could leave them only by crawling through a second story window onto the snow. Many residents of Duluth suffered from cold and hunger and a few met death by freezing in this blizzard.

Another unpleasant incident of the year was the "boodling case." Three aldermen received envelopes containing $200 each. They turned the money over to the mayor. Then came conjectures as to who gave the money and for what bribery it was intended. The matter finally went to the grand jury, but after calling in every group that might have a purpose in bribery (including the newspapers and the Gas and Water Company), the jury could name no corporation or individual as being concerned. The boodling case remains a mystery.

The city had much to be proud of in '92, in spite of slight setbacks. For instance, there was the launching of Captain Alexander McDougall's passenger whaleback, the *Christopher Columbus* at the shipyard of the American Steel

Barge Company. This, the first passenger boat of the whaleback fleet, was built for the World's Fair excursions at Chicago. Luxuriously outfitted, it had five decks and could carry 5,000 passengers at a speed of 20 miles an hour. Bands turned out, and several hundred out-of-town guests as well as local residents attended the launching.

By 1890, Duluth was gaining recognition for its schools. The enrollment was 2808, and there were 65 teachers, four of them college graduates. An additional enrollment of 484 was found in the evening school, which operated five nights a week for pupils between the ages of 12 and 30. It was this year that Duluth inaugurated a free textbook system, leading the state in that action.

With no central school timepiece or bell, few telephones and no radio, dismissals for storms presented a problem which Denfeld suggested could be solved by having the East and the West fire departments give signals.

The present organization of boundaries of districts, co-terminus with the city districts, was adopted in 1891. At the same time the present set-up of the board was organized, a board of nine members, three elected each year.

Ten new schools were built in the last decade of the century - Bryant, Central, Emerson, Glen Avon, Irving, Jefferson, Jackson, Longfellow, Lakeside and Lowell (rebuilt in 1911).

On October 22, 1892, Central High School was dedicated. The building was equipped for teaching manual training, home economics, stenography, typewriting, drawing, vocal music, and physical culture, as well as academic subjects. Although the Westminster chimes were not yet installed, the school with its distinctive Romanesque architecture, 230 tower, elegant chandeliers, and sweeping stairways with wrought iron banisters attracted representatives from boards of education all over the country. When John W. Noble, Secretary of the Interior in President Harrison's cabinet, saw the school, he said, "Your new high school is the finest building of its kind I ever saw. There is no public school building equal to it in the United States."

The emphasis in schools was changing from an academic to a practical education. Manual training and "domestic economy" were already in the school curriculum, and agriculture was soon to be introduced. The high school course dropped Greek, but the principal, John Loman, continued giving instruction in the subject after school hours so that students could complete requirements for entrance to certain colleges. By the turn of the century, the high school had added a commercial and an English course "for some who want to take a high school course without any foreign language." There was growing interest in modern languages, but Latin was extensively elected.

Other local schools were doing a flourishing business, also. The Duluth Yale school was continuing at 926 East Second Street. The Benedictine Sisters, under the direction of Rev. Mother Scholastica, operated a boarding and day academy, the Institute of the Sacred Heart, in rented quarters at Munger Terrace. This academy, founded in 1894, was the beginning of the College of St. Scholastica. In 1898, the academy moved into a new red brick building at Third Avenue East and Third Street, now a section of St. Mary's Hall. From the first catalogue of the Sacred Heart Institute comes this item: "Pupils in the graduating class should wear white Swiss, French lawn, or nun's veiling dresses, neatly and plainly made, with high neck and long sleeves; black or white boots and white kid gloves; all jewelry except brooch and ear-rings is prohibited. Failure to comply with the above will cause a pupil to forfeit her claim to academic honors."

The Benedictine Sisters also established St. Anthony, another parochial school, in 1891.

The Hardy School at Woodland, with its principals Kate Hardy and Anna R. Haire, continued from 1892 to

1895, when it became the Maynard School. According to the bulletin of this preparatory school for girls, the institution had "native teachers in French and German and special departments in arts and music." It offered "training in the Delsarte system of expression through its entire course...It affords instruction of the most careful sort in voice, articulation, gesture (including all movements used in expression, as facial expression, head gymnastics, gymnastics of trunk, of body, etc.), and in walking." Board and tuition were $500 a year.

Plans for a Normal School, forerunner of the Duluth Branch of the University of Minnesota, were being laid.

Newspaper stories in the files of 1892 will show that Duluth reflected the spirit of the "gay 90's."

The Fourth of July was celebrated in fine style that year. The day's schedule included a big parade down town; a program at the Pavilion, at which Mayor d'Autremont gave the principal address: celebrations at Lester Park and West Duluth; a Lutheran Field Day in which 5,000 participated; sports contests by the Duluth Turnverein; boat races in the harbor; and fireworks.

Duluth folks seem to have been sports-minded. A delegation of men from Duluth went to New Orleans to attend the Corbett-Sullivan fight September 1. Local newspapers devoted three columns - on the front page - to the 21 round fight in which the great John L. lost his title. The papers also gave baseball results in the Western League, as well as racing results at Washington Park, Chicago; Monmouth Park, Long Branch, New Jersey; East St. Louis Jockey Club and South Side Park, St. Louis, and Hamline Track, St. Paul. Much front-page space was given to Nancy Hanks, "Queen of the Turf," as she broke trotting records on the big tracks around the country.

Duluth had a West Duluth Driving Park, where Wheeler Field now stands. This was used for many types of outdoor recreation including Caledonian games. In 1892, the Duluth Driving Park Association, with G.G. Hartley president and R.F. Jones secretary, built another race track on Woodland Avenue. Businessmen closed their stores for the afternoon racing programs, and attended the race themselves, sitting in the opera seats in the grand stand. The track opened September 1, with an attendance of 3,000. Unfortunately, the electric cars had difficulty making the Woodland hill that day, so that many people were late for the first races. Another day, a fog rolled in and the last races on the program had to be canceled. S.L. Rice and Captain Sullivan were local owners of race horses with several entries each day. A special race for local horses only showed entries by owners Paul Sharvy, W.T. Bailey, T.B. Heimback, F.B. Daugherty, T.J. Walsh, J.B. Coulson, and G.W. Spar.

The Turnverein Club was an active athletic organization under the leadership of Max Alletzhauser. Over a thousand visitors came to Duluth for the great Turnfest. A large temporary building was erected on Park Point, where cots were installed for visiting athletes.

Annual regattas were held in the harbor for catboats, sloops and racing shells.

Skiing became more than a means of transportation in 1893, when the Trysil Ski Club was formed. The club was composed principally of Norwegians who were members of a local Norse club known as the "Idun" Lodge. This was the seventh ski club formed in the country, according to the files of the National Ski Association of America. John Iverson was the first president and John Norborg the secretary of the club. Local ski jumping competitions were held at Fourth Avenue West below Fourth Street. Among the early skiers were P. Eliasen, John Engen, Pete Wicklem, A. Syversen and John Aasenhus.

Duluthians were traveling, at home and abroad. Why not? Excursion rates to New York City were $27.50 round trip.

New York could have its Ward McAllister, Diamond Jim Brady, and the "400" - Duluth also had "society". Local papers wrote about receptions, yachting parties, tally-ho parties, and moonlight excursions. The center of society was West Third Street. When the D.G. Cutlers entertained at a reception at their home there, a reporter wrote "The spacious rooms of the elegant home each presented the appearance of a symposium of floral beauty, so tasteful and elaborate were the decorations."

A prize should probably go to the society reporter who wrote in the *Daily News:* "Fairy lamps trembled and twinkled through the evening shadows as the swaying trees nodded in unison with the harmony of the mandolins, which sent forth sweet sounds to the passing stranger as he paused to watch the fair young faces framed in the garlands of green beneath the nodding boughs, as the soft swish of trailing garments was heard amid the glad young voices." The occasion was a "reception tendered Mrs. J.B. Culver and her daughter Miss Ray, by Mr. and Mrs. W.R. Stone, after several years abroad, and also the occasion of the debut of the young lady." The Stone home "was decorated with rare curios, tapestries, bronzes, mosaics, and paintings." And the gowns! "Mrs. Culver was regal in a d'argent moire, one of Felix's most successful creations, with a court train and point duchesse lace." There were other little numbers: a Parisian robe of figured lace over ruby satin; embroidered lace adorned with gold passementerie and bouillon with diamonds; white silk with ostrich trimmings; and black grenediene embroidered with jewels.

Another panic hit the country in 1893, caused by the Baring failure in London and by droughts and invasions of insects at home. In spite of a general lack of employment and money, Duluth rode through - on iron and wheat.

In 1894, Frank Emery as given a contract to light the Park Point oil lamps at a salary of $27.75 per month. A new Federal Government building was constructed at the corner of Fifth Avenue West and First Street. New car barns were built at 26th Avenue West. The Omaha depot was erected. St. Mary's hospital moved from the present St. Anne's Home into new quarters at Fifth Avenue East and Third Street. The new building could accommodate 300 patients, and had "every appointment and arrangement known in modern hospital science." A Curling and Bicycle Rink was constructed on First Street at Third Avenue East. Improvements were made to the harbor and piers. The city took possession of a site for a new Carnegie library. The links and clubhouse for Northland Country Club were under construction. The Great Northern Power Company constructed a dam at Thompson to furnish electric power for Duluth. The Fosston railroad branch was opened, placing Duluth on a direct line with the Pacific Coast. The new water system with a pumping station at Lakewood was put into operation. And the *Northwest* arrived.

The *Northwest* was the first of four steel exclusively passenger steamers to run between Buffalo and Duluth in connection with the Great Northern railroad. It was a luxury boat. "The woodwork is of a rich mahogany finish with spirited carving, soft coloring, and a judicious use of gold. The grand saloon is an immense long apartment with sweeping lines and a lofty roof. The amber-tinted glass sheds a mellow light on the highly polished and carved mahogany; the relief work picked out in gold; the luxuriously upholstered furniture and sumptuous carpets. It has been the endeavor of the artist to impress one with a sense of refinement and elegance rather than show and glitter." The ship had 178 staterooms designed to carry 400 passengers. Its white sides stood up as high as a two-story building, and the ship made a speed of 22 miles an hour. Its great refrigerating plant was one of the features of the ship.

The *Northwest* arrived June 8, 1894. Over all public buildings in the city and all boats in the harbor, flags and colors were flying. Early in the morning, engine no. 1 of the

Great Northern Road, President James J. Hill's private iron horse, pulled into the Eastern Minnesota depot bearing his party of fourteen. Hill and his guests went out on a tug to meet the *Northwest*. At the dock and on the canal piers great crowds were gathered to welcome the boat, and the city band played. "At 2:30 the great boat steamed through the canal and blew her sonorous whistle. This was the signal for the greatest screaming of whistles ever heard in the harbor. Two of the Great Northern freighters were in the harbor and led the tooting." At 3:30 the ship steamed out on an excursion for its guests. In a ceremony on the forward part of the main deck, Colonel C.H. Graves presented a set of colors to Hill, and made a speech in which he said, in part: "Twenty years ago, Duluth rejoiced in its first boat line, which consisted of two small and uncertain boats...Today we see in our harbor the supreme triumph of modern marine architecture."

The following year, a sister ship, the *Northland*, was launched.

In 1896, the harbors of Duluth and Superior were united under the title Duluth-Superior Harbor by the River and Harbor Act of Congress. Since 1893, leading citizens of Duluth and Superior had been cooperating to secure harbor appropriations. In '95, they secured a congressional committee to examine and report on conditions. While making the inspection, the boat conveying the committee became fast on a mud flat. It has never been determined whether this incident was by accident or design. After a dull hour's wait, the vessel was pulled out by a tug. The committee reported, and dredging to a 20-foot depth was authorized.

Duluth residents were unhappy about the fog horn. In 1895, the Lighthouse Board built a parabolic reflector to deaden the sound of fog signals on the landward side. In 1897, the fog signal machinery was overhauled and two new smokestacks erected to replace the old one.

Reports from the history of the life-saving station in the nineties are as follows: "During the year 1896, the station performed 11 rescues, persons in small boats, sailboats or steam yachts. One large vessel assisted was the 38 ton steamer *Pathfinder* (Capt. Brown) which collided, capsized and sank two-thirds of a mile WNW of the station on September 1, 1895. One of the crew of five was lost and the damage was $3,000 to a $7,000 vessel. Five days later on September 6, 1895, the steamer *Samuel F. Hodge* was a casualty in Duluth Harbor with a damage of $1,000 in a total value of $38,000. None of the crew of 20 was lost.

"On July 2, 1896, the station assisted the 77-ton steamer *L.L. Lyon* (Capt. Brickly), which was towed to safety. Seven other smaller boats were also assisted during the fiscal year 1897.

"During the year 1898 the station performed 18 rescues. Most of these were sailboats, sloops or yachts, but the 60-ton steamer *Record* which sunk in Duluth Harbor on June 2, 1898, was a catastrophe in which three lives were lost.

"During 1899 there were 13 rescues, one in connection with the 2,476-ton steamer *Northern King* (Capt. Connors) which got into difficulties on June 3, 1899, one mile SW of the station and was assisted, with no lives lost."

The country was coming out of the panic of 1893, when the United States declared war on Spain, April 11, 1898. Americans had long since sympathized with Cuba, powerless in the might of Spain, and on February 15, 1898, sympathy turned into a demand for action. On that date, the United States battleship *Maine* was sunk in the Havana harbor. Two officers and 264 men of her crew were lost.

Duluth had a battalion ready for the wars. Company A was the original Company K organized in 1884, which had become part of the newly-organized 3rd Minnesota Infantry in November, 1891. It entered the Spanish-American War in command of Captain Hubert V. Eva.

Company G had been organized on February 5, 1892, by Captain S.S. Williamson. Its commander for the war with Spain was Captain Charles C. Teare. Company H was also organized in West Duluth. Company C, organized April 11, 1894, was in command of Captain F.E. Resche, in both the organization and the war. There had been another company, I, organized in West Duluth, February 8, 1892, by Captain W.W. Brown, but it was mustered out of the service of the state in 1897.

The battalion had had a difficult time finding a place to drill. From 1884 to 1896, its meeting places were Hunter Hall, and old skating rink on West First Street, Ingalls Hall, the hallway of the city hall, the upper floor of the police station, and the Howard block on Michigan Street. In 1896 an Armory was built at Second Avenue East and First Street and dedicated October 26 of that year. Here the boys drilled and held their social functions. Company C's account of their costume ball in 1897 declares modestly, "It was perhaps the most brilliant social event Duluth ever had." This was the company that enjoyed camp life so much that they established a camp of tents, in the summer of '95, on the lakeshore between Twelfth and Thirteenth avenues east. "Members came down from town every evening, drill was held, supper was partaken of in the mess tent, and later in the evening friends arrived and a general good time was held."

With the call to arms, such goings-on were forgotten. According to military law the militia could not enter the foreign service, so the battalion went to St. Paul to be mustered into the United States Volunteer Army. The boys left Duluth, April 28, under the command of Major Bidwell. Crowds had assembled at the Armory that evening to bid them Godspeed. At 7 p.m., Company A under the command of Captain Eva, first lieutenant Carey, and second lieutenant Hagenson, led the march from the Armory to the depot. "When the column wheeled into Superior Street, the young soldiers had almost to battle their way through a solid mass of cheering humanity, who had come not only from the city, but from the vicinity for miles around, to give the boys a parting farewell such as they would never forget and cheer them on if they should meet the enemy in battle."

At St. Paul, the battalion went to Camp Ramsey (named for the first territorial governor) at the fair grounds. The general muster by companies was begun May 6 and completed May 8. "So promptly had the whole process of recruiting, mobilization, examination, and must been carried through that Minnesota achieved the distinction of being the first state in the Union to have its full quota of regiments under the first call mustered into the Volunteer Army. Duluth companies were the first ready to be mustered in, and Company A was the first to fill its ranks."

Minnesota furnished three regiments at once, the Twelfth, Thirteenth, and Fourteenth. A fourth regiment was organized later. The Duluth companies with more than 300 men were mustered into service as members of the Fourteenth Regiment Minnesota Volunteers. They were eager to get to the front, but on May 16, along with the Twelfth, they entrained for Camp Thomas at Chickamauga National Park, Georgia. The Thirteenth went to the Philippines. The Fourteenth was assigned with the First Pennsylvania and the Second Ohio to the Third Brigade, Second Division, First Army Corps, under command of Colonel Van Duzee. When he became ill, Lieutenant Colonel Charles E. Johnson was in command.

The boys fought the war at Camp Thomas, battling disease. Before they could get to the front, the war was over, August 12, 1898. The news of the surrender of Santiago came to them at night, and they held "a bare skin parade" with the band playing "There'll be a Hot Time in the Old Town Tonight."

The Minnesota boys were next sent to Knoxville, Tennessee, and then back to St. Paul, reaching there

September 23. Then everybody was given a 30 day furlough. For the Duluth boys, the furlough was meaningless for on October 9, while attending the funeral of John McEwen, Company C who died at Chickamauga, they received orders to proceed to Bemidji to quell an uprising of Leech Lake Indians. On October 10, 100 men were sent out under Captain Resche, and the next day 50 more followed, commanded by Captain Eva. "As about one-third of the Fourteenth regiment had heard of the Indian trouble and with or without orders made way to the scene of action, it was found unnecessary to call on Duluth for more troops." After two weeks, the boys came home again.

A bit of trouble occurred about the place for mustering out. Page Morris, representative of the Duluth district in Congress, had been assured by the War Department that the Fourteenth would be mustered out in Duluth. Citizens from other parts of the state, especially the Twin Cities, objected. They said that Duluth's climate was so cold that it would be a menace to the health of the soldiers to come here, accustomed as they were to the South. Governor Clough telegraphed Washington and got the place changed to St. Paul. The Duluth citizens, touched to the quick by a derogatory remark about their climate, let out a roar of protest. The *Duluth Herald* blamed the Twin City merchants for wanting the regiment there for financial reason, and Duluthians planned to bring the Duluth companies home in a special train immediately after the mustering out. The Twin Cities wouldn't get any of their money! The *Pioneer Press* came back with a classic: "The three Duluth companies will...inherit from their Uncle Sam $20,000. But the Cincinnati of Duluth are going back with money enough to buy new plows. No Saintly Capua will enervate the hardy sons of Superior's windswept cliffs. For Mayor Truelson of Duluth has chartered a special train. Citizens of Duluth have paid the fares of three companies. The Zenith City will fall weeping upon the breasts of veterans in no wise shorn of gold or glory. The Hobsonian kiss will smack in touching unison with the clinking of the double eagles."

The Fourteenth was mustered out in St. Paul on November 18, after six months and three weeks of service. Returning home, the boys began the work of reorganization as a National Guard.

Duluth veterans established the John G. McEwen Camp of the National Spanish-American War veterans.

As the year 1898 came to a close, the reports of the Federal Government showed the commercial growth for Duluth in its past 18 years.

	1880	1898
Jobbing interests	$ 12,000	$ 32,000,000
Lumber cut (in feet)	35,000,000	750,000,000
Coal reserve (tons)	60,000	2,549,411
Iron ore and copper shipped (tons)	none	3,511,394
Wheat shipments (bushels)	1,347,679	52,051,256
All other grains shipped	50,000	21,524, 015
Capacity of elevators	560,000	30,000,000
Vessel arrivals	no data	10,870
Flour shipped (barrels)	551,800	7,037,019
Vessel tonnage	302,000	14,135,237

No wonder Mayor Truelson said in his annual message, March 8, 1899: "The future of Duluth never looked brighter than at the present time!"

The rest of the world was reading about Queen Victoria's diamond jubilee and the Dreyfus case. Local interest was in the purchases and manipulations of James J. Hill, Rockefeller, Oliver, Wolvin, and Carnegie in the world of iron and steel.

A strike at the street car company disrupted transportation throughout the month May, bringing with it derailing of cars, placing timbers on tracks, and throwing stones and eggs. One car carrying ten passengers was blown up, but no one was hurt; another car was fired upon. The grand jury found the police lacking in duty during the strike. By June, everything was peaceful again, and in November the cars were being prepared for winter: "The car is taken to the barn, overhauled and the repairs that seem necessary are made. Then the section of the seat in the middle of the car is removed, the stove box and stove are set up, the pipe run up, and the stove is ready for making fires. Weather strips are put in on the lower part of windows...With the addition of the extension of the platform that runs over the steps when the door is closed, the car is ready for winter."

Work was continuing on dredging the canal to make it 350 feet wide. Because of an unusually severe winter the first boat of the season, the *Waldo,* did not arrive till May 2. Other boats were stuck in the ice.

Again there was much talk of gold in this region. There were advertisements for sale of gold stock and property near the mines - Golden Star, Olive, Golden Crescent, Lucky Coon, Alice A., Gold Boy, and Emmet Abbott mines.

A bill passed both the House and the Senate for $75,000 for erection of a building for a Normal School in Duluth. This project dates back four years. In 1895 the legislature passed a bill to the effect that if Duluth would offer a proper site for a normal school and deed it to the state free of all encumbrance, the site to contain not less than six acres, the legislature would appropriate sufficient funds for erections of a building. Duluth did its part, offering the site on which the University Branch now stands. In 1897 the legislature appropriated $5,000 for the school. Some of this amount was spent for clearing a site and testpitting for a foundation. With the passage of the 1899 bill, world could really begin.

No complaint can be made that citizens did not look after the young people. On May 22, the council passed a curfew law for children under the age of sixteen. They had to be off the streets by 9:30 p.m. from May 1 to October 31 and by 9 p.m. the rest of the year. If a child were apprehended a second time, his parents were fined ten dollars.

Duluthians were still interested in sports. Manager Frank Wade had a baseball team that did creditably in the old Western League. The Gun Club was active and captured the interstate cup. The tennis club had tournaments, and the bicycle club had fun. Horse races were run at the county fair held at the Oneota Fair Grounds. And the Boat Club, which had been $2,400 in debt two years before, ended the year with a balance of $150 and 100 members. In a regatta with Superior, Duluth scullers were F.J. Carey in a single scull; D. Mahoney, B.M. Peyton, Thompson, and H. Peyton in four oared heavyweights race; and G.C. Calhoun and F.W. Heimick in the double scull.

The big event of 1899 was the visit of President McKinley to Duluth on October 13. He was met on the train Superior by A.L. Ordean, Page Morris, Bishop McGolrick, Bishop Morrison, and Major Skars. Leaving the train in Duluth, the President passed between lines of the Grand Army of the Republic drawn up on either side of the platform as his escort of honor. Mrs. McKinley and the other ladies in the party asked to be left out of the parade for the President and his cabinet, so they were taken on a drive around the city.

The presidential carriage was drawn by four dashing dappled gray horses. The parade was headed by Chief John Black of the fire department and a platoon of mountain firemen, followed by companies C and A, in command of Major Resche and Captain Eva. With the city band playing, the parade moved up to Central high school, where school children were assembled on the sloping lawn, all waving flags. Showering the President with flowers were a group of fourteen girls, each chosen from a separate school. The high school students stood on the broad front steps of the building, and A.F.M. Custance led them in singing "There'll be a Hot Time in the Old Town Tonight." Then they gave their school yell, and the President smiled and waved his hat to them. He gave a little talk, and then his carriage moved westward, at a snail's pace because it was practically hemmed in by the crowds. Back to the depot the party went, and "as the train moved slowly out, Mr. McKinley stood on the rear platform, smiling, bowing, and waving his handkerchief." He was the first President to visit Duluth.

So Duluth came to the end of a century. The *St. Paul Dispatch* summed up the general condition and progress of the city at this time by saying: "This Odessa of the West is out of short skirts and has put on the queenly robes of womanhood."

CHAPTER IX

Twentieth Century 1900-1920

IN 1900, the United States census put Duluth in class 7 (cities between 50,000 and 75,000) with a population of 52,869, an increase of 19,754 over the census of 1890.

The twentieth century, ushered in against a background of the Russian-Japanese War, moved along with great developments in transportation - automobiles and airplanes; and bustled with new inventions, including the phonograph with cylinder records and motion pictures.

The first "movies", shown about 1900, were "The Great Train Robbery" and a picture of the Corbett-Fitzsimmons fight at Carson City. They were misty, blurred and flickering, but wonderful. Later, an entire nation loved Mary Pickford; emoted with Theda Bara; sighed sentimentally over Rudolph Valentino, Wally Reid, Francis X. Bushman and J. Warren Kerrigan; and thrilled at Pearl White in the "Adventures of Pauline". When David Griffith produced "The Birth of a Nation" in 1915, it was generally conceded that the pinnacle had been reached in the development of motion picture entertainment.

The *News Tribune* of March 12, 1911, says, "The picture houses, of which the Odeum and the Lyric are the best examples, amuse their patrons with moving pictures of scenes of every phase of human endeavor that is suitable for public spectacle...These picture houses have accomplished one great work for the benefit of humanity - they have driven out of existence the dime museum, with its band of fat girls, bearded women, dog-faced boys, idiots paraded as wild men and other monstrosities."

On Christmas Day in 1902, the Metropolitan Theatre opened just west of the present Soo Station. In 1903, the Bijou (which became the Empress in 1911) opened its doors at Lake Avenue and Superior Street. Here Charlie Chaplin is said to have made his first appearance in America, in 1908, when he presented "A Night in an English Music Hall". On August 22, 1910, the new Orpheum (now the Norshor) opened at Second Avenue East on the site of the old Temple Opera House. Fred Bradbury's orchestra played, and the vaudeville program included the Flying Martinis, Fred Duprez, the Rossow Midgets, Nelly Nichols, a short musical, Lyons and Yosco, and Clown Zertha and his Canines. The show closed with a movie comedy. To the Orpheum and Bijou stages came such stars as W.C. Fields and Will Rogers. Other local theatres included the Grand (later named Lyric), Rex (Garrick), Parlor Theatre, Kozy, Sunbeam and Happy Hour.

Most of the luminaries in the theatre world appeared at the Lyceum - Maude Adams, Walker Whiteside, Ethel Barrymore, Otis Skinner, Nat Goodwin, David Warfield, Sothern and Marlowe, Fred Stone, the Dolly Sisters and Fred and Adele Astaire. When "Ben Hur" was to be produced, customers stood in line for as long as eighteen hours to get tickets. It took three days to reconstruct the stage to accommodate the cast of 350 and the twelve horses pulling three chariots on separate treadmills.

The City Council took on the problem of motion picture censorship in 1911. After weeks of debate, on February 7 it adopted an ordinance to place all motion picture and other theatres under censorship. Persons objecting to a show had to file complaint not more than forty-eight hours or less than six hours before the performance was to take place. A complaint must be signed by five persons of voting age, two of them men.

The week of April 13, 1913, the "talkies" had a premiere in Duluth when Thomas A. Edison's "latest, greatest, and most wonderful invention", the kinetophone, was flashed on the screen at the Orpheum. That afternoon 1600 people crowded the theatre, while some 300 more were turned away. After four acts of vaudeville, a screen was lowered and flooded with light. Then the light became a theatre stage and the picture of a man walked forward. He spoke, and the audience gasped. He picked up a china plate and dropped it with a crash. Another man played the piano, a woman played a violin solo, and another woman sang. Dogs ran and barked, and a bugler sounded a call. End of reel one. The second reel was a minstrel show. The dramatic editor of the *Herald* said: "The possibilities are something hard to grasp. Five years from now an audience may be watching and listening to a production of *Hamlet* played by the greatest stars on the stage of this and other countries at a cost of five or ten cents apiece." Synchronization of sound and picture was no always successful - and neither was the kinetophone. It was merely a forerunner of later sound pictures.

Lest these theatre notes conjure up too metropolitan a picture, here is an item that shows Duluth did not have all the appurtenances of a city. A disgruntled West Duluth citizen, in the *Herald* of November 1, 1900, evinced surprise that the City Council had provided a poundmaster for his community. He said, "Cattle of all kinds have run without restriction at all hours for the entire summer destroying gardens and breaking up more sidewalks than the street commissioner's force could repair. The Irving school has a nice lawn which is always occupied by two to ten cows and a kicking horse that resents any attempt to drive him away to other pastures. It was thought here that the Taxpayer's League had compelled the city to cut off the salary of poundmaster in order to reduce city levy."

Duluth pointed with pride to her parks and drives. On October 1, 1900, when William Jennings Bryan was in Duluth campaigning for the presidency, his hosts, Mr. and Mrs. Albert Baldwin, took him over the boulevard drive. "His opinion so generally expressed that American has no finer drive than this." Even taking into account that Bryan was running for office, he must have found this a colorful drive with its splendid view, fine driving horses, well-appointed carriages, and gay tally-ho parties. In 1903, the Park Board planted 2,000 trees along the boulevard to replace the old broken-down fence.

Those were the days when there was much rivalry among the livery stables. Even returning from a funeral, each hack driver took pride in getting his team back to town first so that the trip from the cemetery had all the atmosphere of a good horse race.

Horses and carriages would soon give way to automobiles introduced to Duluth in 1901. An unpublished manuscript by E.J. Filiatrault tells of the advent of the automobile. He and Emil A. Nelson formed a partnership of the firm, the Mutual Electric and Auto Company, in which Filiatrault took over the automobile part of the business. He says, "Being a partner in the automobile business, with no mechanics available, I had to learn the intricacies of each and every car...No one could tell me anything about these cars, but my former mechanical experiences enabled me in due time to solve all mechanical troubles. I was my own manager, salesman and mechanic."

Mr. Filiatrault's daughter, Mrs. Eugene Orren, is authority for the story that when her father's first car arrived, he met it at the station with his wife and a book of instructions. He would follow the instructions as his wife read them aloud, and thus he got the car started, put it into gear, and advanced in triumph upon the city streets.

Early in 1901, according to Filiatrault, there was only one car in Duluth. B.E. Baker introduced a single cylinder Oldsmobile runabout that year, "and frightened every horse that encountered him chugging along the Board of Trade to his home on London Road." J.R. Zweifel claims that he owned the first car in Duluth, having purchased it earlier in the year than Baker. He bought a Locomobile steamer from the manager of the Weyerhauser Lumber Company in Cloquet and drove it to Duluth and down Superior Street, "which was then paved with those nice round cedar blocks, no two of which were the same length." He kept it that night in a livery stable. Next morning, the owner made him push it to the street before he tried to start it. He says, "I knelt in the street and reached under the car for the faucet and turned it on. Nothing happened; I turned on another faucet, and still nothing happened. Then I turned on everything that could turn, looking for a nice, fat, stream of gasoline pouring into the little brass cup. Still nothing happened. Then I lit a match - and everything happened." Gone were Zweifel's Kaiser Wilhelm mustache, eyebrows and hair. The fire department horses dashed up, "got one look at my horseless carriage and galloped on in terror." Bystanders saved the car, but Zweifel lost interest in it, and when he got out of the hospital he sold it.

The next year, Filiatrault contracted for the sale of four Oldsmobiles at $800 each. Two more cars arrived. W.C. Brown purchased a single cylinder rear-entrance tonneau Thomas Flyer, painted a vivid red. It had an 84-inch wheelbase and a maximum speed of twenty miles an hour; it cost $1,700. Ward Ames' two-cylinder Winton, making its debut that fall, was guaranteed to do twenty-eight miles per hour. It weighed 4,000 pounds, and each tire cost $100. In 1903, Filiatrault, Victor Huot, and Al Ribenack had new two-cylinder model-K Ramblers with canopy tops.

The engine was under the body, so the whole body had to be lifted to oil the motor. Filiatrault says he sold forty-nine Ramblers in 1907, a banner year for him.

As more cars were being bought on the range, there was a clamor for opening the Miller Trunk highway. Mr. Filiatrault drove the first car through to the range in 1904; it took two and a half days to make the trip. Cars swayed across a long pole bridge and got stuck in the sand. A motorist always carried a three-quarter inch rope to wind around the wheels to prevent skidding, but these ropes lasted for only about fifteen miles of travel. In 1906, non-skid chains came in.

Early in 1905, a census showed sixteen automobiles in the city. "Probably the most conspicuous car is the aluminum colored Winton owned by Al Ribenack." Touring cars could attain a speed of forty-five miles an hour, but seldom ran over thirty-five or forty. Steam and gasoline cars had practically the same speed, but electric runabouts used in the city had an average speed of twelve miles and hour. As a result of the increase of automobiles, Duluth owners organized an Automobile Club, with officers: president, William Dalrymple; vice president, Al Ribenack; secretary, A.H. Smith; and treasurer, Victor Huot. These officers, with W.J. Stephenson, constituted a board of directors. The object of the organization was the promote interest in automobiles and to assist in getting better roads throughout this part of the state. The club made a map to show all roads in the vicinity of Duluth, which stated whether or not they were suitable. It advocated speedways on London Road and Park Point for automobiling. It also sent circular letters to all owners of cars suggesting rules to follow: "Do not run along the bus portion of this or any city or town faster than eight miles an hour"; "Whenever you see a horse or team that is showing fear of your machine, slow right down, or better still, come to a dead stop and let it pass you"; "Never run past a horse or team on the road without letting the driver know of your approach by blowing your horn. He will appreciate it and then if anything happens you may be excused."

On July 14, 1906, the first successful trip from Minneapolis to Duluth by automobile was completed, when J.M. Arnold arrived in the city after seventeen hours and fifteen minutes of actual driving time. He was sent by the Minneapolis Auto Club to report on conditions of the roads. At the same time, representatives of the automobile clubs of the Twin Cities and Duluth were making an accurate chart of the road (traveled by wagon) as the initial step in the construction of an automobile highway.

An official road guide published by the Automobile Club of Minneapolis in 1912 gives directions in detail. Here is an excerpt from Trip No. 291 - Duluth to Eveleth.

> 0.1 Leave Court House on Fifth Avenue. Go southeast one block and turn right (southwest) on First Street. Paved.
> 0.2 Turn right (north) on Mesaba Avenue under incline trolley. Macadam.
> 0.4 Church on left. Winding road.
> 0.8 Straight ahead. Park on left.
> 1.0 Straight ahead.
> 1.3 Bear left (northwest)
> 1.7 Top of heights. Clay.
> 2.0 Bear left, then right (northwest)

By that time the driver had reached Duluth Heights. Perhaps cars had such slow speed that one could read directions and drive at the same time.

One bit of information given in the guide book is that the registration fee for automobiles in Minnesota was $1.50 every three years. Non -residents were exempted for thirty days. Speed laws were: "business section, 10 miles;

residence portions, 15 miles; outside city limits, 25 miles." So far as ascertained, there were no "hot rods".

In 1903, the editor of the *News Tribune* declared: "The automobile is neither practicable nor practical in Duluth." In 1905, the editor of the *Herald* said there were only thirty-five automobiles in Duluth, "not because people cannot afford to buy cars, but because of the hills and poor roads." On July 20, 1906, at a meeting of the Lakeside Club, John Jenswold, Jr., led a complaint that motorists were ruining London Road. By 1911, the Duluth fire-fighting forces had added motor equipment - a salvage corps and a chemical and hose wagon drive by a "powerful six-cylinder engine". The *Herald* said: "The officials of the department recognize that the horses can never be done away with entirely because of the heavy snows of the winter." By 1916, Duluth automobile owners were instigating a concrete highway from here to the Twin Cities. In 1919, congestion of traffic on downtown streets was so great that Bentley P. Neff, suggested an elevated street from Eighth Avenue West to Third Avenue East.

By 1913, O.A. Rosto had built an airplane, a monoplane that was exhibited in the auditorium for a time. He intended to make a flight over the city, taking off from the ice, but records are hazy on that project.

Robert W. "Bill" Watt, now living in Detroit, and Leonard J. Bemke, publisher of the local *Steel Plant News* claim they made the first plane flight in Duluth. The date was March 22, 1914. Inspired by the Wright Brothers, the boys had made their own plane, working nights and Sundays. They used a second-hand 40-horsepower motor that had formerly been used in an airplane, and a second-hand propeller. The plane was of the Curtis biplane pusher type. It lacked some of the refinements of later craft; if the pilot, strapped in a seat in front of the motor, wanted to drop a wing to turn the contraption, he had to lean over sideways. Bemke made a trial ground run on the ice near the Northern Pacific railroad bridge, and then, since there was room for only one man, generously let Watt take her up. Watt covered about 300 feet on the take-off, and then the plane lumbered in the air. Bemke says it rose about fifty feet, but newspapers say it was fifteen or twenty feet. Then it came down - suddenly. Watt jumped out just as the plane hit the ice. The motor broke from its mountings, and the whole thing was a wreck. It was estimated that Watt's airtime was about five minutes.

Major city improvements in the first score of year in the new century included: the Garfield Avenue viaduct, paved with creosoted blocks "the same material that had been used in the principal streets of Paris and London"; new pavement of sheet asphalt on downtown Superior Street between Eighth and Sixteenth avenues east; the "Great White Way" on East Superior Street, light for the first time the night of April 21, 1910; in 1915, installation of eighty-four incandescent lights and twenty arc lights where gas had formerly been used. In 1913, land for a boulevard drive on the North Shore from Duluth to Two Harbors was offered as a gift to the city by Chester A. Congdon, but it took years to complete the highway.

In 1902, two new banks were founded, the City National Bank and the Duluth Savings Bank, which later became the Northern National, presently the Northern Minnesota National.

The first cablegram from Honolulu to Duluth was received over the new trans-Pacific, January 4, 1903. It was sent to Ward Ames, president of the Board of Trade, by O.G. Traphagen, former Duluth architect, and read, "Cable connected. Greetings."

A new era in photography was announced in 1905, when Louis Dworshak's Studio announced the installation of a new lamp, the "Aristo", "which makes it possible to take pictures regardless of weather, and even at night."

Among serious problems confronting the country was a coal strike. Headlines on January 9, 1903, announced that the price of anthracite coal had jumped to $9.50 a ton. It had steadily risen from $6.75 a ton the previous May. What was the world coming to with such high prices?

Wages were rising. On May 1, 1903, Duluth "white wings" demanded an increase from twenty-two cents to twenty-five cents an hour for cleaning city streets.

A survey of wages of women in Minnesota, made by W.E. McEwen of Duluth as state labor commissioner, investigated the employment of women in 32 industries, employing 7,537 women. It showed that 25 per cent of the women received less than six dollars a week; 47 per cent, from six to eight dollars; 18 per cent, eight to fifteen dollars; and ten per cent, over fifteen dollars. McEwen reported: "Seven dollars a week, $1.17 a day, seems to constitute the minimum wage of efficiency, decent comfort and self-respect for self-supporting females in Minnesota."

It is interesting to note that in 1900 three of Duluth's largest buildings, valued at $400,000, were owned by a nine-month-old baby. John Nicholas Brown, of Newport, Rhode Island. The little boy's father and uncle had died that year, leaving him a fortune of between seven and eight million, including the Lonsdale, Stone-Ordean-Wells Wholesale and Patrick-Granger buildings in Duluth.

From newspapers of the period come these items of information to show the growth of the city: 1906 - In June, Duluth led all American cities in the increase in building operations for the month, and ranked fourth in the nation for the year; 1909 - All former building records were broken this year - more than 1,300 permits were issued, covering $3,700,000 in work; 1913 - Duluth ranked first among all American cities in building operations for the first ten months. The two corner lots which Rice had offered to exchange for a pair of boots in 1857 were sold for $18,000 in 1910. The site of the Lonsdale building sold for $1,200 in

1874, for $11,000 in 1884, and was valued at $100,000 in 1909.

The Duluth Children's Home at 1515 East Fifth Street was opened June 4, 1904. This project had its beginning back in 1887, when a group of women started a small home for six babies and several unfortunate girls. Mrs. O.P. Stearns was leader of this charitable movement, assisted by Mrs. J.H. Crowley, Mrs. J.B. Smith, Mrs. M.R. Baldwin and other ladies. The group built the first home at 1722 East Superior Street. Money for the project was raised through a Charity Ball, held in 1887 at Ingall's Hall, where Albenberg's store is now located. Mrs. A.M. Miller and W.C. Sargent led the grand march at this colorful event. An annual ball was held, usually the Tuesday preceding Thanksgiving, up to about 1935. The Children's Home Society assumes responsibility for the maintenance of the home.

Duluth's first skyscraper, the Altworth building, then the tallest building in the state, was officially opened January 15, 1910. Among other new public buildings were the Soo line depot; Lenox and Holland hotels; the Bethel, with modern accommodations for about 200 men; the Fidelity building; Patrick Knitting and Garment Factory; and Zinsmaster's Bread Company. The Duluth *Herald* moved into its new plant on First Street on February 11, 1902, holding a reception for 6,000 guests and publishing a special edition commemorating the event.

New clubhouses were built by the Kitchi Gammi, Curling and Boat clubs. On January 1, 1903, the 755 members of the Commercial Club formally opened their new building where the Duluth Athletic Club now stands. "Flaaten's orchestra, stationed in the palm-lined card room on the third floor gave rendition of an excellent program and Secretary Preston threw open the doors."

The first stone was heaved in the new curling house on January 4, 1913, by Jack McGregor, lead on President Stephen H. Jones' rink, in an informal game against D.B.

MacDonald's lads. The club was opened on January 11, when 2,500 people visited the new quarters at Fourteenth Avenue East and London Road. "Hundreds of skaters, circling in swaying rhythm to the lilting music made a scene that brought to mind the final belief that at last Duluth has achieved its long-harbored desire to be the home of winter sports...Nowhere in the United States is there a curling house or a skating rink that can compare with the magnificent structure."

The new Masonic Temple at Lake Avenue and Second Street had its housewarming on March 24, 1905. The crowd of 2,000 people was so large that the musical program had to be given twice, first in the Blue Lodge room and repeated to those in the Scottish Rite theatre. Past Grand Master W.A. McGonagle gave the address of welcome.

New residential districts were being built up with the beautiful homes for which Duluth has become noted. These included the Congdon estate on London Road and the Ward Ames estate on Vermilion Road. Mansions on West Third Street were being given up to be turned later into rooming houses, and the Duncans, Brewers, Fricks, Hanfords, Bradleys, Richardsons, Marvins, Millers, Crowleys, McDougalls, Stones, Graveses, Ripleys, Uphams, Barnums, Rays and Markells were building new homes in eastern sections of the city. Because of the number of Scotch people living in Hunter's Park, that district was often called "Oatmeal Hill".

By 1907, there was no question about it - St. Louis County had to have a new courthouse. The commissioners had been looking over locations in the downtown district and wrangling over a project since 1905. The unique eyesore on Sixth Avenue East was beneath the dignity of a progressive city. A Chicago architect, D.H. Burnham, was engaged by the courthouse commission to draw plans for the new building. He was later retained to study actual plans not only of the actual building, but also of its grounds and surroundings. In engaging Burnham, Duluth was getting the top man in his profession, for it was Burnham with two others who had been appointed by the national government to visit and study the large cities of Europe and then to draw plans for Washington D.C. The Burnham Company evolved a municipal grouping plan for Duluth, a civic center between First and Second streets, and between Fourth and Sixth avenues west. They designated the present site for the new courthouse and planned for a city hall and a federal building on either side. The Federal government agreed to go along with the idea, so on October 18, 1907, the city council endorsed the Burnham plan.

The first of the three buildings to be constructed was the present St. Louis County courthouse, completed in 1911. The exterior of this magnificent building is of New Hampshire granite, and the spacious, vaulted halls are marble-lined. From its eminence on the slope, it looked down arrogantly on the Federal building, which appeared small and dingy in contrast.

Duluthians became conscious of the advantages of city planning. Architect Robert Loebeck published a plan in the March 30, 1913, issue of the *Herald* which was in keeping with Duluth dreams. It included Cascade Park with a huge fountain flowing down wide stone steps. Mr. Loebeck suggested that since the avenues were too steep for traffic, they should be used for buildings, playgrounds and gardens, supplied by diagonal streets throughout the city. Minnesota Point would be a reserve of Duluth harbor, built up with docks and warehouses, and connected to the city with a tunnel underneath the channel. Plans called for several tunnels, elevated roads, and elevators. There would also be a new union station. To counter-balance the civic center, an art gallery and museum would be built on Second Street between Fifth and Sixth avenues east, connected by a triumphal arc. An educational center was in the plan, with opera house, orchestral hall, auditorium and university, with the crowning feature of the high school tower. To pay for all this, Mr. Loebeck suggested redeeming part of the lake by filling in between the channel wall and shore, and selling lots to wholesale merchants. He said, "The low-lying ground would afford double-decked streets, the lower one reserved for rails and out of town trade and the upper one for city traffic." That's that.

The largest single construction project in Duluth, and the one which upped the real estate record was the building of Morgan Park. It was in 1907 that the United States Steel Corporation sent a committee to Duluth to examine the location for a new plant. Members of the committee liked what they saw here. The company set aside $14,500,000 for the project at Gary and formed the Minnesota Steel Company (the present American Steel and Wire Company) a subsidiary to carry out the work of building a small city. One thousand acres of land were acquired on the St. Louis River, opposite Spirit Lake, a location where lake vessels could come to deliver their cargoes. Actual work on the village was begun in 1910. The "model city' was modern in every respect. Besides the buildings used for industry, there were houses for workers, office buildings, a clubhouse, hospital, store and school. The latter was turned over to the city public school system. A Catholic church and one church for all other denominations completed the village.

A mild boom had struck Ironton, Spirit Lake and Smithville, just east of the Morgan Park site, in 1893. Among the pillars of the communities were Victor Dash, Albert Overton, A.G. Renstrom, Albert and Edward Swenson, Wolf Siegal and Dennis T. Sullivan. The boom faded out, but with the building of Morgan Park, about 1913, realty companies beat the drums to sell lots in this area. Advertisements claimed that Ironton, Spirit Lake and Smithville already had stores, a school, a Finnish college, a hotel, two railroad stations and a steamer dock, with a 20-

foot depth channel. With the completion of the model city, all city improvements would be forthcoming in this section.

The Universal Portland Cement Plant, a two million dollar project, was built adjacent to the steel plant in 1915-1916. The community of Gary sprang up as workers bought land nearby the plant and built homes for themselves.

Morley Heights was developed in Hunters Park in 1919. Marshall-Wells Company built this new section, moving to the property 100 houses purchased at Barksdale, Wisconsin.

Utilizing the lake and railroads, jobbing increased from practically nothing in 1880 to a sixty million dollar asset to Duluth by 1910. Among the well-known firms were Marshall-Wells, Stone-Ordean-Wells, Kelly-How-Thomson, L.W. Leithead Drug Company, Knudson Fruit Company, American Heating Company, Fitzsimmons-Palmer and Wright Clarkson Mercantile Company. In the first part of the twentieth century, there were established F.A. Patrick and Company, DeWitt-Seitz, Schulze Brothers, Thwing-Stuart, Rust Parker Martin, Klearfax Rug Company, Patrick Duluth Woolen Mills and Zinsmaster Bread Company. In 1909, according to the *Herald* of December 8: "The largest shipment of paint in the world, has been consigned to the Marshall-Wells Hardware Company. The shipment consists of forty carloads of 40,000 pounds each, totaling 1,600,000 pounds."

West Duluth was teeming with industrial plants. By 1900, three iron ranges had been discovered in Minnesota - the Vermilion, Missabe and Cuyuna. (Shipments from the latter were first made in 1911.) With iron ore not only at the back door but also passing through Duluth to the lake at the front door, companies were manufacturing steel and pig iron before the advent of the big steel plant. About 1893, the Ironton Structural Steel Company was in operation at Ironton, about a half-mile north of Spirit Lake. This plant contained several large brick buildings occupying an area about three blocks long and one block wide. The plant produced steel beams and structural shapes, with the help of a blast furnace on the site of the present shipyards. The company rolled a 42-inch I beam, known as the largest I beam ever rolled in the world, which was sent as an exhibit to the Chicago World's Fair. However, the Ironton had a short life.

Blast furnaces manufacturing pig iron before the U.S. steel plant were the Clyde, the National, the Imperial and the Marine Iron Works, and the Zenith Blast Furnace. The Clyde was the original Northwestern Manufacturing Company, reorganized in 1901. It had exclusive manufacturing rights under the Decker and McGiffert patents. The Zenith Blast Furnace, organized by A.B. Wolvin in 1904, took over the West Duluth Blast Furnace and extended the plant, building a huge wooden coal dock and fifty coke ovens. Gas, a by-product of the ovens, has since then been sold to the city. In 1915, the first manufactured shipment of U.S. steel was sent by rail to Gary, Indiana. Duluth's largest industry was in progress.

The American Carbolite Company plant, Duluth Brass Works, Duluth Crushed Stone Company and Union Match Company were among other West Duluth industrial plants. In 1903, the Northwestern Steam Boiler and Manufacturing Company, which turned out nearly everything in the general machine line, incorporated. It was the outgrowth of M.A. Ryan's plant in 1894. There were sundry foundry and machine shops in this section of the city.

One of the great industries which helped to bring wealth to Duluth, but which has passed almost into oblivion, was lumber. The huge logs, brought out of forests on sleighs, were transported by train to Spirit Lake, where they were dumped into the water. Sawmills lined the shores and the big lumber boats loaded there. Mrs. Philip M. Hanft recalls how, as a child, she would go to Spirit Lake with her father, Captain Walter Green, to see his ship, the *Ada Barrett*, being loaded. Sometimes he would take her with him on the slow trip to Buffalo on the ship with its tail of tow barges trailing after it. Captain Green was with the Mitchell McClure Company. The Edward Hines Lumber Company was acclaimed the largest in the world. By 1904, the lumber industry was steadily dwindling. Reports show: 1902 - 414,328,000 feet; 1903 - 407,416,000 feet; and 1904 - 387,824,000 feet. The maximum lumber estimate by mill managers at the Head of the Lakes for 1905 was 196,000,000 feet. Mills in Duluth and Superior were Alger-Smith, Red Cliff, Murray and McCann, Scott-Graff, Merill and Ring, St. Louis Lumber Company, and J.C. Mullery.

First steps toward organization of a Duluth Retail Merchants' Association were taken at a banquet, April 7, 1905, at the Commercial Club. Fifty merchants were in attendance. The banquet committee was J.M. Gidding, R.R. Forward and A.B. Kenney. A committee appointed to investigate similar organizations was composed of E. Silberstein of Silberstein and Bondy, C.E. Bassett of French and Bassett, and W.F. Quayle of Kelly-How-Thomson. I. Freimuth, A.B. Stewart and Jacob Grueson were appointed on a membership committee.

Extensive improvements were being made in the Duluth-Superior harbor. At noon on April 16, 1900, the last spike was driven in the new piers at the Duluth ship canal. These concrete piers, replacing the old wooden ones, were constructed at a cost of $200,000. The cribs, 24 feet wide, were 22 feet below low-water level and the top, 10 feet above low-water. The width between parallel portions of the piers was 300 feet, but they were 316 feet 5 inches apart at the center line of the bridge, and 540 feet apart at the inner end. The length of the canal was 1,650 feet and of each pier, 1,734 feet. Lamp posts were placed at 50-foot intervals. The general depth through the canal was 32 feet, with the deepest spots, near the ends, about 48 feet and the least depth, 27 feet. Improvements were made through the three million-dollar appropriation of 1896.

With the new piers, the Lighthouse Board went to work at the lights. Work was commenced in June, 1900, and completed in August, 1901, on the erection of the permanent rear range tower. This tower was a skeleton iron structure, about 70 feet high, forming the frustum of a square pyramid, surmounted by an architrave, supporting an octagonal gallery, a circular parapet, and an octagonal lantern. It was accessible from below by a spiral stairway.

A combined light tower and fog signal building was also completed on the outer end of the pier in August, 1901. "The building is a one story brick structure, 22 feet wide and 45 feet long, with a tower eight feet square and 11 1/2 feet high, surmounted by a cast iron circular lantern erected on a cast iron deck, 29 feet high to the focal plane. The building is provided with a parabolic sound deflector. A duplicate fog-signal plant is installed in the structure with coal bunkers, wood racks, iron roof and concrete floor." A steel door to the fog signal building and heavy shutters for the windows as protection against the seas were provided in 1903. On September 1, 1901, the 4th order lights were first exhibited. Since Lake Superior's storms send powerful waves dashing over the piers, a tramway 1,150 feet long was laid in the gallery of the superstructure of the new concrete pier. It extends from the gallery to the manhole at the base of the front range and is provided with a car to enable the keeper to reach the outer light in stormy weather.

Three additional fixed red lights were to be established at the harbor entrance when the city furnished the electrical connection for the lamp posts.

In 1902, the two lights and fog signal were cared for by a keeper and two assistants. The frame house, built in 1874, was occupied by the keeper and his family, and assistants rented quarters at their own expense. The Board recommended purchasing a site for a double dwelling for the assistants. In 1907 and 1912, the site was acquired, opposite the keeper's dwelling on Lake Avenue on the Point. During the storm of November 27-28, 1905, the station was damaged by waves. The frame oil-house and brick structure protecting the entrance to the tunnel of the south pier leading to the front beacon and fog-signal house were carried away. The oil house was rebuilt and a water heater was provided for the fog-signal building.

The 1908 report of the Lighthouse Board states: "The approach to Duluth Harbor is one of the worst and most dangerous on the whole chain of lakes. The entrance piers are only about 300 feet in width, and the north pier is so close to the shore that a vessel making a mistake in judging the width would be immediately on the rocks. The Lake Carrier's Association consider this matter of such importance that it has made arrangements for the exhibition of private light for the balance of the season of navigation in 1908."

A new light was initially shown on April 7, 1910, built on a steel shell tower on the north pier at a cost of $4,000. The light was a lens lantern (electric incandescent) fixed white, 46 feet above lake level. It shone two seconds and was eclipsed two seconds and could be seen for 11 miles. The white cylindrical steel tower supporting it was 31 feet high, surmounted by a black lantern.

The Duluth Life Saving Service still had work to do, in spite of these improvements. The crew assisted fourteen vessels during 1900. Between the years 1901 and 1915, when the service became part of the Coast Guard, however, there were only ten cases of assistance recorded. The first name of a keeper of the station on record is that of M.A. McLennan in 1916.

Strangers coming to Duluth inevitably go down to the pier to watch the big ships glide majestically through the quiet waters of the canal. Then they hear the story of the wreck of the *Mataafa*.

In happened on November 28, 1905. In one of the worst storms on the lakes, the outward bound *Mataafa*, with the barge Maysmyth in tow, cut off the barge to lie at anchor near Sandy Island, and turned back to Duluth harbor to wait out the storm. At 2:15 p.m., as she reached the canal, mountainous waves crashed her against the north pier, smashing her bows. She swung to the south pier, and again to the north, striking amidship. The wheel and rudder were carried away, leaving her completely at the mercy of the storm and waves. There the *Mataafa* swung till the stern struck the rock cribbing of the old pier. The ship broke.

The life saving crew brought apparatus to the beach, but huge waves made it impossible to launch surfboats. Life lines were shot out against the howling wind, but only once did a line reach the stricken ship. It caught in some way and frayed in two on the rocks.

Thousands of Duluthians went down to the beach, where, through heavy snowfall, they watched the men on the *Mataafa* and tried to give some solace by their presence. They saw three men in the stern make a hazardous run of 250 feet to shelter forward - saw them and cheered as the men battled the wind and mighty waves, which at times left water ten feet deep on deck. They saw a fourth man start and turn back. The trip became too perilous for the nine men left in the stern. Frantically, men on ship and shore tried to speak to each other through megaphones, but the wind carried away their words. As night came on, those on shore built huge bonfires.

By ten o'clock, there was no sight of the men in the stern, but figures could be seen in the pilot house moving against the lights. At three o'clock the lights went out. It was later learned that the captain kept his men dancing Indian fashion that night, blankets wrapped around them; if a man would doze off, others would wake him and keep him moving - and living. At five o'clock in the morning, they walked through three feet of water to the wheelsman's room, where they huddled around a small fire.

At dawn the storm began to subside. The life saving crew launched the surfboats and brought to shore the fifteen men from the pilot house - men who were exhausted, little able to help themselves, but still alive. Three trips were made to bring in the survivors, each trip greeted with the cheering of thousands. The bodies of the nine men aft, not over 100 from the pier, were frozen fast in beds of solid ice, their faces turned to the warmth and comfort ashore.

Nine ships were wrecked on Lake Superior in that dreadful storm. The steamer *Crescent City* hit the shore at Lakewood, where she lay against the rocks, pounded by waves and wind; the steamer *England* was beached on Minnesota Point; and the freighter *Elwood* sank in the harbor. There was no loss of life on these ships.

Another lake accident occurred at the inter-state bridge in 1906, which cost money, but no loss of life. Early in the morning of August 11, the steamer *Troy*, package freighter, approached the big draw of the bridge, whistling for it to open. Mechanism on the draw had failed, so the bridge-tender could not open it, and as there was no signal system at that time, he could not warn the ship. By the time the captain of the *Troy* realized the situation, it was too late to avoid a crash. The huge span fell into the bay, blocking the channel and tying up thirty-five boats. The span was out of commission for over two years.

Newspaper items taken at random help to tell the shipping story: 1906 - The largest fleet of boats navigating the Great Lakes are from Duluth, with 352 vessels registered; 1907 - Coal tonnage exceeds that for sixteen of the largest cities on the Great Lakes. The Duluth-Superior harbor is the foremost American port, its tonnage record having exceeded that of New York by approximately 400,000 tons; 1908 - The Duluth harbor shipped out over 11,790,000 bushels of grain; 1910 - The navigation season broke all previous records. 10,908 vessels arrived and departed from Duluth; 1912 - All previous records for the local harbor were broken, when 41,474,776 tons of freight were handled.

So the story grew, each year's record of shipping surpassing the previous year. The Statistical Report of the Marine Commerce of the Duluth-Superior Harbor shows that the total receipts and shipments (short tons) in 1900 were 11,725,245, and in 1920, 46,808,613. The 1920 figure was a drop from the peak year of 1918, when the total receipts were 53,746,358. The valuation of cargo in 1918, $537,514,906, has been exceeded only once. This was in 1920, when the valuation was $552,900,033. Shipments of lumber have dropped, so that the bulk of commodities - iron ore, grain, flour and coal, constitute ninety-five per cent of the total commerce of the harbor.

More than six million dollars was spent in 1912 on improvements to docks and dock property, and seven new docks were being planned. Disregarding the outer harbor, since Stuntz's lone merchandise dock at the end of Minnesota Point in 1853, 119 docks and wharf's had been built by 1900, and thirty-nine more were erected between 1900 and 1920.

In 1901, the Pittsburgh Steamship Company was organized by a merger of the principal transportation fleets on the lake. A.B. Wolvin of Duluth was made general manager of the company, which operated 112 vessels. It is said that Wolvin began his career at the age of ten as a cabin boy on a Great Lakes ship.

The first of the freighters with hatches spaced twelve feet apart, the *James H. Hoyt*, appeared on the lakes in 1903. In 1906, there were two 600-foot freighters; in 1908, self-unloading bulk carriers were introduced.

On May 25, 1903, between six and seven thousand persons visited the Anchor line *Tionesta* at N.P. dock No. 4 in Duluth, "one of the most magnificent examples of modern lake passenger and freight ships now afloat." It was a steel ship, 360 feet long, carrying 350 passengers and 3,500 tons of freight. Beginning in 1907, the luxurious passenger ship, the *Hamonic,* made regular trips, followed by the *Noronic* and the *Huronic* of the Northwestern line. The peak of passenger service was in 1902, when 121,292 passengers arrived and departed. Statistics are not available prior to 1895, but it is not likely that there were more passengers traveling on the small vessels in those days.

All this talk of ships brings to mind a satire written by Mark Twain, which ranks with the Duluth speech of J. Proctor Knott. In a book "Following the Equator", which Mark Twain wrote in 1897, he says:

"In the afternoon we sighted Suva, the capital of the group, and treaded our way into the secluded little harbor - a placid basin of brilliant blue and green water tucked snugly in among the sheltering hills. A few ships rode at anchor in it - one of them a sailing vessel flying the American flag, and they said she came from Duluth! That's a journey! Duluth is several thousand miles from the sea, and yet she is entitled to the proud name of mistress of the commercial marine of the United States of America. There is only one free, independent, unsubsidized American ship sailing the foreign seas, and Duluth owns it. All by itself, that ship is the American fleet. All by itself, it causes the American name and power to be respected in the far regions of the globe. All by itself, it certifies to the world that the most populous civilized nation in the earth has a just pride in her stupendous stretch of sea front, and is determined to assert and maintain her right as one of the great maritime powers of the planet. All by itself, it is making foreign eyes familiar with a flag which they have not seen before in forty years, outside of the museum. For what Duluth has done, in building, equipping and maintaining at her sole expense the American foreign commercial fleet, and in thus rescuing the American name from shame and lifting it high from the homage of the nations; we owe her a debt of gratitude which our hearts shall confess with quickened beats whenever her name is named henceforth. Many national toasts will die in the lapse of time, but while the flag flies and the republic survives, they who live under their shelter will still drink this one, standing and uncovered: Health and prosperity to thee, O Duluth, American queen of the alien seas!"

Duluthians who pin their faith on the St. Lawrence Waterway have felt that this is another satire that may come true. Commenting on the passage in an editorial in June, 1923, the *News Tribune* says: "Very evidently Mark thought that it was a delicious absurdity that Duluth, `several thousand miles from the sea,' should have the only `independent American ship sailing the foreign seas.' But if Mark were alive five years from now he might see Duluth make a most substantial contribution to the American merchant marine. He might see ships from all the foreign nations in the Duluth harbor. And he would see Duluth ships sailing the ocean lanes as freely as those hailing from New York. His toast, `Heath and prosperity to thee, O Duluth, American queen of the alien seas,' could be drunk again in all seriousness. The title of `mistress of the commercial marine of the United States' may yet be applied to Duluth in all truth and without a tinge of satire."

Departments of the Federal government moved into their own new quarters during the early days of the century. In 1905, the office building at the Duluth Ship Canal Park was completed for the Duluth District Corps of Engineers.

The Weather Bureau, after traveling around the city for thirty-four years, finally found a permanent home on top of the hill in 1904. When established in 1870, it was located in the Edmonds Block, later called the Miller Block, at Lake Avenue and Superior Street, with the Army Signal Corps officers in charge. In 1882, the bureau was moved to the St. Louis Hotel, on the site now occupied by the Medical Arts building. Two years later, it was shifted to the Metropolitan Block, and in 1895, to the new post office building on Fifth Avenue West and First Street. H.W. Richardson moved his equipment to the present location and made his readings there on January 1, 1904. The new station was considered one of the best equipped in the country. The two-story building contained eleven rooms, but since there were no city water connections, a windmill pumped the water supply from a well. Evidently, Duluthians were complaining about the unreliability of the weather reports, for Richardson explained in the newspaper that the combination of hills and lakes - an abrupt drop from a table of 1,400 feet above sea level to 602 feet at lake level - caused extreme weather changes in various parts of the city, so that a report for one section was not necessarily correct for another section of Duluth.

The fish hatchery, one of the largest hatcheries in the northwest, was completed at Lester Park at a cost of $40,000 in 1910. It was abandoned in 1948, and the buildings were turned over to the University of Minnesota, Duluth Branch.

The advance the cause of science, John H. Darling began construction of his Astronomical Observatory at Ninth Avenue West and Third Street in 1916. This too, was given to UMD.

Duluth has had its share of disasters, large and small. It was in 1900 that car 56 of the street railway company ran wild coming down Third Avenue West. Pulling two loads of ties, it got out of control on First Street, jumped the track at Superior Street, and smashed into the car starter's office. No one was injured, and motorman William Kirkland had his hand on the brake when the car came to a halt.

A disastrous fire occurred in 1908, in which five men and thirty-eight horses perished. The fire started late in the afternoon of June 19 in the Board of Trade livery stable, located where the Steele Lounsberry store now stands. Men went to the basement to lead out the horses and were trapped. Nobody realized the men were in the building until the fire was over.

While on the subject of disasters, one must mention the night of July 21, 1909. The day had been humid and sultry, following a heavy rain. The downtown streets were crowded that evening when a fierce electrical storm hit, followed by a cloudburst. At the Bijou Theatre, a full house was listening to a virtually unknown blackface comedian who came to Duluth each year - Al Jolson. The audience was more than mildly startled to see water rushing down the aisles. They stood on the seats, while Jolson waded offstage, getting his only costume soaking wet. One woman in panic, dashed outside, where the force of the water on Superior Street knocked her down. She was rescued by Manager Joe Maitland. Gil Fawcett, in his Old Timer radio program, says "Maitland effected the one and only rescue from drowning on Superior Street." At Ninth Avenue East and Second Street, two small children were swept from their mother's arms and drowned. Superior Street was a raging torrent. Life lines were stretched across intersections to enable people to cross the street in safety. Added to the force of the water, there was danger of being struck by the beer kegs and cases and other miscellaneous articles carried along with the flood. Street cars stopped running and it was almost impossible to find a cab. There was not a vacant hotel room in Duluth that night. All trains stopped, with the railroad yards under four feet of water. Pavements were ripped up, basements were flooded, and streets and avenues damaged as storm sewers broke. The next day, only the young fry were happy - there being swimming holes all over town.

A tragic disaster occurred in San Diego, California, July 21, 1905, when the gunboat U.S.S. Bennington blew up in the harbor. Oscar F. Nelson, now employed with the Duluth District Corps of Engineers, was on the ship. Amid

174

blinding steam and cries and groans of the injured and dying, he gave such valiant assistance to his shipmates that he was awarded the Congressional Medal of Honor. Out of 182 officers and men on the Bennington, there were fifty-five dead and forty-nine injured.

Back in Duluth, city utilities were being expanded. The Great Northern Power Company bought from the Jay Cooke estate riparian rights on both sides of the St. Louis River and installed an electric power plant at a cost of more than five million dollars. The old Thomson Dam was removed and replaced by a new concrete dam.

In 1900, with the organization of the Zenith Telephone Company, Duluth had two telephone systems. Then came a succession of sales: in 1918, the Zenith was sold to the Duluth Telephone Company; in 1920, the Duluth sold out to the Northwestern Telephone Exchange Company; and in 1921, the present organization was formed and named the Northwestern Bell Telephone Company. In 1903, when the Spalding Hotel installed 185 telephones, one in each room, it was said to be the only hotel in the Northwest with this convenience. On June 7, 1910, the company announced that free telephones would be discontinued. Up to this time, the company had provided free resident telephones where the owner was a subscriber to a special line business telephone.

The local transportation company had had financial difficulties. Up to 1909, the Duluth Street Railway Company had never paid a dividend. "Roadways had to be blasted out of rock, almost impregnable bluffs had to be climbed" as lines were extended over the fast-growing city. This was expensive business. In 1898, the company had gone into the hands of receivers. In 1900, it reorganized, acquired the Superior street railway system, and became the Duluth-Superior Transit Company. In 1901, the system operated 2,258,884 car miles and carried 9,000,000 revenue passengers. The year 1919 was the peak year in rail operation, with 5,538,842 car miles operated; 38,475,440 revenue passengers; and 670 employees.

A human interest story appeared in the January 4, 1903, issue of the *Herald*. It said that August Halgren was the oldest man in the employ of the Duluth District Railway Company. From May 1, 1889 to November 1890, his post had been behind the business end of a pair of mules. Then he took out the first electric cars as motorman. For over a week, he gave free rides to all who cared for the adventure of riding in the new car.

Railroads continued to make news. In 1900, the Northern Pacific took over the old St. Paul and Duluth road. In 1901, there was a meeting in Minneapolis for a proposed Duluth to New Orleans railroad, and the Duluth, Red Wing and Southern road extended its tracks from Red Wing to Duluth. By 1903, fifty passenger trains were arriving daily. Still another line came to Duluth in 1910, when the Soo entered the city. Controlled by the Canadian Pacific, which built the Brooten branch, the Soo pulled into the Omaha depot until its own station was completed. In 1912, the first Soo train left on its own tracks for the Twin Cities. The Great Northern extended its lines into Canada, doubling the importance of the Duluth terminal. By 1913, Duluth had nine railroads: Minneapolis, St. Paul and Sault Ste. Marie; Great Northern; Northern Pacific; Canadian Northern; Chicago, Milwaukee and St. Paul; Chicago, St. Paul, Minneapolis and Omaha; Duluth, South Shore and Atlantic; Duluth and Iron Range; and Duluth, Missabe and Northern.

Seasons still existed for railroads at the turn of the century. On October 28, 1900, the North Coast Limited of the Northern Pacific was discontinued for the winter. It had been put into service in May and had had "a very successful summer season". The Northern Pacific used to put on special trains to Fond du Lac for the summer. This village and Spirit Lake were popular resorts where Duluthians had their summer homes. Passenger excursion boats that ran to

Fond du Lac stopped at Spirit Lake, where the city had built a dock. Among these boats were the *Henrietta* (a stern wheeler), *Lucille* and *Columbia*. They did a thriving business, especially on Sundays.

Speaking of transportation, about 1911 a proposal was first made to construct a canal between Lake Superior and the Mississippi River, from Duluth to Minneapolis. Duluth bitterly opposed the project, and by 1913 feeling was high. At a meeting at the Commercial Club, a board of engineers of the United States army, and men from Stillwater, St. Paul and Minneapolis appeared in advocacy of the canal. The Duluth contingent was not silent. Julius H. Barnes referred to the general failure of internal waterways in the United States and the impropriety of the advocates' comparing the Great Lakes, a deep waterway across the continent, with any casual project. F.W. Sullivan made an eloquent talk defending Duluth's position as "opposed to any canal that would be merely a means of perpetuating the railroad discrimination in favor of the Twin Cities at the expense of the whole Northwest." Other meetings were held, in Minneapolis and in Duluth, but nothing came of the project.

Another daydream was a Duluthian's suggestion that steam pipes be laid in Lake Superior to keep the lake open for navigation all year. This project did not merit a meeting.

A time-honored mode of transportation was abandoned in this period - the ferry to Park Point. On March 24, 1905, the aerial bridge was completed and regular service on it was begun. After suggestions for various types of bridges and tunnels were studied, the aerial bridge was patterned after one at Rouen, France, the only other one of this type in the world. The new bridge was 186 feet at its greatest height, and from the top was suspended a platform which moved across the canal on cables - if a boat were not entering the canal. The platform accommodated six vehicles on the unroofed middle part, and "enough passengers to fill two large street cars" in the enclosed cabins on either side. It could move from one shore to the other in one minute and forty seconds. This bridge was one of the "musts" in the tourist's list of places to see, although one felt an element of danger when driving a vehicle to the front edge of the platform. Only two accidents are recorded, however. One was the time a brewery team drove off the platform, plunging into the canal. Then there was the time H.L. Dresser, chief engineer for the Duluth, Missabe, and Northern railroad, drove his car off the platform. Jim Ten Eyck, coach of the Duluth Boat Club crews, was on the bridge, and in an instant shed his pants, dived into the canal, and brought Dresser to shore.

With the aerial bridge furnishing transportation to Park Point, that community came in for some big plans. The *Herald* of April 5, 1905, ran an architect's drawing for a summer hotel to be built that year on the Point, a sumptuous four story building of forty rooms, complete with verandas, cupolas, a summer pavilion, a bathing pavilion and an observatory. The "Long Beach Hotel" was to be constructed on a site where it would overlook both the lake and the bay. Joseph W. Reynolds, attorney, T.J. Bunting, real estate dealer, and outside capital were interested in the building which was never built.

The *Herald* of April 10, 1905, states "Duluth has an automobile course equal to Ormond Beach." It was planned to have a speed course on the Point. The beach was tried by E.J. Filiatrault, who drove the first automobile on the new ferry bridge, and who was the first to operate a car on Park Point. He drove a light electric Studebaker-Stanhope, since heavy cars could not negotiate the soft sand.

The streetcar company on the Point maintained an amusement park, the "White City" at the end of the car line for a few years at the beginning of the century. Here were presented vaudeville and other entertainment features.

Another place of entertainment was Lester Park, where the proprietor, L.A. Gunderson, had a dancing pavilion and a small zoo.

The Point also had a volunteer fire department. A dress rehearsal startled the citizens early Sunday morning, October 20, 1907, when the fire laddies dashed to the White City grounds.

Park Point became a popular place because of the Duluth Boat Club, the center of social and athletic activities. The club had almost ceased to exist during the Spanish-American War, but in 1900 an intensive membership drive and the interest and financial help of Julius H. Barnes resulted in a vigorous organization. In 1902, the club built a new clubhouse on the Point, and in 1906 the Oatka branch was opened, giving a two-and-a-half mile water course between the two clubhouses. In 1917, Mr. Barnes gave the club a $75,000 natatorium, and Matt Mann of Yale University was hired to coach Duluth swimmers to national championships. The main clubhouse had a dance floor, space for shells, living quarters for crew members, a dining room with windows on four sides, and bleachers, from which customers could view regattas held in St. Louis Bay.

The "Carnival of Venice" given on the night of July 25, 1910, was a brilliant water carnival with 140 craft beautifully illuminated. The committee for the affair was composed of men whose names were constantly linked to the Boat Club: J.D. Mahoney, B.C. Church, John MacGregor, W.B. Cross, Elbert Dresser, Walter McCarthy, and Bentley P. Neff.

The blue and white colors of the Duluth Boat Club flew over winning crews in the major races of the country. In 1887, the club was admitted to the Minnesota-Winnipeg Rowing Association. In 1906, a junior four and a junior eight won the Northwestern Rowing Association regatta at Lake Minnetonka, Minneapolis. By 1909, the club boasted a junior eight in charge of Dr. Frank Lynam, and a senior eight and a bantam four coached by Murray and John Peyton. The club began attracting national attention in 1911, when Jim Ten Eyck, son of the famous Syracuse coach, came to instruct the crews. That year, the bantam four won its first major race in the Northwestern regatta. Members of the crew were Eddie Walker, Meda St. Pierre, Ernie Refus, and Ted Mapp. In 1914, Duluth won the Sir Thomas Lipton trophy, the first time it was offered in competition.

Probably the most famous Boat Club crew was the senior four which was never defeated: Phil and Doug Moore, Max Rheinberger, and David S. Horack. They rowed together for four years as a four and as part of the senior eight with A.R. Kent, B.J. Hagberg, Charles Whiteside, Frances Hall, and Lincoln G. Brown, coxswain. At the national regatta at Springfield, Massachusetts in 1915, this eight set a record that still stands.

From 1911 to 1923, the Duluth Boat Club had the outstanding crews in the nation. With A.R. Kent coaching in 1921, the boys won twelve out of thirteen races at the national regatta in Buffalo, New York. One Eastern sports writer complained of the monotony of seeing Duluth win. Another suggested that if the Duluth crews would wear their medals they would be so weighted down they would not have a chance to win. In all, the crews entered fifty-eight races, won forty-seven including twenty championships, and took nine second and one third place.

In 1922, Walter Hoover, single sculler, won both the Philadelphia Gold Challenge Cup, emblematic of the world's championship for amateur single scullers, and the Diamond Sculls at Henley-on-Thames, England. When Hoover returned to Duluth from England, most of the town was at the Omaha station to welcome him. Led by the American Legion band, the townsfolk escorted Hoover through the downtown streets. That night, a mammoth parade was held in his honor, and there was dancing on the new pavement on Superior Street.

When the Duluth Ski Club was organized in November, 1905, another sport was developed to bring national honors for Duluth. The club was formed, with a charter membership of forty-two, under the direction of Aksel Holter, secretary of the National Ski Association of America, which had been organized the previous year. The officers were: I.A. Iverson, president; Adolph Lunde, secretary; Dr. H. Hovde, vice president; and H.G. Borgen, treasurer. H.B. Knudsen, Odin Halden and L.A. Larson were elected board members.

According to Harold A. Grinden, who has been a promoter of the sport both locally and nationally, "Duluth has played a very prominent role in the development of skiing on a national basis and has been recognized many times by its citizens winning national titles and citizens selected for national association official representation." Odin Halden served the national organization as treasurer in 1906, and H.G. Borgen in 1911 and 1912.

Ole Feiring in 1907 and John Evenson in 1908, 1909, won the national class A title; and H. Trannum in 1908 and Sig Bergerson in 1915 won the national class B championship. Top flight ski jumpers of Duluth around 1906 were Ole Feiring, Oluf Larson, John Evenson, Gustave Bye and John Mangseth, whose victories are listed over a period of years in the early records.

Duluth entertained the national jumping classic in 1908 and 1915 at Chester Bowl.

Beginning about 1902, ice horse races were run on the lake back of Fitger's Brewery. Race meets were held every Saturday and Sunday, promoted by R.B. Whiteside, Captain James Sullivan, Dr. John McKay, P. Sher, William McCullough, Lawrence Duplaise, L.R. Totman, Charles Armistead, A.A. Campbell, C.R. Rust, John Runquist, H.R. Elliot, Dr. Davis and George Gamble. In 1914, Captain Sullivan's horse "Captain S", driven by Billy Randall, established a world's record for the one-half mile on ice, a record that has never been broken. Events were decided on a best of three out of five heats. Horses were equipped with special calks to pull the two-wheel sulkies.

Although the daily papers of 1900 had a sports section of only three columns per week, Duluthians seem to have been interested in a variety of sports. The Bicycle Club had held annual bicycle races since 1891. All state records were made on the course from Fifth Avenue East on London Road to the fish hatchery at Lester Park and back to Ninth Avenue East. Gold watches, cups, and bicycles were prizes for winners. J.R. Zweifel was Duluth's star in early days. He has the trophy, which had to be won two years in succession, for the five-mile race which he won in 1896 and '97. The 1898 race was a ten-mile affair on the half-mile track at the present Wheeler Field. Sixty-eight riders were here from all over this part of the country. Handicaps ranged up to seven minutes but Zweifel had to ride from scratch. In that race he won three first prizes - for Duluth riders, for Head of the Lakes riders, and for the best time of all. His time was 26 minutes, 45 seconds. About 1906, the popularity of bicycle racing faded.

The Northern Baseball League was organized in 1902, with teams from Duluth, Superior, Crookston, Winnipeg, Fargo and Grand Forks. In 1906-1907, this league changed to the Minnesota-Wisconsin league, familiarly known as the "Minnie" league, including Duluth, Superior, La Crosse, Winona, Fargo, Grand Forks, Winnipeg and Brandon. The Northern league reorganized in 1908, with Duluth, Superior, Minneapolis, Winona, Red Wing, Grand Forks and Winnipeg. For a period the Duluth White Sox were one of the great teams in the league. Owned by A.W. Kuehnow, real estate dealer, and managed by Darby O'Brien, the "Irish orator", the team won the league pennant in 1909 and in 1910. It sent more players to major leagues in these years than in any other period of Northern League baseball: George Dauss to the Detroit Tigers, where he was the greatest curve ball pitcher of the American league; Elmer Miller, outfielder, to the Cleveland Indians, where he distinguished himself by being the first major league player to hit a home run with bases loaded in a World Series game; Elmer Smith, outfielder, to the New York Yankees; Otto Mueller, catcher, to the Brooklyn Dodgers; and Rube Marion, pitcher, to the St. Louis Cardinals. A third baseman of the White Sox also made a name for himself, though not in baseball. Frank J. Lausche became mayor of Cleveland and is at present governor of Ohio. From 1910 to 1925, history of the Northern league is sketchy, but by 1928 it had resumed something of its old standing.

Besides league teams, Duluth had several independent teams with players of note. In 1910, the Big Duluth team defeated Artie O'Dea's Superior Northern league team, 7 to 2. A sports item in a newspaper said: "`Babe' Bennet pitched well for the winners. `Scotty' Macaulay, Tom Taylor, and Frank Summers starred for Duluth." In the same summer, in the West End the "Chippewas" were organized by Frank Mork, George Wollin, Paul Lyman, Russel Broman, Ray Olson, John Seglem, Arnold Olson, Andrew Anderson and Fred Lund.

Duluth had a lacrosse team in the early days of this century. On May 31, 1903, a crowd of 700 witnessed a game at Oneota Park, where St. Paul defeated Duluth 5 to 3.

A crack shot rifle team brought honors to the city. Charles Helmer, L. Berger, A.E. Ritzman, P.W. Perrigo, H. Spitvold, F.E. Resche and E.G. Simpson, representing the field staff and band of the Third Infantry, Minnesota National Guard, won the indoor championship of Minnesota in 1909, and the battalion trophy, the A.B. Siewart trophy and the Superior trophy in 1912, besides numerous other matches. Nearly every member of the team won a large number of individual medals and honors.

John L. Sullivan, "the strong boy of Boston", whose publicity read "He was always on the level and he never threw a friend," appeared at the Lyceum in April of 1905 to give a talk and exhibition bouts. About his talk, the *Herald* reporter wrote: "Nothing but his nerve and determination saved him from a knockout long before time was called on him. Several times the English language landed a solar plexus blow that had John gasping and taking the count, but he always came back with a handful of disconnected grammar and decomposed pronunciation that kept him going until his second got busy with his prompter's book...Along, with only the aid of his second at times, John stood there and conquered that monologue in full sight of over 2,000 people who packed the Lyceum to its doors. It was superb! It was heroic! It was grand!...But when John had the monologue down and out and bought chips in a gentleman's game, where it was give and take, he was there with the goods."

Not all sport was competitive. A free skating rink was prepared and maintained by public subscription on the south side of London Road at Twelfth Avenue East. East End boys made a house to house canvass for funds, under the direction of J.H. Davis. On fine afternoons 300 to 500 people of all ages could be seen skating on the new rink. There were also rinks at Lakeside and Glen Avon.

With shorter working hours, people had more time for recreation, and Duluth was not behind other cities in providing recreational facilities. In 1908, a Public Playground Association was organized. It formulated plans for a playground at Lakeshore Park, the first in the city, followed by Lincoln Park playground. The next year, playground apparatus was installed at West Duluth at Fifty-first Avenue on Wadena Street. In 1910, Portman Square was made into an athletic field and work was begun on Congdon Park. In 1912, the Park Board began to build shelters for the larger playgrounds. In this year the Board of Education and the Playground Association combined forces.

In 1915, T.S. Settle of New York City, field secretary for the Playground and Recreation Association of America, drafted plans for an all-year recreation program in Duluth - fourteen playgrounds, municipal golf links, bathing beaches in public schools, tennis courts, children's motion picture theatres, and playgrounds near every schoolhouse. J.R. Batchelor, physical director of the Boys' Y, was appointed recreation director. Duluth's all-year playground and recreation system was officially opened at Chester Park in June, with a band concert, an address by Mayor Prince and a sports program. Miss Pauline Stode of Chicago became assistant director, and Roland B. Reed was lifeguard and swimming instructor, stationed at the Indian Point bathing beach. By the end of the first year, 260,487 Duluthians had participated in the recreational activities. In 1916, the city had ten playgrounds and rinks.

A new community tradition was begun on Christmas Eve, 1912, when twenty-five choristers paraded the streets of suburbs, carrying lanterns and singing carols. In 1914, a community Christmas tree was erected in the Courthouse Square. In sub-zero weather, the park department built huge bonfires, and the courthouse doors were left open so that people could enter the building for warmth. The Third Regiment band played, school children sang carols, and the Svea Male Chorus, Orpheus and Swedish choruses gave vocal numbers. Souvenir cards were passed out on which were printed a verse by O.J. Williams, which had won first place in a city contest. War raging in Europe, but that was far from Duluth that Christmas season.

One generous, anonymous Duluth citizen had a Christmas tradition of his own. This item is found in the *Herald* of December 24, 1912: "This is the night when the `newsies' who sell the *Herald* get their papers free, and the night when income is velvet. Each year a mysterious benefactor sends the *Herald* a check for the papers and asks the public in general to buy from the boys, give more than the price of the paper, and tell the boys to `keep the change.'"

One of the builders of Duluth died March 14, 1913 - Roger S. Munger. Among his activities, he had built the first grain elevator, the first sawmill, the first coal dock, Munger Terrace and an opera house in the city. He had an interest in the Spalding Hotel, held the contract for digging the canal, and supplied ties for the Northern Pacific. Mr. Munger was the grandfather of Mrs. Warren S. Jamar, who lives in Duluth.

Probably no man at any time had a greater interest in the welfare and development of Duluth than had Mr. Munger. His wife used to say that he had an obsession that no one should speak ill of his beloved city. She told the story that at a dinner party at their home one evening, they were entertaining some Easterners. Although Mr. Munger had briefed his wife on the praise she was to give Duluth, he valiantly endeavored to listen to the conversation at both ends of the long table, to be sure that all went well. It was something of a feat to keep up his end of the conversation and listen to the other end as well. He failed to hear the gentleman ask Mrs. Munger, "Do you have typhoid fever here?", but he heard his wife answer "No, we don't have it in Duluth." Indignantly, Mr. Munger boomed out, "Well, we can get it!"

Another respected Duluth citizen who was a power in the development of the city, Colonel Charles Graves, was appointed Minister to Norway and Sweden in 1905. He was the first Duluthian to have a foreign ministry. Before he left for his post, prominent Scandinavians gave him a party at the Commercial Club. Dr. J.M. O. Tufty was master of ceremonies, and John Uno Sebenious presented the Colonel with a handsome silk American flag. Flaaten's orchestra played Scandinavian and American airs, and there were speeches galore. The affair ended with toasts around the champagne punchbowl.

Debates and informal arguments were a prelude to the city election of December 3, 1912, when the citizens of Duluth voted to change from the aldermanic to a commission form of government. The new charter was the third for the city, the first one adopted in 1870 and readopted in 1887. The charter provided for a mayor and four commissioners, who "shall devote their entire time, during business hours, to service of the City, and shall not hold any other public office during their terms of office." It was designated that the mayor would be commissioner of public affairs. Other divisions of the government were departments of finance, public works, safety, and utilities. After a bitter campaign, the new elected city commissioners met for the first time at noon on April 14, 1913. W.I. Prince was the first commission mayor; old Fred Voss, W.A. Hicken, Roderick Murchison and 69-year-old Leonidas Merritt were commissioners.

Commissioners Fred J. Voss called up the past when he introduced in the council a resolution for appointment of a canal and dike commission to collect a claim with interest, approximately $450,000, against the Federal government for the construction of a ship canal and of the dike subsequently built and later destroyed by order of the government. Uncle Sam did not agree with Voss about payment.

Miss Edith Scovell is authority for a story about the remains of that dike. It seems that when it was destroyed, parts of it were left submerged, a danger to sailing boats in which young people went for the equivalent of an evening's drive. It was a common excuse for a girl coming home late (after nine o'clock) to say the boat got stuck on the dike. Some of our best people had that experience, and one couple had to remain fast to the dike all night. That dike seems to have been just as efficacious an excuse as a flat tire or running out of gas.

The commissioner of public safety had inherited a problem of cleaning Duluth streets. A month before he was elected, it was stated unequivocally, that Duluth streets were in the worst condition in history. The *Herald* of March 11 says: "The prevalent opinion is that the municipality should not wait for the sun to do the bulk of the work, but that the winter's accumulation of snow, ice and dirt should be loaded in wagons and carted away at once."

William A. Hicken, in campaigning for commissioner of public safety, promised to clean up the city and see that laws were obeyed. He did just that, but not without receiving vigorous complaints, threats and anonymous letters. Declaring that the first Sunday of the commission administration should be a pattern for future Sundays, he had the whole force out to see that liquor was not sold. His crusade included observing laws about no liquor served in public dining rooms and about saloons closing at 11 p.m. Three hundred bartenders endorsed him in this by sending him a huge bouquet of American Beauty roses. By the end of May, the notorious segregated red light district on St. Croix Avenue had practically passed into oblivion, the 130 fancy women having left the city.

As a campaign measure for the city selection of 1917, volume 1, number 1 of the *Duluth Ripshaw* was published March 24, 1917 by John L. Morrison. In June, it became a weekly paper. The *Ripshaw* guarded morals of the city by exposing SIN, CORRUPTION and city and county officials. The mystery of how the chief of police had obtained his Marmon car, "King Odin" and his activities as county auditor and school board meetings were stand-bys in every issue. "The great family journal" used stock phrases: "Firoved, member of the "sly old board of education", was always "the little commoner" in an organization which was "a struggle between democracy and autocracy"; teachers were "nuns without cloister"; any member absent from a school board meeting was "conspicuous by his absence"; the courthouse was "the marble-lined courthouse"; the eastern section of the city was "the snobbish East End"; women were "pulchritudinous". The paper abounded in stories of "love pirates" and generally contained an article in "ye olde style". It used lurid headlines: "Wide Knocks Out Olson's Teeth", "Superior Opens Hotel de Jag", "Virginia is as Beauteous as a Virgin". The *Ripshaw* was read, not so much because of its scandal stories as because of its satire. Its reputation was such that when a woman bought a copy the newsdealer would wrap it up for her in plain paper. The original *Ripshaw* lived about four years and died with the editor, although there were sporadic efforts to revive it.

The days of referring to "the high school" came to an end in 1914, when Denfeld high school (now West Junior) was built. The new school was very modern, with thirty classrooms, a gymnasium, and woodworking, manual training, domestic science, and laboratory rooms. In 1901, a new manual training high school was organized and located in the Washington building.

At the turn of the century, the Duluth public school system was comprised of thirteen elementary schools and one high school. Between 1900 and 1920, the city erected twenty new buildings: Monroe, 1900; Nettleton and Washburn, 1905; Ely, 1906; Ensign, 1908; Fairmount, 1910; Lowell, Merritt, and Washington, 1911; Cobb, 1913; Munger and the old Denfeld, 1914; Lincoln and Stowe, 1915; Morgan Park, 1916; Lester Park, 1917; Grant, 1918; and Bay View Heights, Liberty and Park Point, 1919. The total original cost of these buildings was about two million dollars.

Duluthians showed a deep interest in even the little details of education in the public schools. In 1904, a controversy arose about penmanship. Citizens sent petitions to the Board of Education requesting that their children be taught slant writing. Denfeld, superintendent, championed the cause of vertical writing, claiming that vertical had shown the best results in regard to speed and legibility. The argument was carried into the newspapers. In these days, when a child uses his individual style of writing, such a controversy seems unimportant, but to citizens who built twenty schools in nineteen years, everything about the education system was important.

Among the school facilities of which the city was proud was the night school for foreigners, established at Central and Irving in 1912. Finns predominated in the classes, with Swedes and then Germans next in number. At the Industrial High School in West Duluth, the 1913 graduating class published their first yearbook, the *Oracle*, which is still published by Denfeld. Duluth boasted the best equipped manual training school in the state and the first school system in the state to teach physical culture, a course instituted in the nineties.

The State Normal School, established by an act of the State Legislature in 1895, opened its doors for its first students in 1902. Dr. E.W. Bohannon, the first president, served in that capacity continuously for thirty-six years. In 1905, the name became the Duluth State Normal School, and in 1912, the Duluth State Teachers College. Its chief mission was the education of teachers for public schools in Minnesota. As the school grew in enrollment, a dormitory was completed in 1910, and other additions in 1911 and 1914.

The first Commencement Day at the Normal was June 3, 1903, when seven girls received the first diplomas awarded by the institution. Graduates were Bessie E. Bowman, Amanda E. Ellefsen, Esther Levy, Elizabeth Merritt, Helen Bowyer, Agnes R. Holt, and Willena Marshall. "The members of the class were gracefully gowned." G.A. Morey of Winona, President of the State Normal Board, handed out the diplomas, and the Rev. A.B. Marshall, Minneapolis, gave the commencement address.

In 1909, the first unit of the Villa of St. Scholastica, outgrowth of the Sacred Heart Institute, was built on a 160-acre tract in Kenwood. The high school became accredited, and in 1913 a junior college course was started with eight students. The curriculum was centered around religion, philosophy, mathematics, Greek, Latin, English and the natural sciences. The following year, the college was accredited to the University of Minnesota. A new wing with accommodations for a chapel, dining room and kitchens was erected in 1919, and a combined gymnasium and auditorium in 1921.

Cathedral school grew out of the old St. Thomas in 1904. In 1907, the Christian Brothers established a high school for boys, and in 1910, Girls Cathedral high school was established. These two schools were combined in 1940 t be known as Cathedral high school. Other Catholic schools organized in this period were St. Peter and Paul, 1901; St. Jean Baptiste, 1905; and St. James, 1913. The St. James Orphanage was founded in the old St. Mary's Hospital (now St. Anne's Home) in 1900 and moved to the find building at Woodland in 1910.

Closely associated with education in the Duluth public library, a gift of $75,000 from Andrew Carnegie made possible the present building. On July 4, 1901, the cornerstone was laid as part of the holiday celebration. Photographs show a great crowd of people present, partially obscured by umbrellas; the occasion as well as the crowd was dampened by a cold rain. The library board was composed of Robert E. Denfeld, president; R.C. Mitchell, vice president; Dr. Charles L. Codding, secretary; Giles Gilbert, William T. Thompson, W.M. Hubbard, Mrs. C.R. Keyes, Dr. S.M. Stocker and S.T. Harrison. The new library was opened, April 19, 1902. The following year, a report showed that Duluthians were partial to western writers. Branches were established in West Duluth in 1912; West End, 1915; and Morgan Park, 1917.

Another cultural organization was the Little Theatre, founded in 1914. Mrs. S.R. Holden was the guiding spirit for this group.

In 1904, the Svea Glee Club (Swedish) and the Normanna club (Norwegian), the two principal singing societies, held their first annual contest for the Carlson trophy...The Third Regiment band, directed by J.H. Flaaten, made several concert tours in 1905...January 29, 1913, saw the introduction of a Duluth symphony orchestra at the Lyceum, with guest Mischa Elman. There were forty-two musicians directed by Gustav Flaaten...In 1915, Fred H. Bradbury organized the Duluth Concert Orchestra, which gave its first concert, January 10, in the Central high school auditorium.

The present central building of the YMCA at Third Avenue West and Second Street was erected in 1908. Duluth citizens subscribed $180,000 for this building, which included the most modern equipment and every opportunity for healthful recreation. That year, 2,675 men joined the association. The West Duluth branch building was a gift of Julius H. Barnes in 1920. The Y center at Gary was established in 1919 through the efforts of Watson Moore, but was abandoned in 1924.

In 1916, the Boys' Y building was erected, the gift of Julius H. Barnes and his partner Ward Ames Jr., as a memorial to Ward Ames Sr. This is a real club, distinguished from most institutional buildings by its iron railings and green shutters on the exterior, and beamed ceilings and huge fireplace in the lobby. The Boys' Y had been organized in 1903, when Norman D. McLeod came from Ottawa to be the first secretary.

When speaking of the Boys' Y, one thinks of Camp Miller, a permanent camp which grew out of an outing of fourteen boys in about 1900. In 1914 Camp Miller was started at Sturgeon Lake, with a clubhouse and tents for cooking and living quarters. J.R. Batchelor, city recreation director, built the first cabin, named in honor of Watson Moore. Other cabins named for men active in Y work are Barnes, Ames, McCabe, Wade, Mitchell, Harvey Williams,

Walker, McGonagle, and Congdon. Frank Hathaway gave one of these cabins. Mrs. Williamson and her daughter gave Williamson Lodge, and Minot and Rotary built lodges named for their donors. The hospital was a gift from the Kiwanis Club and was furnished by Dr. W.A. Coventry. The Exchange Club built and donated a craft shop. The first boats were given by Henry F. Salyards and G.A. Priest back in 1919.

The Young Women's Christian Association, as it is today, was established in 1902. This was really a reorganization, for the institution had had a start in 1893, when a group of civic-minded women rented a room where young women could have exercise and a cheerful place for recreation. However, because of hard times, the first organization existed for only two years. The new YWCA employed Miss Maude Culver (Mrs. Robert G. Dunlop) as general secretary and gymnasium teacher. By 1908, the building now in use was completed, offering a home for approximately seventy-five girls. It has served transients of all races and creeds from all over the world.

In 1914, the Girl Reserve department of the YW was started at Central high school, with Miss Mary McGonagle (Mrs. Mark Tibbets) the first president. In 1945 this department adopted the new name of Y-Teens.

In the first year of reorganization of the YW, a deaconess was engaged as a Travelers' Aid at the Union depot. By 1911, a second worker was employed to help strangers coming to Duluth. Posters in several languages were put up in the stations. The women who do Travelers' Aid work accomplish everything from finding lost relatives to helping with wedding plans.

The next branch of work of the YW was the International Institute, established in September, 1919, with the opening of the "little gray house" in Gary. This department became a separate organization in 1946.

The Associated Charities was organized on October 18, 1909. According to an annual report, "For a year, quiet and efficient work was done in completing the organization of this society and in securing the cooperation of thirty different social and civic organizations represented on its central council." Courtney Dinwiddy, the first general secretary, took up his duties in November, 1910. The founders of the Associated Charities set up an agency devoted primarily, not to relief-giving, but to friendly visiting and counseling. The aim was not so much to relieve poverty as to prevent it.

Another type of organization was the Naval Militia. The year 1910 was a banner year for the men of this organization. They built a boathouse and headquarters, put themselves in uniforms, and won boat races. The Militia had entered crews since 1903, and in 1910 they "cleaned up". In a 28-foot whaleboat, they won a trophy presented by the Buffalo Chamber of Commerce and Manufacturers Club, won over the Motor Boat Club's militia at Motor Island near Buffalo and won the executive's trophy. It is said they never suffered a defeat until they met a regular Navy crew from the *U.S.S. Wolverine*.

The Naval Militia was organized in 1903, growing out of a local movement in 1898. Instrumental in the organization was Captain Guy Eaton, who became the first commander. The Militia consisted of two divisions with a total of twelve commissioned officers and eighty-three petty officers and enlisted men. Members had to supply all their own equipment except 100 rifles, which were furnished by the state. The first drill hall was the Shrine auditorium.

At first, the men had two 30-foot navy cutters for training purposes, but in 1905 the *U.S.S. Fern* was acquired for practice cruises and renamed the *U.S.S. Gopher*. The Naval Reserve base at Twelfth Street on Park Point was established in 1910.

Two new divisions were added to the Minnesota Naval Militia in 1913, one at Duluth and one at Pine City; in 1916, Bemidji, Crosby, Lindstrom and St. Paul had divisions. By January, 1917, there were twenty-eight officers and 511 enlisted men. By an act of Congress, August 29, 1916, National Naval Volunteers were organized to be recruited by enlistment or draft from membership of Naval Militia organizations. These were the first men to be called up in World War I.

The country had a rehearsal for war in 1916, when a punitive expedition was sent into Mexico to hunt the bandit Francisco Villa, whose gang of cutthroats acquired the irritating habit of murdering Americans. A new National Guard company, Co. A, was mustered in Duluth by Colonel F.E. Resche, January 25. Elmer McDevitt, local attorney, was elected captain. By February, the company had a complete roster.

On March 15, two columns entered Mexico, commanded by Brigadier General John J. Pershing and Colonel George A. Dodd. In Duluth, on March 23, the Spanish-American War Veterans organized a company, on order of their national commander. Villa was a cagey cuss who had no intention of being found in the mountains of Mexico, and he led the Americans a merry chase. The Mexican government finally grew weary of seeing American soldiers cluttering up their landscape. The fracas ended in November, when the National Guardsmen returned to their respective states to be mustered out of Federal service. Villa was not found.

By this time, America was more concerned over the war in Europe, which had seemed so far away, when begun in the summer of 1914.

The *Herald* reflected the general attitude of America at the beginning of the war, in an editorial on August 25, 1914: "What the war means to us and to them is simple enough; it means that we shall keep out of it, and that we shall go about our business just as though the world were at peace, except that the war in Europe opens up to our farmers, our manufacturers, and our ship-owners a rare opportunity to do a great business...Let's dedicate our days to the business we have to do, and thus win the prosperity that is our due and the profits that are ours for the grasping."

It seemed a simple thing to stay out of war until the sinking of the *Lusitania* in 1915, followed by torpedoing of other American ships. American began to question the slogan "Peace at any price," and think of preparedness. The following year, Germany announced that it would sink ships without warning, but Woodrow Wilson was reelected president that fall on the slogan, "He kept us out of war."

In January, 1917, Germany proclaimed a policy of unrestricted submarine warfare, and in February, Wilson severed diplomatic relations with Germany. By this time armed neutrality was a burning question and hundreds of American young men had joined the French and English armies.

On April 6, 1917, America declared war on Germany - a "war to end war".

Within two days, seven Minnesota divisions of the Naval Militia were in Duluth, twenty-two officers and 326 men, to entrain for the Navy Yard at Philadelphia. "Duluth staged the first of those ceremonious, noisy, and heartbreaking last farewells from the people of Minnesota that were to become so familiar in months following."

In Minnesota, there were four regiments of National Guard units, three of which made up a brigade of infantry under the command of Brigadier General Frederick E. Resche. Colonel Hubert V. Eva was in command of the Third Infantry with headquarters at Duluth. Companies A and E, and a detachment of C of this Infantry were placed temporarily on guard over mills, docks and bridges at Duluth, Two Harbors and International Falls. A new machine gun company was organized here. By the latter part of July, 7099 men and 222 officers were mustered into state service. In the recruiting campaigns, Duluth's quota of volunteers was 1,550 men. In August, the National Guard, as the Third Infantry, pulled out for further training at Deming, New Mexico. The Third was reorganized in September as the 125th Field Artillery. In full strength, it was composed of 1,462 men and included Batteries A, B, C, D, and E. Most of the Duluth men were represented in A, C, and E, and in the medical department.

In April, the Home Guard of Minnesota was established to replace the National Guard in the city under Captain Roger M. Weaver. In May, Duluth organized a Citizens' Training Corps.

Men between the ages of twenty-one and thirty registered for the first draft on June 5. On July 20, the drawing of serial numbers took place in Washington. Men with the serial numbers drawn reported for examination and induction.

All Duluth carried on the war in one way or another. Women served on Red Cross committees, and devoted themselves to such tasks as knitting and rolling bandages. A general committee carried on Americanization work to help foreigners to become neutralized citizens. Solicitations were made for relief work in Europe and for welfare agencies in the war - Red Cross, Salvation Army, National Catholic War Council, Jewish Welfare Board, Y.M.C.A., Y.W.C.A., War Camp Community Service and American Library Association. "Wheatless days," "meatless days" and "heatless days" were observed to conserve food and fuel. There were great parades, with industrial units, marching units, military units, bands and units of captured German war equipment.

Minute Men were organized to carry on bond sales. Duluth's record in that activity is magnificent. In the first Liberty bond sale, the city doubled its quota of $2,000,000; in the second, it raised over $7,000,000, oversubscribing the quota by about $1,500,000; in the third, $7,000,000 again; in the fourth, $8,448,300; and in the fifth, the Victory Loan, $6,500,000, and oversubscription of $1,000,000.

In 1916, Julius H. Barnes and Alexander McDougall had constructed one of the largest ship-building plants on the Great Lakes. At Riverside, it built dry docks to provide for sixteen freighters at a time. Sixty homes were erected for workmen and their families. The first ship to be launched was the *Robert L. Barnes* of Duluth, a new square type of ship which Captain McDougall designed, adapting for it the seaworthy qualities of the whaleback ship. The vessel was sent to the Atlantic in 1916, and it was taken by the Navy in 1917. It served the Navy for twenty-five years, and then - but that is another story.

The McDougall-Duluth Shipbuilding Company made an astounding contribution to the war. It could construct eight vessels at a time, great seagoing steel freighters that went through the canal in their weird coats of camouflage. Here were manufactured the huge boilers for the ships, while steel parts were supplied by local foundries. The St. Louis River was widened at places so the first big ship, the *Lake Portage*, could be floated. Launchings were kept secret, but they were accompanied with bands and the traditional christening with champagne. The shipyards built thirty-seven vessels in 1917-1918.

The Superior Shipbuilding Company and the Globe Shipbuilding Company were also working twenty-four hours a day to build ships for war.

Ore boats fairly paraded through the canal, as hundreds of millions tons of iron ore were shipped down the lakes. In 1917, the Lake Superior district produced nearly 85 per cent of the total amount of ore mined in the United States. Some of this remained in Duluth to be manufactured into war-time products, but the records show that through the harbor went 37,892,382 tons in 1917, and

38,213,498 in 1918. Shipments of 200,000 tons of ore a day were not unusual. The old wooden ore docks were replaced by steel and concrete docks, where four or five vessels could be loaded simultaneously. Railroad dump cars now ran on to the docks and opened directly into the hoppers. The hoppers, spaced as hatches on boats were spaced, poured ore into the hatches by spouts, loading all hatches at the same time. One man could dump a carload of ore in about fifteen seconds. The record is more than 12,000 tons in sixteen and a half minutes.

By the autumn of 1918, armistice terms began to be discussed in newspapers. It was near the end of the war that a Spanish influenza epidemic struck the country. In Duluth, there would be as high as forty-five new cases reported in a day. On October 11, public gatherings were forbidden, and all schools, theaters and churches were closed, to remain dark for about six weeks. About 1,500 cases of flu and 100 death were the toll in Duluth.

The day following the ban, Saturday, October 12, came the worst forest fire in the history of Minnesota. Smoke was in the air most of the day, but Duluthians were accustomed to smoky October days and had no premonition of impending disaster. In the afternoon, a crowd attended the annual Central-Cathedral football game at the old ball park. When the game was stopped for a call for volunteers to fight the forest fire, there was a moment of surprise, and then the game continued.

Meanwhile, the fire was racing along, as hundreds of little fires, creeping through the dusty swamps and feeding on dry leaves, combined into a sheet of flame. The weather was unseasonably warm and the land was dry; in twenty months, the area was twenty inches short of rain. The wind rose steadily, and by 3:30, the sun burned red through swirling smoke. By six o'clock, when the fire was at its height, the wind had increased to gale proportions, and word reached Duluth that the Pike Lake district was in flames. Many Duluthians were on their way for weekends at the lakes and were caught in the fire. By early evening, cars were dashing down Superior Street, bringing in refugees. The fire had struck swiftly, so families had no opportunity to save their belongings. They came into hotels, empty-handed and stunned. One small girl stood in a hotel lobby carrying a tired-looking doll, while her brother clutched a piece of apple pie.

Flames jumped from one locality to another, cutting off escape. Some settlers sought safety in roothouses, where they were smothered by smoke and gasses; others took boats into the lakes, where huge waves overturned their crafts. Thousands lined the Pike Lake road. The Home Guard, Motor Corps, and National Guard requisitioned cars and trucks for rescue and dashed out the Miller Trunk road. Returning before a 60 to 78-mile wind, many cars were overtaken by flames and abandoned by the roadside. On a curve in the road, one driver, blinded by smoke, swerved into a ditch, and others, following the tail lights of cars ahead, piled up in the ditch. Drivers with passenger cars carrying ten to twenty people, wept as they passed refugees standing with hands outstretched imploringly.

In early evening, the fire reached Duluth. Homecroft school burned down; then the Cobb, as the fire swept Woodland. Northland Country Club burned; the Alger Smith Lumber Company on Garfield Avenue went up in flames; and the approach to the interstate bridge was wrecked. In Hunters Park, Woodland, and Lakeside, fire-fighting groups were formed to save schools, churches, and dwellings. A sudden change of wind at night was all that saved Duluth from destruction.

On Sunday, news was brought to the city of the extent of the tragedy; Moose Lake and Cloquet were completely wiped out; in Moose Lake there were 500 dead; 8,000 people were evacuated from Cloquet in one hour before the trains stopped running; morgues were overcrowded with unidentified bodies. It was later estimated that more than 1,000 people were lost, many of whom were never identified.

The National Guard Armory was thrown open Saturday night and the Red Cross began its work of caring for refugees. A huge dining hall was set up in the basement. Churches and schools were also fitted out with cots. Governor Burnquist appointed Colonel Hubert V. Eva general manager of a relief commission, with W.A. McGonagle chairman. Doctors and nurses volunteered their services. Men left their business to spend long, arduous days in helping. Since schools were closed for the influenza epidemic, teachers helped to distribute clothing, serve meals, or assist in crowded hospitals. Housewives came to help, and clubs pooled their resources. The commission had at its command about 1,500 private cars and between 400 and 500 trucks loaned by manufacturers and wholesalers. The railroads carried freight and passengers without compensation for about four months. Contributions came in from over the country. Long tables were set up in the Armory, where was piled a vast amount of clothing sent in by the people of Duluth.

Poignant scenes were common at the National Guard Armory, as members of families, separated in the fire, were reunited. One man and his wife, coming to seek help, were on opposite sides of the office, registering. Each thought the other dead; then, suddenly, they looked up and saw each other. Another man insisted upon his Scotch collie dog's accompanying him; the dog, he said, was all he had left. His wife and six children had perished. There was stark tragedy in the Armory those days.

The commission report states that 11,382 families registered for aid, and 9,016 farm animals were fed and cared for. There were 2,100 injured who received treatment, and 106 who died of flu and pneumonia. Actual needs were provided for. Material was given for one-room houses and barns, and volunteer workers assisted in construction. Generous individuals gave livestock as well as money. The vast extent of the rehabilitation work may be appreciated when one reads in the commission report: "All who desired were able to return to their land with their stock during the winter." A sum of $3,150,000 was expended in relief to victims of the fire.

The work, heartaches and suffering which make up war came near an end on November 11, 1918, when the armistice was signed. No celebration had been planned for the great day, but crowds milled around the Commercial Club most of the night, waiting for the signal. About 4:30 in the morning, the whistles began to blow up to announce the armistice had been signed. Shouts went up on the downtown streets and, as if on a prearranged schedule, automobiles converged on Superior Street in an impromptu parade that lasted into the night. The sidewalks were jammed with people waving banners and yelling with joy as they marched up and down. Adding to the din of screaming whistles, cars trailed noisemakers of all kinds, chiefly tin cans, garbage cans and kitchen utensils. One sedate black limousine, complete with chauffeur and white-haired dowager (sitting alone in stately grandeur on the back seat) dragged behind it all day a big copper wash boiler. Some people went to work, but business houses and industrial plants were closed. However, open trucks stood by, ready to be filled with workers to join the parade. They sang the war songs, "Over There", "Oh How I Hate to Get Up in the Morning," "Keep the Home Fires Burning," and "It's a Long Way to Tipperary."

News of the armistice lifted the pall of gloom and despair. Fire refugees were ready to begin life anew; the flu epidemic was diminishing; and the war was over. One dared, again, to look toward the future.

Headlines in the *News Tribune* of January 23, 1919, read: "Duluth welcomes the 125th Field Artillery men today.

All Duluth will be downtown today to greet heroes home from France." The Marshall-Wells whistle screamed the announcement when the trains reached Superior. The Northern Pacific brought in the first contingent at 2:20 p.m., and the Great Northern arrived a half hour later. The boys were met by the town, including representatives of the Commercial Club, Motor Corps and all lodges and clubs. For sheer noise, there was probably never a homecoming to equal it. Whenever the din subsided enough so that they could be heard, Charlie Helmer's band played. At night, there was a dance in the National Guard Armory.

The *big* homecoming celebration, however, was held on August 16. The dead, as well as the living, were remembered. A Temple of Victory was erected, where friends and relatives placed wreaths and bouquets for the boys who would never come back. The Temple closed at noon, and Marine scouts stood guard over tributes to the heroic dead.

Festivities for the returned soldiers began in the morning with a lake excursion. This was followed by a gigantic parade of decorated floats and costumed groups and individuals. At one time, in planning, it was suggested that the soldiers march in the parade, but this idea was vetoed on the grounds that the men were guests - and besides, they had had enough marching to last them the rest of their lives. Carnival was the theme, with music on every corner, tons of confetti, and street dancing at night at the Court of Honor; and everything was free for the men in uniform. The *Tribune* states that there were present "the insignia of 40-odd overseas divisions, colors of every branch of the service, and hundreds of uniforms of allied nations."

Over in Paris, France, March 15-17, veterans of World War I Expeditionary Forces had effected an organization that would be a force in Duluth as in the nation - the Foreign Legion. This non-political, non-sectarian organization stated its purposes in the preamble to its constitution: "to uphold and defend the Constitution of the United States of America; to maintain law and order; to preserve the memories and incidents of our associations in the great wars; to inculcate a sense of individual obligation to the community, state and nation; to combat the autocracy of both the classes and the masses; to make right the master of might; the promote peace and good will on earth; to safeguard and transmit to posterity the principles of justice, freedom and democracy; to consecrate and sanctify our comradeship by our devotion to mutual helpfulness."

The first organization of the American Legion in Duluth was David Wisted Post No. 28, formed June 24, 1919. It was named in honor of David Gilbert Wisted, the first Duluthian killed in combat in World War I. Wisted had fought in the battle of Chateau Thierry and was killed in the Battle of Belleau Wood. Charter members of the Post are Elmer W. McDevitt, John H. Truax, Donald S. Holmes, Gordon M. Clark, G.A.W. Henberg, Whitney Wall, Jr., Russell A. Mather, John Clark, Jr., Burt C. Hubbard, George B. Sjoselius, Leslie C. Gilbertson, C.C. Beeth, Carl Haglund, Douglas C. Moore, Lawrence E. Duby, Thomas W. Doan, James S. Elder, L.A. Robert, R.L. Mayall, J.E. Coates, Leonard McHugh, Lawrence Jacques, W.H. Sanford, Lewis Bolin, Frank F. Foster, Thomas E. Williams, Clarence T. Burke and Oliver B. Worcester.

Post-war life in the United States saw some changes. Two amendments to the Constitution were added in 1919: the eighteenth, prohibiting the manufacture and sale of intoxicating liquor; and the nineteenth, giving women the right to vote.

At an "over the top dinner" in 1919, a national movement was started on the St. Lawrence waterway, with Charles P. Craig of Duluth a director in the organization. Again, Duluthians could envision ocean liners in the harbor.

A glimpse of things-to-be was given when the landing site committee of the Head of the Lakes Club announced its selection of the Superior Country Club grounds as an official landing field for Duluth and Superior. People had come to the conclusion that the automobile was here to stay; now attention was turned to the airplane.

The first mail was sent by airplane from Duluth to Minneapolis and St. Paul on February 21, 1919. Lieutenant Walter Bullock was pilot. Mayor C.R. Magney sent the following message to Mayor J.E. Meyers of Minneapolis: "Greetings from the great port of the Northwest. As modern inventions annihilate distance, continents, countries and cities are brought close to one another and their common interests increase. The machine which carries this message is merely `blazing the trail' which will in the future be the most traveled highway between Duluth and the Twin Cities." The same idea was expressed in Magney's letter to Mayor L.C. Hodgson of St. Paul. Among letters sent were greetings from acting postmaster of Duluth, Colonel W.F. Henry, to the postmaster at Minneapolis and from Colonel Roger M. Weaver to Adjutant General W.F. Reinow in St. Paul.

The J.B. Culver Post of the National Guard Armory of the Republic in 1919 erected on Courthouse Square the statue "Patriotism". This statue is a commemoration to soldiers and sailors.

The nation was jubilant over victory in the war and was confident of a lasting peace and prosperity, as Duluth entered "the roaring twenties."

CHAPTER X

Twentieth Century - to the Mid-Century

THE year 1920 was the fiftieth anniversary of the chartering of Duluth as a city. Jay Cooke's town had survived three wars, three depressions, and one village and two city forms of government. It was entering upon ten years of unparalleled prosperity in the roaring Twenties, ten years of depression in the frenzied Thirties, and another war that made previous conflicts seem like back-alley fights.

The Twenties recall gangsters of the prohibition period, resurgence of the Ku Klux Klan, vamps turned to flappers, dance marathons, crossword puzzles, and a general spirit of excitement.

Duluth commemorated her birthday in August of 1920, with a six-day celebration including dances, parades, concerts and an historical pageant. The latter, the North Star Festival, was held at Barnes' Field in Hunters Park, with the American Legion in charge and Rodney Paine general chairman. T.W. Hugo wrote the script and A.F.M. Custance composed the incidental music. A.R. Burquist took the part of Daniel De Greysolon Sieur du Luth. Among the notable guests were Vice President Marshall and Herbert Hoover.

The pageant, depicting glories in the progress of Duluth, helped the citizenry to forget the skeleton in the closet. This was a happening on June 15, 1920, a tragedy foreign to the north country - a lynching. Three Negroes from the Robinson shows were alleged to have assaulted a seventeen-year-old West Duluth girl on the night of June 14. Six Negroes from the show were held in the city jail. The following evening, about six o'clock, hundreds of angry young West Duluthians plied the streets in trucks recruiting a mob. Police, called in from all sections of the city, mobilized at entrances to the jail and placed heavy hose lines there, but the mob cut the hose and effected an entrance to the cellrooms by breaking down two heavy steel doors. In a highly informal trial, the gang decided three of the Negroes were guilty and dragged them from the wrecked jail to the corner of Second Avenue and First Street. The victims, all from Virginia plantations, were Isaac McGhie, Elmer Jackson and Nate Green. As a rope was thrown over a telephone pole to hang the first man, McGhie, Rev. W.J. Powers stepped out of the milling crowd and climbed the pole to implore that the law be permitted to take its course. He pleaded, "In the name of God and the church I represent, men, I ask you to stop." He was pulled down from the pole. Another priest, Rev. P.J. Malony, and various sane businessmen tried to reason with the mob, but it was completely out of control, in a frenzy of vengeance. With a searchlight from a car highlighting the gruesome scene, the three Negroes were hanged. Police cut down the bodies at one o'clock.

As an aftermath of the lynchings, there were days of unrest and an undercurrent of lawlessness in the city. Fourteen Negroes were brought back from the show for questioning and held in the county jail, and threats were made of more lynchings. On June 19, Sheriff Magie asked the governor for troops, and a battery of state militia and a machine gun detachment arrived. Five squads of the state militia were stationed in and about the jail. Members of the tank corps and Minnesota naval militia were mobilized and posted in the corridors of the jail. In the face of the troops and of American Legion "minute men", the state of lawlessness subsided.

At subsequent court trials for leaders of the mob, no one was found guilty.

Duluthians prefer not to hear the rattle of the skeleton in the closet. They dwell upon the worthwhile aspects of the city's history and future.

A group interested in "the discovery, preservation and dissemination of knowledge about the history of St. Louis County and the state of Minnesota" organized the St. Louis County Historical Society in November, 1922. Officers were: W.E. Culkin, president; W.A. McGonagle, Mrs. Julia M. Barnes and A.E. Bickford, vice presidents; J.D. Mahoney, treasurer; Mrs. Ada Mauseau, secretary; and Miss Alice Lindquist, assistant to the secretary. The board of governors included Edward C. Congdon and W.C. Sargent, Duluth; J.C. Poole, Eveleth; Peter Schaefer, Ely; and W.N. Tappan, Hibbing. Mr. Culkin served as president from 1922 to 1938 and Otto E. Wieland, from 1938 to 1943. Dr. Richard Bardon has been president since 1943.

The society had its headquarters in the courthouse until 1947, when it moved into its present building, the magnificent old Savage home at 2288 East Superior Street. Here school groups, including university students doing research, come to see a butter ladle made by Lewis H. Merritt for his wife about 1834; a chisel supposed to be the first used in drilling iron ore on the Mesabi Range; and axe used by George R. Stuntz in blazing the state line between Minnesota and Wisconsin; a spinning wheel; an ox yoke; a collection of Indian articles; and hundreds of other relics of the past. Here also are thirty-two oil paintings and charcoal drawings of Chippewa Indians that artist Eastman Johnson made at the Head of the Lakes in 1857; and old photographs of the city - the Clark House, Superior Street with its plank sidewalks, Minnesota Point before the canal was cut, the old lighthouse at the end of the Point, the first schoolhouse and the first post office. Here are copies of the *Minnesotian* and the *Morning Call;* diaries of Edmund F. Ely and his wife Catherine, begun in 1833 when they were missionaries at Fond du Lac; and manuscripts of historians at the Head of the Lakes. Filed in cabinets are early shipping records and deeds; manuscripts, clippings and pamphlets on 520 subjects, covering the early fur trade, lumbering, shipping and mining; biographical documents; and hundreds of reminiscences of pioneers.

The St. Louis County Historical Society, in 1947, was one of six such organizations in the country to receive the annual award from the American Association for State and Local History, in Washington D.C. The citation was made "for collecting historical material, including manuscripts and artifacts, including a biographical file of citizens of St. Louis County, and for opening a new headquarters and museum August 1, 1947, and for sponsoring the erection of bronze markers at Indian Mounds." The mounds, at Lake Eshquagama, were marked in June, 1946.

"The Society," says Miss Corah L. Colbrath, secretary, "seeks to preserve not only the history of the past, but also records of the present for future historians."

Duluthians had cause to remember the past in 1925. One of the oldest coal docks in the country, a mud-filled structure built in 1883, was torn down at 300 Garfield Avenue. It was 1,560 feet in length and 300 feet wide...The land office, which had opened in Duluth in 1861, was moved to Cass Lake, designated the consolidated land office for Minnesota...Wrecking crews razed the first church building in Duluth, St. Paul's Episcopal, at Lake Avenue and Second Street. This was the building erected in 1870, which Jay Cooke and General Sargent helped finance. It had been vacated in 1912...The old trading post well at Fond du Lac, dug about 1865, was discovered, cleaned out and returned to use in Chambers Grove Park...The Astor trading post with its stockade came into the news again on August 4, 1935, when it was rebuilt at Fond du Lac. Into the structure went portions of the original building, logs bearing the Astor stamp.

In 1927, when crews of the Minnesota Power and Light Company were digging a trench in which to lay a new conduit at Second Avenue East and Superior Street, they found old wooden water pipes laid in an earlier day. It is thought the pipes were the ones that led from a spring (once located about the middle of Second Avenue East above Second Street) to the J.B. Culver home, where the Shrine auditorium now stands.

Duluth is proud of her heritage and frequently reviews the past when celebrating progress. In a special edition published for the Exposition of Progress, the Board of Trade gave bits of history about itself. The Duluth grain trade was handled through individual grain dealers from the beginning until 1881, when the Duluth Board of Trade was organized under state law. A.J. Sawyer as president and W.W. Spalding, secretary, served until 1883, when W.T. Hooker and A.C. Arveson were named to those offices. In 1884, the board first employed a paid secretary and moved from their first quarters, the old Metropolitan building on the site of the present Lonsdale. In 1894, this building was destroyed by fire, and the present quarters on Third Avenue West and First Street were built and occupied in April, 1895. In 1908, an addition was erected.

When the national convention of the Knights of Columbus was held in Duluth in August of 1925, charter members of Duluth Council No. 447 recalled the organization of September 4, 1899, the initiation into the order of fifty-eight men from Duluth and nine from Superior at Elk Hall over 118-120 West Superior Street. On September 30, 1925, the Council opened their new club rooms at Fourth Avenue West and First Street, with George W. Atmore, Sr., past grand knight and past district deputy, presiding.

A new Builders Exchange building on Lake Avenue reminded Duluth that this organization had operated since 1902, when M.A. Thomson was president. There had been a former Duluth Builders and Traders Exchange in 1893, with B.F. Howard president, but it operated only a year.

In 1921, Aftenro Home ("the evening repose" in Norwegian) was completed, and in 1926 an addition was built. This organization had been established, October 1, 1910, when eight women met at the home of Mrs. J.J. Moe to form a society to provide a home for aged persons. The first officers were Mrs. Moe, president; Mrs. H.H. Hovde, vice president; Mrs. Odin Halden, treasurer; and Mrs. H.P. Bjorge, secretary. Others active in the organization were Mrs. I.N. Sodahl, Mrs. J.H. Stenberg, Mrs. Theodore Odegard, Mrs. H. Holmboe and Mrs. O.M. Pihlfeldt. The society was incorporated in 1915 and received its first big gift, $40,000, from an anonymous donor in 1916.

The Bethany Children's Home at Thirty-Ninth Avenue West and Ninth Street was opened September 15, 1922. This home first occupied the old Merritt house on that side, built in 1892, one of the handsomest residences in the West End. The children occupied that home from May 1, 1916 to October 19, 1920, when the house burned to the ground. Families in the community took in the children until the new building was completed. The home is maintained by the Swedish Lutheran Church. Miss Anne Sundholm has been superintendent since 1929. By 1949, the Bethany had cared for 853 homeless children.

Duluth not only appreciates her history; she also erects monuments to it. On June 14, 1923, Greysolon du Luth and Daughters of Liberty chapters of the Daughters of the American Revolution erected a memorial tablet at Fond du Lac. The inscription on a huge granite boulder reads:

"Fond du Lac, Minnesota, site of an Ojibway village from the earliest known period. Daniel Greysolon du Luth was here in 1679. Astor's American Fur Company established a trading post on this spot about 1817. The first Ojibway treat in Minnesota was made here in 1826. This monument was erected by the Daughters of the American Revolution, Duluth, Minnesota."

Merritt Memorial Park at Forty-Sixth Avenue West and Superior Street, a gift of Leonidas Merritt and his nephew Thomas, was formally dedicated October 26, 1924. A bronze tablet was placed to mark the spot on which the first church in Oneota was built in 1890. The tablet reads: "Rev. L.F. Merritt Memorial Park, dedicated A.D. 1924 in memory of Lucien F. Merritt, pastor, Merritt Memorial Methodist Episcopal church erected on this site during his pastorate A.D. 1892."

Soldiers' Monument at Oneota cemetery was dedicated on May 30, 1925. The monument, a gift of the people of St. Louis County by action of the county board, was unveiled by Miss Anna Louise MacMullen, former Red Cross nurse with the A.E.F. in France during World War I. The dedication took place on a plot of ground given by the cemetery association to the West Duluth American Legion as a burial ground for soldiers. A national salute of twenty-one guns was fired by members of the 125th Field Artillery, and taps was sounded by T.J. Bernhardt, bugler.

In spite of these glimpses into the past, Duluth, in the prosperous Twenties, was chiefly interested in the development and progress of the city.

A White Way was opened in the business section of West Duluth on the night of September 21, 1922. There was a parade to the accompaniment of bands, horns and general hilarity. Miss Grace Seymour, chosen Queen of the White Way, switched on the lights at eight o'clock. Henry Grono, chairman for the celebration, introduced the speakers: Rev.

W.J. Barr; P.G. Phillips, city commissioner; and L.A. Barnes, president of the West Duluth Commercial Club.

Business organizations west of the Point of Rocks were getting into high gear. On April 1, 1922, the West Duluth Business Men's Club was founded with Thomas J. Doyle, president; E.G. Kreidler and L.A. Barnes, vice presidents; and D.C. Wakeman, T.F. Wieland, Amol G. Swanstrom and Charles Kauppi, directors.

The Duluth Business Men's Association, organized in 1902 with C.O. Nelson president, changed its name in 1905 to West End Commercial Club. On June 8, 1922, it organized as the West End Business Men's Club, with Emil S. Gustafson chairman of the organization committee and Blu D. Lutz, secretary. In 1935, the name became West End Business and Civic Club.

Downtown, the Junior Chamber of Commerce was organized in 1926. Charter members were Warren S. Moore, A.W. Wilson, L.E. Sundby, Arthur C. Pearson, P.R. Pascoe, D.H. Breitenbach, Edwin J. Chalk, H.D. Bush, Harold A. Bergquist, L.O. Anderson, Julius M. Nolte, T.A. Webster, O.L. Ulvang, S.J. Nelson, F.E. Mackey, O.L Coleman, M.F. Crosby, Jr., W.L. Fredrickson, D.A. Bakke, J.R. Pratt, Lloyd Bergset, Joseph L. Kelly, Henry W. Hanes, James J. Willesen, John A. Stephenson, Jr., E.G. Field and R.B. Reavill.

This area and the Northeastern Minnesota Civic and Commerce Association adopted a new name on January 19, 1925 - Minnesota Arrowhead. The name was selected by directors from entries in a world-wide contest in which every state, Canada, Hawaii, the Philippines, Europe, and Mexico responded. Winner of the $500 prize was Odin Mae Crickart of Pittsburgh, Pennsylvania.

All civic organizations joined in revivals of the Winter Frolic, in charge of F.H. Marvin, city recreation director. The week-long celebrations included parades; snow-modeling, snowmen, and store window contests; hikes, sports and horseshoe pitching. Each organization had its own costumed marching unit, reminiscent of the old Duluth Toboggan and Snowshoe Association of 1885 to 1889, whose members wore elaborate heavy white woolen suits with white caps and blue tassels. James A. Bogg was captain of that group which each year attended the Winter Frolic in St. Paul and also built in Duluth the long high trestle for the toboggan slide from the foot of Seventh Avenue East down to the ice on Lake Superior. The 1926 edition of frolics was slightly different; it had bathing beauties at the Chester Park ski meet. In the light of a myriad of bonfires, Miss Dorothy Jones was crowned queen at Lakeshore Park, after a coronation parade in which 5,000 costumed persons participated. The Frolic was repeated in 1927-28, when the queens were respectively, Miss Helia Nauka, and Miss Bernice Derbyshire. The frolics were succeeded by Winter Sports Week.

Celebrations were also held to open new paved highways. Duluth and the Range joined in a ceremony, October 14, 1922, to dedicate the newly paved fifty-four mile Miller Trunk highway, Minnesota's longest stretch of paved roadway completed under the Babcock system. Honored were Charles G. Miller, Duluth businessman, who had been the founder of the highway when he was county commissioner in 1898, and John S. Lutes, Duluth mining man, "to whom," says the *Herald*, "goes the distinction of having driven the first automobile over the Miller Trunk road in 1904." (This bit of information does not agree with E.J. Filiatrault's statement that he drove the first car to the Range.) C.M. Babcock, state commissioner of highways, placed in the center of the pavement a small brass plate on which was inscribed: "Miller Trunk Highway, State Highway No. 11, Opened October 14, 1922."

Pavement from Duluth to Esko's Corner was opened to traffic at 6 p.m., July 3, 1924. This was the first paved link at the northern end of Minnesota Trunk Highway No. 1, beginning at Worden Street and Fifty-ninth Avenue West.

The new highway eliminated steep Thompson Hill which had struck terror in the hearts of plains people as they came into the city. Some said it was bad enough to negotiate that sudden drop, but the added insult was a sign at a garage at the foot of the hill: "We reline brakes." The new pavement was dedicated on July 16, with W.A. McGonagle, president of the Duluth, Missabe and Northern, giving the chief address. Other speakers were Andrew Miles, chairman of the dedication committee of the West Duluth Commercial Club and P.H. Martin, president of the club; J.R. Stack, donor of the road standard; J.H. Mullins of the state engineer's department; Mayor S.F. Snively; county commissioner Joseph Becks; James Harper, president of the Chamber of Commerce; and A.C. Pearsons, chairman of the Kiwanis committee and originator of the idea of Rest Point. After exercises at Sixty-Fifth Avenue West and Kingsbury Creek by the West Duluth Commercial Club, the cavalcade of cars moved to Rest Point, where the Kiwanis Club tablet was dedicated.

Festivities dedicating the North Shore Drive pavement took place on the new Lester River bridge, September 17, 1925. The Duluth Automobile Club had charge of this celebration and the Naval Reserve band furnished the music.

Along with paved highways came another boon to automobilists - balloon tires. The first ones arrived in Duluth on October 26, 1923. They were Firestones installed on a new 1924 model Cole Aero Eight, on display in the show rooms of the Johnson Motor Company.

"The greatest civic demonstration in the history of the city" was the Exposition of Progress and Iron Ore Golden Jubilee, held July 20-25, 1925. Arches, pylons and statues lined London Road, John Philip Sousa's band was here, and the Great Lakes fleet of the United States Navy. The National Guard Armory, Curling Club and Amphitheatre were used for exhibits and entertainment.

Fred W. Beecher was manager of the exposition with a committee composed of B.J. Culbertson, E.P. Fisher, Guy E. Hibbs, C.J. Snyder, Frank Parker and Edward L. Paterand. There were fleet maneuvers, band concerts, a regatta, a public wedding and dancing. An historical pageant, directed by Fay H. Marvin, was written by Spencer Searles, Mrs. C. Harris Roberts and W.E. Culkin. Mrs. Stanley Butchart directed the chorus of 1,500 voices. Other members of the pageant committee were Mrs. J.O. Pary, chairman, Mrs. Edward Hatch, Rev. Charles W. Ramshaw, Rev. William J. Powers and R.A. Grady. The title for the pageant, "The Spirit of Kitchie Gammi," was selected in a contest won by Thelma Webb, student at Central High School.

The next big city whoop-de-doo was the Fall Festival, held in 1949, in celebration of the Minnesota Territorial Centennial. Sponsored by the Duluth Ambassadors, the festival included a mammoth parade; luncheons; banquets; presentation of the Bob Hope radio show, sports events; coronation of Lorry Walsh, as the Duchess of Duluth; and an historical pageant written by Miss Louise Brennan, directed by Norman C. Johnston and Miss Ellen Smith, and presented by music students in the public schools.

The public works and safety departments were turning their attention to motorization and mechanization. Files in the public works department show that street cleaning started in 1908, with man power and horse drawn equipment. First oiling of the streets to settle dust was done in 1912 by the Standard Oil Company. By 1913, the department owned two automobiles, and in 1915 it purchased a 14-ton Locomobile truck. In 1924 an electric street sweeper began operations, replacing the old-time horse drawn sprinkler and street sweeping machinery and its attendant crew of "white wings." The early equipment would look archaic along side the Sno-Go, a rotary plow unit purched in the Forties, which cuts off great drifts of piled up snow, chews it up into fine particles and throws it through a funnel in a shower into trucks. A new front end of this fantastic equipment cost $3,383.70 in 1949. The department owns trucks, tractors, sweepers, diesel tractors, graders, and semi-trailers as well as a few assorted cars. Duluth needs equipment to care for its 700 miles of street. The city has an area of approximately seventy square miles, as compared to St. Paul's fifty-five and Minneapolis' fifty-eight square miles, although population of the latter cities is three to five times larger. Duluth is ninetieth in order of population in the country and thirteenth in order of area. The size of the city, combined with winters which are hard on pavements, presents problems which can be solved only with plenty of first rate equipment.

The New Duluth fire station, on May 11, 1923, retired Jim, the great bay horse that for twelve years had galloped along accompanied by the clang of the fire gong. Jim and his buddy Tim were supplanted by a Stuntz triple combination truck. On May 19, 1924, a motorcycle patrol was organized with "bathtubs" for passengers, to be used for responding to small roof and grass fires. In 1941, a streamlined aerial ladder truck replaced the old style hook and ladder equipment - an 85-foot telescope ladder that can be hoisted in sixty seconds, and in thirty seconds can be maneuvered into position.

A sign of the times in the winter of 1923 was the fact that for the first time in the history of the Duluth police department, the traffic bureau functioned throughout the winter. The electric automatic traffic signal at Second Avenue West and Superior Street was used all winter. On September 9, 1926, the first arterial highway stop sign was installed at Thirtieth Avenue West and First Street, the first of 100 to be placed in the city. A study of a police radio system was made in 1935.

The present sewage disposal system was completed in 1940 at a cost of $2,700,000.

A City Planning Department was established in 1922. A.B. Horwitz was the first permanent planning engineer, serving from 1926 to 1944, and succeeded by John C. Hunter. In 1925, Harland Batholomew City Planning Consultants of St. Louis, Missouri, were engaged to prepare a master plan for Duluth streets, transit, recreation, railroads and harbors, and civic art plans. This report is used on a consulting basis. In 1943, a Citizen Planning Association was created, which consists of about 150 citizens representing seventy organizations, along with members selected for their special abilities in city planning. One of the biggest projects confronting the two organizations (which work together) is planning a limited access expressway to help solve transit and traffic problems in Duluth.

In 1920, the Duluth Telephone Company sold to the Northwestern Telephone Exchange Company, and in the following year, the present company was formed and called the Northwestern Bell Telephone Company. It serves over 1,500,000 telephones in five states - Minnesota, North and South Dakota, Iowa and Nebraska. Duluth has over 900 telephone employees to serve more than 41,000 telephones. It ranks forty-fifth in 211 cities as to the number of telephones, with eighty per cent of the families having service. The company reports that Duluthians place 250,000 local and 2,750 long distance calls a day. Work now underway to convert sixty per cent of the city telephones to dial service is expected to be completed by the fall of 1950.

The Minnesota Power and Light Company was formed in 1923 to reorganize the old Duluth Edison Company and to consolidate into a single operating system the facilities of several nearby electric light and power companies. The company is owned by its share holders, more, more than 6,000 of whom live in Minnesota and in

Superior, Wisconsin. Between 1888 and 1923, about ten different companies engaged in the light and power business in Duluth.

Instead of from a single source, as in 1882, Duluth now draws its electric power from an inter-connected system, giving it many sources of power and numerous paths or circuits over which the power is transported. The seventeen separate generating stations have a combined generating capacity of 213,790 kilowatts, or 286,581 horsepower. Five are powered by steam and twelve by water power. A fourth generating unit of 44,000 horsepower has been authorized for addition to the M.L. Hibbard Steam Electric Station at Duluth, scheduled for completion in 1951. The company makes extensive use of water power. Twelve hydro-electric generating stations, located on three different water sheds, at dams along the St. Louis, Kettle and Upper Mississippi rivers, have a total capacity of 143,351 horsepower. This includes an additional 16,000 horsepower unit at the Thomson Hydo-Electric Station, completed during the spring of 1949.

Since 1923, the use of electricity for domestic purposes has almost quadrupled, now that housework can be done electrically. During the same period, the average rate per kilowatt for domestic use has decreased about fifty per cent.

Each attempt to furnish electricity to the people of Duluth has been undertaken by groups of citizens who helped to finance the various ventures. Among those whose early efforts are particularly outstanding are Alex H. Hartman, Curtis E. Van Bergen, R.A. Costello, C.R. Haines and Franklin Paine.

By 1929, the single mile of street railway used in 1882 had increased to 113.64 miles in Duluth and Superior. A gasoline bus service was started in December of 1924, operating between Morley Heights and the Woodland streetcar line at Lewis Street. The first trolley buses were put in operations on October 4, 1931, on the Lester Park line from Forty-Fourth Avenue East and Sixty-First Avenue West. This service was extended to Piedmont at Tenth Street in 1934. By 1939, the changeover from streetcar to bus service was completed. A few days before the incline was torn down, a big sign was put up over it, "Last Chance." In 1949, radio service was installed in many of the buses.

The Duluth Street Railway Company went into receivership in 1930 and was reorganized under the name of Duluth-Superior Transit Company. By 1948, the company owned thirty-two trolley and 154 motor buses; served ninety-five miles of streets; operated 6,277,527 miles; and carried 25,670,030 revenue passengers. It has 426 employees.

Aviation became a major civic project, starting in the Twenties. In 1926, Bert Wheeler, commissioner of public safety, requested Mayor Snively to appoint a committee to get all available information on the necessity and requirements of a municipal airport. Civic organizations, particularly the American Legion, Chamber and Junior Chambers of Commerce, were also making studies along this line. Duluth was not satisfied when Twin Ports flying field was established, May 23, 1927, at the Superior entry of Arrowhead bridge by the Arrowhead Airways Company, Inc. A bill was passed by the state legislature that year for issuance of city bonds for a Duluth municipal airport.

In 1928, an airport committee was appointed, composed of Julius M. Nolte, F.G. Germaine, A.B. Horwitz, John A. Wilson, and J.A. Scott. A $100,000 bond issue was passed June 4, 1928.

Every organization in the city seemed to advocate a different site for the airport. The chief spots were the ones located at the foot of Sixty-Third Avenue West, Wheeler Field, Maple Grove and Haines, Vercellini, Proctor, and Work Farm sites. The Sixty-Third Avenue West and the Work Farm sites had the most advocates. The Department of Commerce, Aeronautics Branch, Washington, D.C., advised the Work Farm site; the airport board recommended it; Leonard Macomber, airport engineer and builder of Chicago, gave a favorable report and survey of it; and in 1929 the city purchased it at a cost of $70,000. The County Board contributed $20,000. Ground was broken for the airport on August 2, and by November, two runways, 2,650 feet long, were completed. The site consisted of a tract of land of 640 acres, of which seventy-seven acres were available for a landing field. It is situated about seven miles from the post office and is about 1,400 feet above sea level.

In the meantime, Anderson Field at Pike Lake was used as a landing field. On June 23, 1928, daily airplane service between the Head of the Lakes and the Twin Cities started here with the arrival of a six-passenger plane of the Mid Plane Sales and Transit Company. On July 28, Duluth was officially linked in a sectional airmail line.

Seventeen-year-old Margaret DuPrey, the first Duluth girl to complete a solo flight, flew from the Pike Lake field. With her instructor, Pilot A.J. Pfaender of the Great Northern Airways, she circled the field several times, then took the plane up alone, circling the field for about fifteen minutes.

To Miss Anne C. Macdonald (Mrs. E. Victor Filiatrault) goes the distinction of being the first aviation student to solo from the municipal airport. On October 2, 1929, she made the flight in a Standard plane, local training ship for the Arrowhead-International Airways, after only eight and a half hours of preliminary instruction by J. Warren Smith. Miss Macdonald was a teacher at Washington. Says the *Herald:* "There were no preliminaries. She appeared at the field shortly after school was out and after a few minutes the plane was rolled out and she went up."

Carl A. Lindberg made the first glider flight in Duluth, May 10, 1930, from Hartley Field to Northland

Country Club. The glider was made by members of the pioneer Glider Club: Lindberg, Guilford Hartley, Dr. A.J. Huderle, John Prinz and Cass Avery.

On September 11, 1929, Mayor Snively and his party established Duluth as a naval port of entry for airline passengers, when they inaugurated a new airline between the United States and Canada. They used two cabin planes, equipped with pontoons, piloted by William S. Brock and J. Warren Smith, traveling over a route established by the Schlee-Brock Aircraft Corporation.

In December of 1929, the city took over the Duluth Boat Club. On May 30, 1931, airmail and passenger service was established at this seaplane base when a huge Sikorsky amphibian of Northwest Airways, Inc., landed there. A band played and thousands of Duluthians were present to cheer the plane. In July, the city entered into a long-term contract with this company for use of the Boat Club hangars as a municipal seaplane base for operating amphibian service between Duluth and the Twin Cities.

The municipal airport was formally dedicated, September 13-14, 1930, the ceremony in charge of the American Legion and the Junior Chamber of Commerce. The dedication committee was composed of George W. Welles, Jr., chairman, Glenn Locker, Kenneth Skoug, Ellis Butchart, E.F. Converse, E.R. Cluett, Joe Boggio, A.B. Kapplin, John Harrison and A.W. Wilson. Kapplin, State Commander of the American Legion, gave the dedicatory address, and Miss Zelda Snively, niece of the mayor, dedicated the field. The program included a visit by the National Air Tour for the Edsel B. Ford Reliability Trophy; exhibitions by Charles "Speed" Holman, "the Northwest's own speed demon of the air", A.T. (Jake) Pfaender, dean of Duluth Commercial pilots, and R.L. (Rube) Bloom; a model plane contest; balloon and glider flying exhibitions and a bomb-dropping contest; army plane maneuvers by the 109th Aero-Squadron, Wold-Chamberlain Field, Minneapolis; an

222

aviation banquet at Hotel Duluth; a band concert and fireworks display at Leif Erickson park; and an aviation ball at the Amphitheatre.

The field was christened the Williamson-Johnson Municipal Airport, and a marker was placed to memorialize these two Duluth aviators. Harvey Francis Williamson, Jr., former ensign in the Naval Air Reserves, was a pioneer of commercial aviation at the Head of the Lakes. Through his efforts, the first air line between Duluth and the Twin Cities was established. He was made general manager of the local branch office and laid out runways at the Pike Lake airfield. He was killed August 23, 1928, while flying over Duluth harbor, when his seaplane took a sudden nosedive into the bay. Lieutenant Conrad Gilbert Johnson was Duluth's first flier to be killed in World War I. He was shot down by an enemy aircraft gun while flying over German lines in Argonne, October 23, 1918. He was buried by the Germans.

In 1932, the Duluth Aviation Club was organized, the idea originating with H.A. Lindberg. Its objectives were to stimulate local airmail and passenger service; to instigate airport improvements; and to sponsor airmeets and tours. The first officers were: Howard D. Bush, president; Stephen R. Kirby and L.O. Anderson, vice presidents; Guilford Hartley, secretary; and E.J. Soukup, treasurer. A women's unit included two pilots, Misses Margaret DuPrey and Geneva Clark, and Misses Anne C. Macdonald, Doris Roswell, and Linnea Willman.

On April 30, 1932, a *News Tribune* reporter, in a plane 5,000 feet in the air, talked to his office as Northwest Airways inaugurated a two-way radio communications system of Duluth-Twin Cities and other divisions in the organization.

A city ordinance providing for a municipal airport board of five citizens to serve without pay was passed in 1939, and members were named: John W. Woodfill - one year; Halvar Haugen - two years; Howard D. Bush - three years; George W. Welles, Jr., - four years; and Harold A. Lindberg - five years. The Airport Advisory Board, which held its first meeting, November 27, 1939, elected Bush president and Lindberg secretary. In 1944, an ordinance made the board a division of the city's affairs and enlarged it to seven men, who have the responsibility of the airport management, construction, control, and operation.

At present, the Williamson-Johnson Municipal Airport has a total acreage of 1,243. It has three runways, two of them paved, two 5,700 feet in length and a third (paved) 4,000 feet long. In 1950, a new $200,000 administration building will be completed, with a permanent control tower, to provide facilities for airline offices, customs, and immigration headquarters and a restaurant. According to Ernest A. Bodin, Commissioner of Public Utilities, about $3,000,000 has been expended on the airport, all money paid by the Federal and State governments except $700,000 from city tax money.

Duluth Radio, the omni-range station two and a half miles southwest of the airport, sends four beams to help guide planes into Duluth, to Minneapolis, and toward Fargo, Rhinelander, and Canada. CAA has announced it will install a $121,000 instrument landing system at the field.

Records show that in 1932 there were 309 plane arrivals and 318 departures. The 1949 records show 25,673 flights by all categories of planes, with 3,206 movements of private aircraft.

Two commercial airlines have offices at the airport. Northwest Airlines, operating 36-passenger planes, gives mail, passenger, express and cargo service in flights terminating in Minneapolis and in Chicago. Wisconsin Central Airlines has two flights daily, to Hibbing and to Chicago, operating nine-passenger Lockheed Electras for passengers, mail, and express. The company is planning to include DC-3's and to extend service to International Falls, Houghton, Alexandria, and Fargo.

Three charter plane service companies have headquarters at the airport: Twin Ports Airways, Inc.; Lakehead Airways, which is also equipped for ambulance service; and North Star Airways. These companies run a taxi-service to areas not served by regular airline runs, and rent planes to pilots flying for their own pleasure. Augmented by the Zenith City Company, they give instruction to about 75 student fliers.

A weather bureau was established at the municipal airport in 1941, and on March 1, 1950, the city weather bureau was transferred there. However, an observing station continues downtown to satisfy the needs for temperature and precipitation observation within the city. At the airport, twenty-four full and twenty-four partial observations are made a day, as well as observations under special changes, while only two observations are made daily in the city. According to Laurel Dahlin, first assistant meteorologist at the airport, Duluth's lake and hills present special problems in forecasting. The wind direction is particularly important, because if the wind shifts just a few degrees to the northwest, for instance, air might not come over the water, so will not be cooled. A few degrees in the shifting wind makes a greater difference than in many localities. It also determines fog and low clouds. The hills are steep and high enough so that we get a mountain effect with fog on the hill and not downtown. Kenneth Nicolson is meteorologist in charge of the airport weather bureau and its many gadgets and charts for accurate forecasting.

An Indian at Isle Royale, by the way, is noted for the accuracy of his forecasts without the paraphernalia of modern science. In the summer of 1948, a group of professors from the University of Minnesota, on a fishing trip to the island, relied on him each morning for the forecast. His predictions were uncannily accurate. The sixth day, however, when one of the professors went to get the daily report, the Indian refused to give it. The professor was puzzled, but insisted on hearing the forecast. The Indian remained silent. The professor thought he wanted more money than the amount daily paid, so dug into his pocket. The Indian remained silent. Exasperated, the professor asked what was the matter. The Indian replied, "Radio broke."

Sky Harbor-Duluth, privately owned seaplane base on Park Point, was begun in 1946, the result of dreams of Jack C. Brockway when flying the Himalayan "hump" and William Neukom, helping to keep the Navy flying as an Aviation Machinists Mate 1st class in World War II.

Back home from the war, the men selected the present site - a cove in the sheltered inland harbor on the bay side of the Point, just 4.5 miles from the center of town. The final organization included Neukom to handle maintenance and base operation; Bob Matheson to head an instruction program; and Bob Bergum, with Brockway, general manager, to head the charters. With many sidewalk superintendents, the men did hard labor in building the ramp and dock. They moved and patched up an old barge to make the dock. Brockway says, "All tackled any job from digging a trench for the underground power cable to painting, carpenting, cement finishing, bulldozing and dishing out `two hamburgers with'."

The first purchase in the charter aircraft line was a Noordyn Norseman UC-64, bought from the War Assets Administration ad converted for passenger service. The first flight was made on August 21, 1946. A Piper Cub on floats and an Aeronca Champion for float plane instruction were purchased that summer.

With a 6 x 8 foot shack as office and a pilot's lounge, the men obtained their formal seaplane base license on August 24. Then they built a full-sized office, two light plane hangars and shelters to house six ships. The winter operations consisted of flights of the Norseman on skiis with ice-fishing parties to the Canadian border lakes.

In May, 1947, a full scale seaplane operations were begun. Acquisition of a State Flight School license paved the way for flight training approval under the G.I. Bill. Three Champions and the Cub on floats were soon averaging more than six hours a day in the instruction program and charter promotion began to pay off. A Grumman Widgeon was added.

The base became Legal Port of Entry for seaplanes clearing customs Canada bound. Pilots opened the famous Albany River country of northern Ontario for sportsmen. They provided air service to existing fishing camps and resorts throughout the Minnesota Arrowhead, Manitoba and Ontario. The longest charter trip was a 4,400 air mile one for a white whale hunt on the Churchill River at Hudson Bay.

A state license as an airport was obtained in 1947, opening the way for land-plane activity. By 1948, instruction was being given to well over 100 students. The base has four full-time instructor pilots, four full-time mechanics, and a secretary-receptionist.

Sky-Harbor Duluth stands as an example of Yankee ingenuity and American industry. It is veterans' dreams come true.

Now, to get back to the Twenties, when prosperity was the keynote of the nation. Building went on at a great rate in Duluth, with apartments and small hotels rising quickly.

In 1920, the largest office in the world opened, when employees of Marshall-Wells Company moved into quarters of the seventh floor of the new Lake Avenue building...United States Steel spent $9,000,000 for extensions at its plant and additions to its housing accommodations...The Lyceum Theatre was completely remodeled into a motion picture theatre, and the great stone steps and lions were removed.

A story went the rounds about those lions. They were a landmark, so nobody wanted them destroyed. Still, it was problem to dispose of them, since such massive things need plenty of space. Al Anson, theatre manager, had a bright idea. He called the zoo and said he would donate two lions if zoo officials would pay the cost of transportation. Would Mr. Anson provide the cages? Everything would be taken care of. The offer was enthusiastically accepted, and the lions were sent to the zoo, where caretakers awaited them, probably with chunks of raw meat. Officials placed the lions at the entrance and exit to the zoo.

By 1922, the total assessed value of land and buildings in Duluth was $65,440,842. Petitions were on file for $5,000,000 for the next year's building program. A fifty-foot lot on the lower side of West First Street brought a record price - $85,000.

St. Mary's hospital opened its new building, September 1, 1922, "one of the finest and best equipped hospitals in the northwest." The addition supplied seventy-seven new private rooms. The top floor was planned for children, with a roof garden and playground equipment.

It was estimated that $15,000,000 was spent on building operations in 1923. About 650 homes were built, averaging $5,000 each.

Two new synagogues were built, Tifereth Israel at Fourth Street and Third Avenue East, and Temple Emanuel at Fourth Street and Nineteenth Avenue East, which had been a place of worship for the congregation for thirty years.

The McDougall Terminal Warehouse Company was opened in 1923, "the most complete structure of its kind in the world, with 350,000 square feet of general storage space and 1,000,000 cubic feet of cold storage space." A. Miller McDougall was president of the company and its subsidiary, the Minnesota-Atlantic Transit Company, with its Poker Fleet - the Ace, King, Queen, Jack, and Ten.

Hockey became so popular that almost as many people were turned away from the Curling Club as could gain entrance. To accommodate the crowds, the Amphitheatre was built, opened December 4, 1924, "the most modern artificial ice-skating rink and auditorium in North America." The main arena had an ice surface of 90 by 215 feet and a seating capacity for about 5,000 spectators who jammed in to see near-mayhem. "All requirements of the building code regarding exits, exit lights and building construction have been carefully observed." One Sunday afternoon, February 12, 1939, the building was packed for a hockey game between Duluth's policeman and Virginia's firemen. Boy Scouts, Girl Scouts, School Police, and youngsters from the Children's Home were guests. During the intermission, while many people were milling about in the lobby, an ominous sound was heard overhead. The vast roof, weighed with snow, began to sway and sag. Police and firemen immediately went into action and calmly herded the crowd out of the arena, just as a large section of the roof crashed to the ice, its concussion breaking windows. Leland McEwen, playing the organ during intermission, kept at his post until the last person was out of the arena. There was pandemonium in the lobby, but Police Chief Oscar G. Olson and George Lane, manager of the police hockey team, directed the terrified mob and got everyone safely out of the building. The Amphitheatre has never been rebuilt.

St. Luke's nurses moved into their five-story home, November 22, 1924, recalling the first graduating class in 1892 - Miss Fanny Shephard, Miss Isabella Latta, Mrs. Gould (later Mrs. S.F. Boyce), Miss Christine Davidson and Mrs. Edith Spencer. The following year, a million-dollar addition to the hospital was completed. In 1950, another huge addition is being built, connected by a second-floor overpass above Tenth Avenue with a new County Hospital. St.

Luke's is the hospital that was started in 1882 with five dollars in cash.

The new St. Louis jail was opened in 1924, "in all respects a model penal institution." One hundred prisoners were transferred to this building, which can house 194 guests of the county.

The formal opening of Hotel Duluth was held May 22-23, 1925. Ninety per cent of the work on this $2,400,000 structure was done by Duluth firms. A few minutes before the doors were first opened, May 8, room clerks, office staff, bellboys, porters, and waitresses marched into the lobby, and on signal went to their respective stations. The hotel register and the front doors were opened by L.L. Tipple, manager. George H. Crosby, "father of Hotel Duluth," who had secured $350,000 in subscriptions for the building, was the first to sign the register. The first out-of-town guest was John F. Scott, St. Paul, president of the Minnesota Building and Loan Association, who was assigned room 1003.

In the next two years, among major building projects were the Gary-New Duluth fire and police station, the zoo building, the Duluth Clinic and Webber Hospital Clinic.

The story of the building of the city hall covers several years. In Duluth, such projects are not completed without study, contemplation, and argument. In 1916, the city had purchased the present site from St. Louis County. In 1919, the state legislature authorized the council to issue a million-dollar bond issue for the building. In 1922, the firm of German and Jenssen was by resolution employed to design the city hall. In 1923, the preliminary drawings were approved as to the exterior design, but the interior had to be changed, since there was no provision for quarters for the police department. In 1924, the firm was paid for the drawings, and the Taxpayers League came into the picture, opposing construction of a city hall. In 1925, there was much controversy about the type of building to be erected and the council canceled arrangements with the firm formerly employed. Meanwhile, the city divided into camps. One, lead by the *Herald,* wanted the Burnham plan followed; the other, with the *News Tribune* as its spokesman, recommended that the city council disregard the plan, on the grounds that the expense was out of the question. Editorials were hot and bitter. The *Herald* declared that the city could not break faith with the Federal government, which had agreed to build a new Federal building according to plans for a civic center. The *Herald* faction won, and in September, 1925, the city council approved following the Burnham building plan. In 1926, the council adopted an ordinance providing for the selection of an architect by means of a competition. Thomas J. Shefchik's plan was given the first award, and the Taxpayers League congratulated the city on the success of its first competition. On July 9, 1927, the cornerstone of the building was laid, preceded by a parade and witnessed by an audience of 5,000. The city hall was dedicated on November 12, 1928. The *Herald* and *News Tribune* had to look for other matters on which to disagree.

Residents of Park Point, in January, 1927, informed the city council that the famous 23-year-old Aerial Bridge was near the end of its usefulness. By March, for the second time that year, a cable had broken, putting the bridge out of commission for half a day. Residents had to make a perilous boat trip across the canal through floating fields of broken ice, and they not relish participating in a scene reminiscent of *Uncle Tom's Cabin.* A survey was made for remodeling the structure, and in March, 1928, formal application was made to the War Department for a permit to alter the Aerial Bridge to a lift-type span.

The old bridge made its last trip on July 1, 1929. "With its battered old warning bell tolling, the whistle of the Park Point street car bleating mournful accompaniment, and ships tooting, the car made the last trip of twenty-four years at 8:45 a.m. with city officials, pioneers and crowds of interested persons." It is said that tears stood in the eyes of James Murray, veteran bridge car operator, as he started the bridge back to the mainland. He said, "It was a good old car and I hate to see her go." Just as the bridge was starting on its last trip, the *Ellen D.*, the city's "navy", started from the Park Point side. It was used along with a tug and a scow for transporting passengers until the new bridge was completed.

The present structure, called the Aerial-Lift Bridge, was first operated on March 19, 1930. The original towers and overhead span were retained, and a solid lift replaced the moving platform. The bridge has a length of 510 feet and a vertical clearance of 138 feet. The span of the bridge is 383 feet, 9 inches long; 172 feet 7 inches from the water to the lower edge of the truss; and 222 feet 7 inches from the water to the top of the truss. The 900-ton lift is counterbalanced by two 450-ton concrete blocks. The bridge is electrically operated at an annual cost of about $20,000. This lift is one of the fastest in the world, rising 150 feet in about fifty-five seconds.

The new $500,000 Arrowhead bridge was first used on March 11, 1927, when J.B. Finch, president of the bridge company, was the first to drive over it. It was formerly opened on July 16, in a celebration charge of the West Duluth Commercial Club. This bridge connects Duluth and Superior by way of Grassy Point and Belknap Street.

It was on March 28, 1922, that the city council granted the Duluth Central Heating Company a franchise to operate in the city.

Another city project was the zoo at Fairmount Park. The story goes that in February of 1923, the Pittsburgh Steel and Wire Company requested that the city return some wire the company had donated for the zoo. City commissioners, averse to returning anything that it got for nothing, decided it would establish a zoo. Bert E. Onsgard, West Duluth printer, had a little fawn he had found along the Canadian border, when it was cold, lonely and lost. The West Duluth Business Men's Club pushed plans for the zoo and appointed Onsgard as chairman to obtain animals. A *Herald* reporter jocularly remarked, "Any citizens having mountains lions or other pets they would like to give the city, see the city commissioners." Starting with the fawn "Rainbow" and a few animals donated, Mr. Onsgard began to build a zoo. School children contributed pennies to purchase animals. In 1925, bear dens were added, and in 1928 the large animal house was completed. By that time Rainbow was one of some 400 animals and birds at the zoo. Facilities are provided for waterfowl, goats, deer, flightless birds, elk, moose and small animals. A pool has been constructed in the creek by taking advantage of natural rock formations. In the main building are the big cats. There is also an aviary for birds of prey. Beginning in 1929, the zoo was a separate department of the city, but in 1945 it became known as the Park Department.

The zoo had no difficulty in acquiring bears - for nothing. Nearly every summer one or two bruins roam into the city. In August of 1929, there was a bear hunt in the East End, which resulted in killing a 250-pound beast on the lawn at the Julius H. Barnes home at Twenty-Sixth Avenue East. Four days later, August 18, came the most famous bear of all, making a story that has become a legend. At 6:10 a.m., a 350-pound bear plunged through a fifteen-foot plate glass window into the coffee shop of the Hotel Duluth. Albert Nelson, night watchman, was more than mildly startled to see the animal ready for such an early breakfast, and he called the police. When police sergeant Eli LeBeau and patrolman John Hagen arrived, they found Nelson throwing a bombardment of chairs at the bear, which had upset tables and chairs and run along the top of the short order counter in a vain attempt to escape. LeBeau shot the animal and a large crowd gathered to look in awe at a bear lying in the coffee shop of a first class city hotel. Some of the guests were a bit wary about going out on the streets that day. It is thought that the bear had followed Arvid Peterson, truck driver, into town, as Peterson was bringing a load of fish. A delightfully humorous account of this story is given in H. Allen Smith's "We Went That-a-way".

The real "Bear Year" was 1949. The first animal was seen on July 28 and the last stragglers scampered for the woods late in October. August was the busiest month, when police answered 210 calls to "come get a bear". Animals were cornered in garages, trees and fenced-in back yards. As soon as a bear was sighted, a crowd would gather to watch the police try to get him. Sympathy always seemed to lie with the bear as he would try to elude his captors - especially if he were just a little bear. The most exciting incident occurred when a bear was lassoed as he was swimming in the ship canal. Men in a boat were towing him to shore, when the bear decided it would be easier to ride, so he climbed into the boat. That was one of the bears that were shot. Opinion was divided as to the disposal of the animals, some citizens wanting them shot on sight for safety's sake and others wanting to protect them. Some individuals set up feeding stations on the edge of town on the presumption that if the animals got enough to eat they would not invade the city, but the bears seemed to feel that after a good meal they would like a tour of the town. The municipal zoo hung out an SRO sign for bears and sent the beasts all over the country. No zoo had to buy a bear that summer.

Except for an occasional bear on the city streets, Duluth has progressed along the lines of more conventional cities. Take the development of radio, for instance.

The first successful experiments with a radio broadcasting station in Duluth were made on the night of August 4, 1922, at the Paramount Radio Corporation, when music from a Songster talking machine was sent out into space.   R. Helgedick of Kelley-Duluth announced the numbers. Freimuth's store installed a radio room.

The beginning of broadcasting in Duluth was over WJAP, August 23, 1922. The station was sponsored by the *Herald,* the Lyceum Theatre and Kelley-Duluth, and was located in the theatre. A.L. Anson, manager of the Lyceum, was director.   The first program was dedicated to the memory of Jens Flaaten, late director of the Lyceum orchestra. It included an address by M.F. Hanson, publisher of the *Herald,* solos by Mrs. J.E. Barton and Lyman Ackley; a cello solo by Alphin Flaaten; a string trio composed of Miss Esther Manson, J.P. Moody and Alphin Flaaten; and thirty minutes of dance music by Frank Mainella's orchestra. An amplifier in front of Kelley-Duluth attracted a crowd, who danced on Superior Street.   Thursday nights, phonograph music was played from 8:30 to 10:30.   Requests were made for volunteers for Monday and Thursday night concerts. On September 3, Dr. Charles Nelson Pace of the First Methodist Church had the distinction of having his service the first local religious service broadcast.

The *Herald* would not only publish the complete program to be heard on the broadcasts, but would also review them.   By December, Saturday night was added to the schedule, with cabaret entertainment from the St. Louis Hotel from nine to midnight. Advertisements read: "Make this a radio Christmas", as firms advertised the new radios - Tuska, Notsco, Westinghouse, Aeriola, Grebe and Kennedy battery sets with earphones. On Christmas Eve, midnight Mass was broadcast from Sacred Heart Cathedral.   The *Herald* of December 28 first gave other station programs: WOC Davenport and WWJ Detroit.   Radio sets were installed on the Blue Goose and Blue Jay busses operated by the Mesaba Transportation Company.

By 1923, WJAP felt the need of a slogan, so conducted a contest offering a receiver set as a prize. Mrs. W.H. Hautla's entry won: "Duluth to the Sea - See Duluth".

On November 3, John W. Davis, Democrat presidential candidate, closed his campaign with an address over the radio, the first ever made by a presidential candidate on the eve of election day. J. Adam Bede, former congressman from the eighth district, former editor of the *Herald*, and Duluth's own "silver-tongued orator", brought the Republican rally to a successful close in Duluth that night without benefit of even a public address system.

The *Herald* and the Orpheum Theatre opened up broadcasting station WBBZ, March 20, 1926, at the theatre. Paul Earle was announcer for the station, which was under supervision of Noble Watson, United States government operator and radio engineer. In the opening program, D.J. Michaud's orchestra played and the Daziel Sisters sang popular songs. All programs were made up of local talent and "every child in Duluth may broadcast at one of the dinner hour programs." The station was closed with a two-hour program on April 9.

Installation of a wireless station was completed in Duluth on September 8, 1924, putting this port in continuous contact with boats and other ports along the lake. The Inter-City Radio Telegraph Company placed on top the McDougall Terminal one of the steel towers formerly belonging to the Coast Guard on Park Point and installed a high-powered transmitter, with a five-kilowatt spark transmitter for auxiliary equipment.

One of the pioneer radio stations in Minnesota is WEBC of Duluth, founded by Walter C. Bridges of Superior. The station is affiliated with the *Superior Evening Telegram*, has its transmitter in Superior, and maintains studios in both Duluth and Superior. WEBC first took to the air in May of 1924. Its initial broadcast was a program of piano music by thirteen-year-old Fulton McGrath, who has subsequently played with many of the leading name bands in the country. The first phonograph recordings to be played on WEBC were furnished by the Miller Music

Company. It seems that the little station did not wish to invest in records, so Bridges made a deal with the Millers whereby they would let him borrow records if he would announce that they were furnished by Millers. The recordings were carefully wrapped and transported to the studios with a warning that they must be kept free from dust and under no circumstances were they to be scratched. This is the first time any sort of commercialism entered WEBC broadcasting.

Among those who have achieved prominence in the field of radio after serving an apprenticeship at WEBC is NBC comedian Henry Morgan, who startled Duluth listeners one winter morning in his weather forecast by saying, "Increasing cloudiness and snow tonight, followed tomorrow morning by small boys on sleds." Another time, when Morgan was disc jockey, he gave a fifteen-minute transcription program of sound effects only. "Now you will hear a steamboat whistle...Here are two cars coming together...Now for a thunder storm." Charles Persons, director of engineering at WEBC since 1926, can regale one by the hour with the legend of Henry Morgan.

The WEBC studio in Duluth was first on the mezzanine floor at the Spalding. In 1930 it moved to the hotel penthouse and in 1938 to new studios in the WEBC building.

When Coolidge spent the summer at the Brule in 1928, WEBC became affiliated with NBC in order to give the President better news coverage. Previously, it had broadcast special programs from NBC. The station had had its own network, the Arrowhead Network, since 1935, when it added WMFG of Hibbing. The network now includes ten stations, six AM and four FM.

WEBC pioneered FM broadcasting in March of 1940, when it was one of only half a dozen stations in the country to have it. It is the first station in the area to announce its intention of broadcasting television, having filed for a permit with the Federal Communications Commission on June 23, 1949.

Station KDAL, located in the Bradley Building, gave its first broadcast in Duluth on Sunday, November 22, 1936. The studios were thrown open to the public, and the entire day was devoted to a series of dedicatory programs, in which nearly every civic, musical and dramatic group in the city participated. On September 5, 1937, the station became affiliated with the Columbia Broadcasting System, carrying Major Bowes Family Hour for its first network broadcast.

KDAL started operations on 1500 kilocycles with 100 watts later increased 250 watts. In 1941, the Federal Communications Commission approved an application to increase the power to 1,000 watts. Because a directional antenna was required by the change, another tower was needed beside the single 165-foot tower on Minnesota Point. At the foot of Sixty-Third Avenue West, a brick building to house the transmitting equipment and two 300-foot towers were erected. On Friday, October 24, 1941, the switch to 610 kilocycles (from 1500 and then 1490) was recognized by a special broadcast by civic and station officials from a Northwest Airlines plane flying over the stations enlarged coverage area. On August 7, 1947, when power was increased to 5,000 watts, there was a vigorous promotional campaign climaxed by a free show in the National Guard Armory. Governor Luther Youngdahl dedicated the newly widened influence of KDAL to a constructive and forward-looking program of entertainment and public information.

Among the outstanding local programs on KDAL have been "Historic Site Ahead", written and directed by Gilbert Fawcett and "Diary of Duluth", a program in which Fawcett himself as "Old Timer" gives glimpses of Duluth history. Perhaps the station is proudest of two instances of public service in 1949. Directing the operations with a radio sound truck, KDAL recruited and aided searchers hunting a little girl lost in the woods near Pike Lake. A crew stuck to the job all night, until the child was found. Another example of the station's public service was the time it was credited with saving a family from an explosion. An opening warning was broadcast to an unknown service station patron that he had purchased gasoline instead of the fuel oil he thought he was getting. As the patron, with his wife and baby, entered his one-room cabin, he switched on his radio. Just as he raised the can to pour the liquid into an oil stove, he head the KDAL warning. All was safe.

Station WDSM, now owned by the Duluth *Herald* and *News Tribune*, was founded in 1939, by a Superior organization. It has studios in Superior and in the penthouse of the Spalding in Duluth. The station, which is affiliated with the American Broadcasting Company, will change from 250 to 5,000 watts in August of 1950.

Duluth's newest radio station is WREX, which broadcast its first regular program, January 2, 1948. This station is unique in that it is the only one in operation which employs seven towers to control its aerial pattern. The towers are set up in the marshlands of the St. Louis River, where 27 1/2 miles of heavy copper are laid to enhance the soil's conductivity. The transmitter is located at Gary-New Duluth. The broadcasting unit, owned by the Lake Superior Broadcasting Co., Inc., operates on a day power of 10,000 watts and a night power of 5,000 watts.

Policies of WREX are determined by a committee of area leaders representing civic, labor, industry, cultural, church and service organizations. Officers are: Thomas M. McCabe, president; Herschel B. Fryberger, secretary-treasurer; Frank Mahan, vice president; and James R. King, executive vice president and general manager.

In 1924, President Coolidge recommended that the 68th Congress take definite action toward approving the Great Lakes-St. Lawrence Waterway. That was nothing new in Washington. In 1850, eighty-seven pioneer residents of this area had sent to the 31st Congress a "petition of citizens of the United States residing in the valley of the Northwestern lakes, praying the adoption of measures to procure free navigation of the St. Lawrence River." The petition referred to the St. Lawrence as a "great and natural outlet of the lakes which seems designed by Providence as the great commercial channel by which the immense commerce of the lakes should find its way to the Atlantic ocean and the world."

Duluth has never given up the project of a water route to the ocean. Each succeeding year, men have worked diligently to procure action. Each year has seen Duluth and the Midwest hopeful. Presidents have approved it. The seaway was considered a certainty in the interests of national defense in two world wars and a boon in work projects in the depression. Gustaf A. Nordin, managing editor of the *Herald* and *News Tribune*, summed up the status of developments in 1949: "Predictions on what is in store for the St. Lawrence Waterway have come so frequently that Washington looks to it almost as a daily weather forecast.

The Point of Rocks has continued to hold the local public's interest sporadically through the years. In 1923, a 10-ton boulder crashed to the street, smashing the automobile of W.D. Jones, who was driving by. Agitation was again started to remove the potent danger, but the following year there was disagreement: the city planning commission would remove the Point completely; businessmen would remove only enough rock to provide a direct route from downtown to the West End. Harlow W. Tischer presented a plan for the removal, using the rock to construct a municipal dock. In 1925, K.C. Hoxie, chief engineer for the Minnesota Steel Co., presented a new plan. The city accepted bids for work of removal. In 1926, blasting started to remove 3,500 yards of rock forming the most dangerous part of the ledge. More suggestions were forthcoming: the Observation Community Club planned another route on grades to the top of the hill; W.H.

Woodbury, civil engineer, suggested spreading solution of the problem over a long period. The city council adopted the plan of City Engineer John Wilson, but set that aside to wait for recommendations of Bartholomew's study. In 1927, "East and West join hands in celebrating signing of a contract removing Duluth's historic eyesore, the Point of Rocks." That fall, work was begun by day labor. In 1928, a bond issue to provide funds for removing the Point was defeated at election by a 2 to 1 vote. Rocks continued to drop off now and then. Nearly 10,000 tons were removed during the paving of Superior Street in 1928. The present plan is a huge undertaking in parks - a natural park in the heart of the city overlooking the harbor. It would begin at Mesaba Avenue and include the Point of Rocks district from First Street to Michigan Street. This is a twenty-five year development project in which the Duluth Women's Institute and the Citizens Planning Commission are participating. Some citizens say the Point of Rocks is a physical barrier to development of the city; others call it a psychological barrier that cuts the city in two. If the park plan is carried through, it will be an area of beauty.

The American Legion has established thirteen posts in the city. After World War II the Lydia V. Whiteside post was organized for women veterans, named for a Duluth nurse killed in World War I. Other veterans' organizations include Veterans of Foreign Wars and the Order of the Purple Heart, the latter for men wounded in battle.

David Wisted post has brought fame to Duluth with its band, directed by Glen S. Locker, which in 1924 won the national championship and in 1930 and '38 the state championship for Legion bands. The post has also been active in work for young people, instituting an annual Christmas entertainment for children of the Kate Barnes orthopedic classes; sponsoring state and regional junior baseball tournaments; conducting high school oratorical contests; and sponsoring selection of outstanding boys to

Boys' State. The post helped to secure from the War Department establishment of ROTC at the University of Minnesota, Duluth branch, and it annually awards a medal to the outstanding advanced ROTC student at this institution.

The Hall of Fame, sometimes called "Flowers to the living and the community", was the idea of Commander A.B. Kapplin of David Wisted post back in 1924. Every year since then, the National Commander of the American Legion has come to Duluth to attend the banquet at which the award is presented to an outstanding citizen. Duluthians in the Hall of Fame are H.A. Comstock, W.A. McGonagle, Bert E. Onsgard, F.W. Paine, B.J. Enger, J.H. Darling, Julius H. Barnes, George H. Crosby, George G. Barnum, G.A. Andersen, Margaret Culkin Banning, Mary Sherwin Weiss, I.N. Sodahl, S.F. Snively, John H. Hearding, Mrs. J.R. McGiffert, Dr. William R. Bagley, Frank Crassweller, Sr., Mrs. George P. Tweed, C.F. Liscomb, Glen S. Locker, Paul H. VanHoven, Mrs. E.J. Kenny, Arthur M. Clure, Dr. W.A. Coventry and Albert Baldwin.

Duluth's dream of an auditorium dates back to 1925, when David Wisted post began a campaign for such a building as a memorial to Duluth's soldiers and sailors who fought in World War I. In 1927, the Chamber of Commerce announced it would support the movement inaugurated by the Legion "for erection of a memorial auditorium and art institute as well as an athletic stadium." By 1929 all leading civic groups had endorsed the auditorium and a special committee of the Chamber of Commerce had been named to study the project. The proposed auditorium has been a plank in the platform of nearly every candidate for mayor for the past twenty-five years. But it is still a dream.

The Community Fund organization was completed and the first drive got under way in 1922 with S.A. Bowing executive secretary, a position he still holds. The drive began on September 25 with four-minute speakers appearing at schools, factories, stores, shops, railroad yards and all public gatherings. The major committee included Ralph S. Hanson, major general; colonels of divisions; Fred Ash, public employees; Mrs. Kenneth S. Cant, residential; Edwin L. Hanson, commercial; Philip R. Moore, industrial; A.B. Polinsky, unit group; and T.B. Silliman, business. Chairmen of committees were Howard W. Cooper, publicity; Dennis F. Donovon, speakers bureau; E.A. Johnson, radio; and E.A. Marien, "come and see" trips. The first drive resulted in $208,560 from 8,063 subscribers, and in 1949 it was $357,387 from 32,476 subscribers. During World War II and additional $400,000 was raised for the National War Fund and USO.

Duluth organized the fiftieth Community Fund in the country; there are now 1,300. It is credited with being one of the best in the nation for cities of this size, having a high standard of giving and of payments from subscribers. For the past ten years, the Fund has met its goal each year. It is composed of thirty agencies. In 1948, the organization's name was changed to Community Chest.

According to Mr. Bowing, the Duluth Community Chest was the first in the country to use the red feather as an emblem. That was the idea of Wallace Hankins, publicity man in 1928. Six months later, New Orleans displayed the insignia, which is now in general use.

The Irving Moore Memorial building, formally opened on August 1, 1924, is a gift to the city by Mr. and Mrs. Watson S. Moore in memory of their son, who died in World War I. The building, which originally housed a saloon on its first floor, is given over to welfare agencies. It was first occupied by the Associated Charities, Confidential Exchange, Lighthouse for the Blind, American Legion, and offices of the Occupational Therapy department, Boy Scout headquarters and Legal Aid Bureau.

The new Salvation Army home on Third Avenue West was dedicated, November 30, 1924. The Salvation

Army in Duluth operates three major branches, dealing primarily in the field of youth character building and citizenship training. The twenty-four departments of service are in operation and the relief given to destitute and needy individuals continues constantly. It is also serving in the field of training for under-privileged mothers, with home economics training classes and opportunities for social expansion. Major Ernest R. Orchard says, "We are servicing a large segment of Duluth citizens who attend our program of religious emphasis and are thereby receiving church and religious training to good advantage."

The Duluth Council of Churches adopted this name and a revised constitution in 1922. This organization grew out of a "Men and Religion Forward Movement" of 1911, when laymen from the international committee of the YMCA toured the country to arouse Protestant churches to greater religious and spiritual life. Officers in Duluth were W.L. Smithies, Judge Page Morris, Dr. J.J. Ecklund, Andrew Nelson, W.A. Anderson and Phil Bevis. Mr. Smithies was executive secretary from 1913 to 1935 and was succeeded by Rev. J.J. Runyon, the present secretary. According to Reverend Runyon, the organization, headed by a group of ten men who secretly financed the work, in 1918 put the city dry. Duluth was the largest city in the country to go dry before Federal prohibition was passed.

By 1920, the YWCA had opened Camp Wanakiwin, which offers girls an opportunity for healthful summer recreation, and the West Duluth Center in the West Duluth YMCA building. The YW, since 1893, has held to its purpose: "To build a fellowship of women and girls devoted to the task of realizing in our common life those ideals of personal and social living to which we are committed by our faith as Christians. In this endeavor we seek to understand Jesus, to share His love for all people, and to grow in the knowledge and love of God."

The YMCA celebrated its centennial in 1944, with a banquet at Hotel Duluth. One of the features was burning of the mortgage of the Y building. Julius H. Barnes was guest speaker on this occasion, when Bert Wheeler, one of the oldest members, handed the Torch of the First Century to Dick Granquist. Among those who have made gifts to the organization are A.L. Ordean, Mrs. Chester Congdon, the Wheeler Fund, Oscar Mitchell, Miss Laura McArthur and Kirby Jones.

At the fiftieth anniversary of Camp Miller in 1948, Norman D. McLeod retired from his work as secretary, and William Hanson, secretary of the Boys' Y took over. Camp Miller has had a modern dining room, seating 150 boys, since 1941. Called Congdon Hall, it is the gift of Mrs. C.A. Congdon.

On behalf of himself and his two daughters, Mrs. Frederick L. Gates and Mrs. Torrey Ford, W.J. Olcott presented a permanent summer camp to the Duluth Council of Girl Scouts in 1929. The beautiful property on Half Moon Lake was named Fannie Bailey Olcott Camp in memory of Mrs. Olcott.

Kenwood, the last of Duluth's "little red schoolhouses", a two-room wooden structure built in 1890, was town down in 1924 and replaced by the present modern building. In 1921, Riverside was built; and the magnificent Denfeld was completed in 1926, followed by Chester Park and East in 1927 and Congdon Park in 1929. That was the last of school building for twenty years. Temporary frame portable buildings were used as needed in the interim, moved about from one part of the city to another. In 1949, Duluth citizens overwhelmingly passed a $3,000,000 bond issue to provide for two new buildings, at Piedmont and Lincoln, and additions and remodeling of its older schools. There were forty public schools in 1949, with an enrollment of 16,257. The Junior College, established in 1927, will be discontinued in 1950 and an Area Vocational School will be established at the old Salter, using the equipment of the Veterans Vocational School.

The public schools provide special classes for children defective in hearing, eyesight or speech, and the Kate Barnes School is for children needing orthopedic care. Two teachers are employed to give home instruction to pupils too ill to attend school. A reading clinic will be established in 1950. A well-developed adult education program is carried on. The schools have become recognized for their participation in community life.

A museum is part of the public school system. Established by Miss Mabel Wing in the Salter when it was an elementary school, the museum was moved to the A.M. Chisholm home in 1930. The home was the gift of Mrs. Chisholm, and the museum was named the A.M. Chisholm Memorial Museum, although old-timers still call it the Children's Museum. The museum contains a wealth of exhibits, and each year is visited by most classes in the elementary schools. In addition, Miss Wing conducts a loan library of exhibits on definite subjects which are sent to schools.

In the carriage house on the grounds of the museum, the museum board and the Duluth Art Institute conduct a Rental Art Library. Artists submit their work here for exhibit, rental and sale.

The Duluth State Teachers College became the University of Minnesota, Duluth branch by an act of the 1947 legislature. Raymond C. Gibson, president of the college, became provost of the new institution. He will be succeeded in 1950 by acting provost, Dr. John E. King. Historically, the institution's chief mission has been in the education of teachers for the public schools of Minnesota. With the change to a university, approximately one-third of the students enter teaching; one-third, other professional courses; and one-third, liberal arts. The institution gives a bachelor of arts, bachelor of science, and associate in arts (awarded at the end of two years' college work) degrees. In the summer of 1949, it gave first graduate degrees. Tweed Hall and Olcott Hall are mansions given to the university by George P. Tweed and W.J. Olcott.

The College of St. Scholastica has become greatly expanded. A gymnasium was erected in 1921; an extensive college wing, Tower Hall, in 1928; and three new buildings in 1937 - the Chapel of Our Lady Queen of Peace, Rockhurst auditorium, and Stanbrook Hall, which houses the college preparatory school and library. Cloisters connect the main buildings. Facilities for sports include an athletic field, a golf course, tennis courts, a hockey field, a skating rink, a standard archery range, and grounds for soccer and track.

In the autumn of 1924, the junior college of St. Scholastica expanded into a senior college; it was accredited by the University of Minnesota the following year. In June, 1926, it conferred the first degrees on two graduates - Frances Sarazen and Eleanor Solom, both of Superior. By 1949, the college had graduated 1,039 students - teachers, nurses, medical record librarians, medical terminologists, and graduates in sociology, home economics and dietetics. The 1949 enrollment for Stanbrook Hall was 175; and for the College of St. Scholastic, 501.

St. Michael and St. Jean Baptiste elementary schools were established in 1920, and the latter became a high school in 1926. Other parochial schools include Cathedral high school, an organization of the Christian Brothers school and Girls Cathedral high school, which joined in 1940; and elementary schools: St. Anthony and Holy Rosary, 1923; St. John the Evangelist, 1926; St. Margaret Mary, 1927; and Mary, Star of the Sea and St. Clement, 1940.

The Duluth Public Library has extended its services since 1920. Branches were established in the Gary-New Duluth Municipal Building in 1935 and in the Park Point Recreation Center in 1936, while books are available at deposit stations in the Fond du Lac, Riverside, Kenwood, and Norton Park communities. In 1937, through contract with the County Board of Commissioners, service was extended to the southern part of the county, with books in thirty-eight stores, homes and schools. There is also regular service for hospitals and other institutions. The main building has a periodical room; a children's library of 34,350 books; and reference and rental departments which house over 170,000 volumes. It has approximately 3,000 volumes of books in twenty-three foreign languages. Copies of old local newspapers are recorded on microfilm. The library also has a collection of 2,000 phonograph records; it gives a concert from these one noon a week.

Sports have continued to hold the interest of Duluthians. Crowds jammed the streets in front of the *Herald* to watch the electric scoreboard for World Series games before radio. Five thousand fans stood there in a drizzle to get returns of the Firpo-Wills fight megaphoned by Art Champagne the night of September 11, 1924.

The old Duluth Ski Club, which had become dormant toward the end of World War I, was revived in the fall of 1922 by ski enthusiasts Ben A. Rasmussen, Thorwald Seglem, Helmer Sather, Engel Nelson and Fred Tronsdal.

The first tournaments were held on Miller Creek on a part of what is now the Enger Park golf course. The following year, the club built a wooden slide at Chester Park. The giant steel slide, designed by Rasmussen and Seglem, was built at Chester Park in the fall of 1925, and the first competition was held in January 1926. W.W. Spring was the spark plug in raising funds to build this slide.

The huge 60-meter structure at Fond du Lac, engineered by Edward Ronning, was dedicated February 2, 1941, when Torger Tokle of the Norway Ski Club of New York set a record of 203 feet. His record was broken in 1948 by his brother Arthur and was smashed a dozen times in the annual club meet of February, 1949. The present record holder, with a leap of 220 feet, is Matti Pietikainen of Finland.

When Herald Grinden returned from Lake Placid in 1929, he introduced the techniques of downhill and slalom activity. That winter, the club held its first community ski class at Northland. Since then, recreational skiing has been popular in Duluth.

Junior competition for boys began in 1925 and early in 1932 junior clubs were organized in the city. Central High School has won the state high school championship thirteen of the fifteen times entered.

Duluth has held the national jumping events four times - at Chester Bowl in 1908, 1915, 1926, and at Fond du Lac in 1942. It will again stage this event in 1950. The city held the national committee event at Fond du Lac in 1948, and the same year sponsored the first national junior ski jumping championship on the slide at Chester Bowl.

The National boys class championship was won in 1926 by Erling Grinden and in 1928 by George Kotlarek. Peter Fosseide won both the national cross country and combined skiing titles in 1940, while George Kotlarek, in winning the 1948 national senior class titles, became the only man in the United States to win the D.C.A. and senior titles of national association. Carl Holmstrom won a place on the 1932 American Olympic Team.

Duluth has gained national prominence in skiing. Ben A. Rasmussen served the National Association as president in 1926, and Harold Grinden in 1928 and 1929. Grinden has since served six years as national secretary and has twice been secretary of the American Olympic Ski Games Committee.

Another winter sport popular in the Twenties was hockey. The first Duluth hockey team to make a national reputation was the Northern Hardware club about 1906. This team, with such stars as Roy Deetz, Ray Fenton, Ed Furni, Charlie Horn, Coddy Winters, Earl and A.C.

Cummings and Charlie Cargill won the amateur championship of the United States. From then to 1913 there were local leagues, of which the Adams Athletic Club was outstanding. In 1913, Joe Linder, manager of the Curling Club, organized a hockey team that played with clubs in the copper country, Cleveland, Fort William, Port Arthur and Winnipeg.

The heyday of hockey began in 1920, when Gordon Hegardt and Gus Olson took over the American Legion team and entered the United States Amateur Association, composed of Duluth, Cleveland, Pittsburgh and St. Paul. The team was dubbed the Hornets. Various cities entered and withdrew from the league in the following years, and the league changed its name to Central Hockey Association in 1925 and to the American Hockey Association in 1926. Bill Grant, manager of the Hornets, became president of the association. Mike Goodman, Herbie Lewis, Moose Jamieson, Johnny Mitchell and Jim Seaborne of the Hornets and visitors Cree, Conacher, Stuart, Ching and Ade Johnson and Moose Goheen drew a packed house of from 4,000 to 5,000 screaming fans. Those were the days when it was customary for the visiting team to wait for police escort before it dared leave the dressing rooms. In 1926-27, the Hornets captured the league championship, winning the final in three straight games from Minneapolis. Came the depression, and the Duluth franchise was transferred to Wichita in 1933. The great days of a nationally known Duluth hockey team were gone.

Duluth has the distinction of being a member of the original National League of Professional Football Teams, holding a franchise from 1921 to 1929, when it was sold to Orange, New Jersey. M.C. Gebert, manager of the sports department of Kelley-Duluth, and Dewey Scanlon, West Duluth football star and former quarterback on the Valpariso team, secured the franchise and organized a team they called the Kelley-Duluth. Among the players were

Russ and "Smoke" Method, Young Sharkey (whose real name was Art Juntilla), Art Von, Howard Kiley, Kenneth "Bunk" Harris, Oke Carlson, Joe Cobb, Bill Rooney, Bill Stein, Art Johnson, Dick O'Donnell, "Doc" Williams, Wallie Gilbert, Fred Denfeld, Bruce Caldwell, Daniel Coughlan, Hank Daugherty, Ole Wick, George Gibbons and "Doc" Bouchor. John Sternaman, who had been a star for three seasons with Zuppke's Illinois eleven, directed the team. In 1923, Gebert dropped out, and for three years the players took over on a cooperative basis. In 1924, Ole Haugsrud was made secretary-treasurer and Scanlon coached, and in 1926, Haugsrud became manager. Duluth had no stadium, so played at old Athletic Park in the West End, where most of the fans had to stand, frequently in snow, to watch the games. Consequently, gate receipts were low. When it began to cost the players themselves real money to play, a reorganization took place. In 1926 Haugsrud made a road team which played a schedule reached from Portland, Maine to San Francisco. He brought in Ernie Nevers, All-American fullback at Stanford the previous fall, and renamed the team Ernie Nevers' Eskimoes. F.A. Patrick decked the boys out in big white mackinaws adorned on the back with an igloo and the team's name. The boys trained in Two Harbors, the first pro team to establish a training camp. The depression brought an end to that organization.

The history of boxing in Duluth dates legally from 1915 when Minnesota granted franchises to Minneapolis, St. Paul and Duluth, cities of the first class. Later, franchises were extended to all cities of the state. Duluth's first legal show was held at the Orpheum Theatre, Al Wolgast, ex-world lightweight champion meeting Joe Welling of Chicago in the main event. Mike O'Dowd, St. Paul, later holder of the world middleweight title; Fred Fulton, Minneapolis, aspirant for the world heavyweight title, who was put out of the running by Jack Dempsey; and many other boxers of national reputation appeared here.

Among the more prominent world renowned and more popular boxers developed in the Northwest and fighting out of Duluth was Billy Petrolle, welterweight, who fought before all of the leading clubs in the country, including many appearances in Madison Square Garden, New York. He met all the greatest boxers in his division, defeated the big majority of them, but never won a title.

Duluth Boat Club crews had a bad time in 1924 when money could not be raised to finance activities. The following year, however, under Coach Doug Moore, the oarsmen regained the Northwest rowing supremacy. In a regatta of the National Association of Amateur Oarsmen at Philadelphia, the intermediate eight won the coveted $5,000 Fox trophy, one of the oldest trophies offered; Walter M. Hoover again won the singles championship; and the senior eight lost by only half a length. The crews finished second in aggregate scoring. Then came evil days for the Boat Club. With widespread ownership of automobiles, young men lost interest in the rigorous training necessary for oarsmen, and financial backing was slow in coming from others who could now more easily participate in hunting, fishing or golf. From 1929 to 1933, the city leased and operated the Boat Club and natatorium, but because of lack of funds had to drop the project. Small boat builders and a yacht basin are now established there.

Golf has become a popular sport in Duluth. A new private club, Ridgeview, was opened in 1922.

B.J. Enger gave the city a park that bears his name and contributed $50,000 for improvement of the municipal golf course constructed there. Plans for the course were made by a committee of citizens: Elmer Whyte, chairman; W.H. Bruen, J.H. Hearding, Herman Matzke, John C. Neipp and David Duncan. Whyte laid out the first nine holes in 1924, and Dick Clarkson, golf instructor at Northland and ex-player at St. Andrews, was architect for the second nine in 1927. The clubhouse was decorated and furnished by

Mrs. Torrey Ford, whose father, W.J. Olcott, supplemented finances by donating materials. The clubhouse was dedicated, July 2, 1927.

Another 18-hole municipal golf course was opened at Lester Park in 1931. The layout was checked by Thomas Vardon, golf instructor at White Bear Yacht Club and brother of the famous Harry Vardon. Citizens who contributed financially to make the course possible were H.C. Dudley, Robert Congdon, F.W. Paine, R.W. Higgins, Mrs. A.M. Marshall, Mrs. A.L. Ordean, Mr. and Mrs. Franklin Rice, I.S. Moore, B.M. Peyton, Ward Ames and Thomas D. Merritt. The clubhouse was enlarged in 1949.

Although Duluth has developed many outstanding golfers, only two have won the Minnesota state title, R.S. Patrick and Bobby Campbell. The latter won twice. In 1938, in the first international golf match for blind men, Clinton Russel won 6 and 5 over Dr. W.H.J. Oxenham of England. The match was played at Ridgeview.

The city of Duluth owns and operates Longview Tennis Club as well as courts in upper Chester Bowl. It has developed a slalom course at Hartley Field, bathing beaches at Minnesota Point and Twin Lakes and a winter sports center at Fond du Lac. It operates various other playgrounds, skating rinks and tennis courts. In 1926, it acquired possession of a tract of land at Thirty-Fourth Avenue West and Third Street, which it named Henry W. Wheeler Field. Years ago, this was the county fair grounds, race track and site for circuses and carnivals, but it is now a municipal playground. Barney Oldfield once raced there in his Green Dragon and Red Devil racing cars.

Ordean Field, the gift of A.L. Ordean in 1924, a tract of land of approximately twenty-eight acres, is located on Superior Street, across from Northland. Here is a lighted playing field with bleachers and an archery range.

The Minnesota amusement zone of over 197 acres was acquired by the city in 1936. The center includes a dock, bathhouse, horseshoe and shuffleboard courts, a picnic area with tables and fireplaces, and two baseball fields. The city owns two amusement rides there and leases others. Except for three narrow parcels of land owned by the city of Superior, the Duluth property runs all the way to the Superior entry. About a mile and a half from the recreation center, in the midst of pines, there is the caretaker's cabin surrounded by thirteen summer cottages which the city rents. Since there is no road beyond the seaplane base, only a path to the end of the Point, provisions are brought into the cabins by boat.

A municipal All-Sports Stadium, equipped for night as well as day games, was built in 1939-40. Here Frank Wade's Duluth Dukes, a member of the Northern League and a farm club of the St. Louis Cardinals, play baseball.

It has been said the "Duluth people seem to think the hills are a clever device of the Creator to furnish a foundation for their parks." Of the seven streams that rise back of the city and find their way to the lake, six are the centers of city parks - Lester, Congdon, Chester, Cascade, Lincoln and Fairmount. From the three parks dating back to 1865 (Fond du Lac Square, Franklin Square and Lafayette Square) the park system has grown to 107 parks, parkways, boulevards, squares, triangles, playgrounds and skating rinks. The city has one of the largest per capita park and municipal forest areas in America with more than 3,925 acres of recreation areas and 2,148 acres of municipal forests.

The last western extension of the Skyline Parkway was formally opened on October 28, 1927. From West Duluth, it extends around Bardon's Peak, Mission Creek, and through Fond du Lac and Jay Cooke State Park. In 1934, Mayor Snively began an eastern extension on the ridge 650 feet above the lake back of Lester Park, Lakeside and Crosley Park, overlooking residential Duluth.

Lakeshore Park on London Road was renamed Leif Ericson Park in 1927 in honor of the Norseman who discovered the North American continent in 997. B.J. Enger presented the boat which corresponds to the original boat used by Leif and which was sailed in 1926 over the route taken by him. Built in Korgen, Norway, the craft was manned by a crew of three men under Captain Gerhard Folgero. Leaving Bergen, Norway, on May 23, 1926, Captain Folgero touched at the Shetland Islands, Faroe Islands, Iceland, North Greenland, St. Johns and Newfoundland, and arrived in Boston on August 12, covering 6,700 miles in eighty-one days, of which nineteen were spent in various ports. The ship arrived in Duluth, June 23, 1927, and except for a brief sojourn to the Chicago World's Fair it has remained on a permanent base in the park. It is actually smaller than Leif's boat and is believed to be the smallest craft that has ever traversed this route. It measures forty-two feet in length with twelve foot, nine inch beams, and it has a capacity of twelve tons.

Dedication of Leif Ericson Park, on September 8, 1929, consisted of a banquet in honor of Mr. Enger and a program at the park. At the latter, John Midtby, president of the Norseman's League, introduced Mayor Snively, who gave the address of welcome; Judge C.R. Magney gave the dedication address; and Governor Theodore Christianson was the principal speaker. The municipal band played, directed by Charles Helmer, and a united chorus of singers from Duluth, Superior, Cloquet and the range towns gave a program directed by I.N. Sodahl.

At Enger Park, a gift of Mr. Enger, a beacon in memory of him was dedicated on June 15, 1939. The Enger Memorial Tower is built of native bluestone and has a lookout at each of its six stories. At the top is a beacon which can be seen from over the city and from far out in Lake Superior. The tower was dedicated by Crown Prince Olav of Norway.

At Indian Point in West Duluth and Brighton Beach on the lakeshore, the city has established tourist camps. At first, the only accommodations were tents, but in 1926 eight cabins were built on each site and every year the camps have been extended or improved. In 1949, 7,975 cars and trailers were registered at the camps.

The park department has developed an arboretum and nursery at Fond du Lac Park. Here are twenty-eight specimens of evergreens, fifty-nine deciduous trees, eighty shrubs, twenty-seven roses, fourteen vines and nineteen perennials.

Short news items of the Twenties are: Shipping automobiles by boat was a transportation development of 1920...On November 5, 1923, the motorized barge *Twin Ports*, a new type of lake-canal craft, arrived in New York from Duluth with the first unbroken freight shipment to travel the all-water route. Cargo included a tub of butter and a barrel of flour, gifts from Mayor Snively to the Mayor of New York...The first dog show, sponsored by the Head of the Lakes Kennel Club was held in November, 1923. F.C. Tenney's "Kemo Ricky", C.H. Dunning's "Friar Tuck" and "Robin Hood" and J.E. Anderson's "Red Law Redfield" began their careers here...The Duluth Art Association and the *Herald* held the first exhibit of local art in the public library, January 25, 1924...In 1925, the Duluth Day dinner replaced "over the top" banquets and women participated in the event for the first time...On January 27, 1926, Captain Robert B. Miller, native Duluthian, rescued twenty-five members of the crew of the shipwrecked British steamer *Antinoe*. The city council had a gold medal for him...Annually, from 1921 through 1926, the USS *Paducah*, Duluth Naval Reserve training ship, carried off first place honors in squadron cruise and inspection...The world's horseshoe pitching tournament was held at Leif Ericson Park, August, 1927...The Garrick showed "On With the Show", the first all-talking and singing picture to be done entirely in natural color, July 12, 1929...On July 27-28, 1929, with fifteen armed men on guard, $20,000,000 in cash and securities was transferred from the American Exchange National Bank building across Superior Street to quarters to be occupied by the merged First and American National Bank, formerly the First National. Money was divided into small parcels and carried by bank employees...Nine Communists were arrested September 14 and 15, 1929, when police broke up Communist street meetings...Paul Block and M.F. Hanson, owners of the *Herald*, took over the *News Tribune* on December 1, 1929.

The summer White House was established on the Brule in 1928, with executive offices set up in Central High School, Superior. Although Mrs. Coolidge and son John frequently came to Duluth, an official visit was made by the President and Mrs. Coolidge on August 22. W.A. McGonagle was chairman and George Crosby was vice chairman for the occasion. Crowds lined the streets, a reviewing stand was located at Eighth Avenue East, and a twenty-one gun salute was fired by the 125th field artillery battery.

Weather makes news in Duluth. There was Washington's birthday in 1922, "the day of the big blizzard", a storm that raged for three days. Streetcar and train service was paralyzed, and the only sure modes of transportation were skiis or snowshoes...Christmas Day in 1923 was the first green Christmas in Duluth since weather records were kept in 1891...On the night of April 24, 1924, there was a city of lights on the lake, as a large field of floating ice, fifteen to twenty inches thick, propelled by strong winds, trapped thirty-two boats headed for the harbor. W.M. Edmont, amateur radio operator in Duluth, kept in touch with the vessels. The ships stayed there till the night of April 29, when the *North Star* and the *Allegheny* broke through the canal, followed by a parade of other boats...A hailstorm on June 10, 1929, with hailstones "as big as baseballs", wrecked hundreds of cars, including new automobiles on the docks...The year 1936 was a world beater for weather. An all-time cold wave record was set with the temperature below zero for thirty-one consecutive days, from January 7 to February 7, dropping to 35 below twice and in the 20 below bracket a dozen times. Then from July 7 to 13, a new heat record was set. On July 7, the temperature was 100.5 degrees, the hottest day in history (the record had been 99 on July 1, 1882); the thermometer stayed in the 90s till July 12, when it went to 102.2 degrees; and on July 13, it hit 106.2 degrees...There was assorted weather in 1941. On March 16, a 70-mile wind sprang up that did thousands of dollars worth of damage. In fifteen hours the mercury slid from 25 above to 2 below zero. On September 14, a cloudburst cost the city more than $100,000 in damage to buildings, streets and industries. The first four days of December, the mercury rose to the highest points ever recorded for those days - on December 1, 48 degrees above zero, and on consecutive days 52, 51, and 54 degrees above zero.

Such weather stories are unusual and oft repeated. That the city's climate is healthful was proved in 1925, when Duluth had the lowest death rate in the country for cities of more than 100,000, according to a mortality report by the United States Department of Commerce. Dr. L.A. Sukeforth, director of the Duluth Bureau of Health, declared that the reasons for this low mortality rate were "climate, weather, beauty and comfort, and the greatest of these is climate."

The biggest news of 1929 was bad - all bad. Newspaper headlines read: September 27 - Stock market declines. U.S. Steel common dropped $9.25 to 223.50, nearly $40 under its record price of a few years ago. Big stocks lost from $7 to $13...October 23 - Headlong dive registered on stock market...October 24 - Terrific crash slashes values in Wall Street. Great bankers meet hastily when hundreds of millions are sliced from prices...October 28 - Stocks' crash again shakes Wall Street. Bank support proves ineffective and prices tumble to new lows...November 6 - Selling flood pushes stocks down sharply...November 13 - Distress sales force stocks to new lows.

The depression was on. People who were millionaires one day (on paper) found themselves practically paupers the next day. Americans had hundreds of conveniences and luxuries, but they couldn't turn these into cash because nobody would buy. Will Rogers said this was the only country where everybody was going to the poorhouse in automobiles. "Brother, Can You Spare a Dime" became a theme song.

In the depressions of 1857 and 1873, residents had left Duluth for more prosperous communities. Now, there was no place to go, since the whole world was affected. Out of work, older people walked the streets seeking jobs or sat and sighed for "the good old days". Young people crowded the public schools, which organized post graduate work. Short of funds and faced with a vast enrollment, the Board of Education cut teachers' salaries twenty-five per cent in 1932 and cut two weeks of the school year in 1933. The County Board voted a straight pay cut of ten per cent.

In 1930, bank clearings in Duluth were the smallest in six years, down some $14,000,000. Ore shipments dropped more than a million tons.

Duluth might dawdle over a new auditorium and the Point of Rocks, but she rolled up her sleeves in a hurry to try to lick the depression. Business firms signed up to assure no cuts in their personnel. The American Legion made a house-to-house canvass for jobs. In November of 1930, unemployed persons registered at polling places, in one of the first such polls in America. Results of the tri-city unemployment census showed that Duluth had the largest idle floating population, with 4,174 persons out of work - more than half the voters. Minneapolis ranked next, and then St. Paul. The peak of the depression was reached in May of 1933, when 8,295 families in the county were on the relief list.

A joint committee of representatives of the city and civic groups had an unemployment survey made by W.H. Stead, professor at the University of Minnesota, and then planned a method for recovery. The final recommendations of the group, headed by Francis J. Dacey, were approved by the city council and plans were worked out by all public and private agencies in an effort to relieve unemployment during the winter. The plan called for division of all agencies into four groups - city officials, employers, labor and social relief. City authorities organized to speed public improvements, and employers were asked to keep all persons then employed for at least one year. Social agencies consolidated all efforts to maintain indigent, sick and jobless residents of the city.

Judge H.A. Dancer was chairman of a committee which worked out an unemployment bond issue to finance a five year city program of improvements to stabilize employment. Voters approved the $250,000 unemployment bond issue in 1931, and work was begun on such projects as the Miller Memorial Hospital, Lester Park golf course, and the post office. The hospital and Medical Arts building were the first structures of a new type of American architecture in Duluth.

The Miller Memorial Hospital of ninety-two beds is a charity hospital. Funds for it were left to the city by Andreas Mitchell Miller, in memory of his son Athol Morton Miller. Eligibility for admission is determined upon application to the Social Service worker in the hospital or to the County Welfare office. Regularly scheduled clinics are held, including dental, venereal disease control and tuberculosis. A one-year accredited course in practical nursing is offered in conjunction with the Board of Education. The hospital, housed in a streamlined, modern building, is on the approved list of the American College of Surgeons.

It is characteristic of Duluth that some occurrence should lighten the atmosphere, even in a depression. In 1930-31, it was the "battle of the sheriffs". In November of 1930, when Emil M. Erickson was elected sheriff, the former sheriff, Frank L. Magie, claimed he was not a citizen and was therefore ineligible to hold office. Although the State Supreme Court ordered Magie to vacate his office, he sat pat and Erickson set up a new office. Both men sent representatives to Erickson's birthplace in Norway for further evidence, and Magie was granted a new trial. Shortly after it started, Erickson resigned. The District Court decision ordered him an alien. Dr. C.F. McComb, coroner, served as acting sheriff for a few days, until the County Board appointed Sam M. Owens.

With repeal of the prohibition amendment in the 1932 national election, Duluth breweries put men to work preparing for the advent of beer. "Duluthians greeted the new brew at watch night festivities, April 7, 1933."

Franklin Delano Roosevelt was inaugurated as President of the United States, March 4, 1933, and began his national recovery administration. He declared a national banking holiday for March 5. Although banks had been forced to close all over the country, Duluth did not have a single bank failure.

The alphabet got a working over as initials were used to designate new departments of the Federal government.

In April of 1933, the CCC (Civilian Conservation Corps) was organized to give employment to young men. Living in camps, under mild military discipline, boys worked clearing roadsides and forest areas, planting trees and constructing small buildings for parks. Classes were held, stressing vocational subjected, and by 1940, the camps began work to equip men for national defense work.

The National Recovery Administration (NRA) in Duluth began on August 29, with a parade of 2,000 individuals and a mammoth rally. A reemployment campaign committee was organized by the Chamber of Commerce, with Fred W. Buck, chairman, to act as a clearing house for NRA activities in the city.

In the spring of 1933, two new Federal agencies were established; Federal Emergency Administration of Public Works (PWA) to foster employment in civic projects; and Federal Emergency Relief Administration (FERA) to provide relief for the destitute unemployed. The Duluth Port Authority applied to PWA for $3,700,000 for a high bridge linking Duluth and Superior. President Roosevelt signed the bill in July 1938. Plans for the structure are underway.

In November, the Civil Works Administration (CWA) was established to help finance projects initiated and sponsored by local governments. It gave work to 8,000 individuals in St. Louis County, including 3,345 Duluthians, on such projects as the sewage disposal plant and the airport. Twenty-five local CWA jobs were approved. This agency was discontinued in the spring of 1934.

The Work Progress Administration (WPA), a new work-relief program, was established in the spring of 1935. By the time the WPA was discontinued, in April, 1943, the agency had sponsored 459 projects in Duluth, and had spent $9,426,724 in payrolls in Duluth workers and $1,150,000 in non-labor costs. Sponsors' contributions in the city were $2,607,000. An average of 1,500 persons were employed monthly in various projects, including installation of sewers and water and gas mains, farm work, streets, viaducts, parks, the airport and historical and archeological research surveys.

The Federal Housing Administration (FHA) committee began in September, 1934, to foster jobs in the city under terms of the Federal Housing Act.

The National Youth Administration (NYA) was set up in June, 1935, to help young people through guidance and placement, student aid and works projects programs.

By 1934 there was some economic improvement. That year, 5,000 railroad workers got a raise; 500 Federal workers in Duluth had a five per cent pay increase; the County Board voted salary cut restoration to employees; and the County Commissioners voted themselves a ten per cent salary increase. The Board of Education, however, was still in financial difficulties. It ordered five schools closed, but on pressure reopened two of them and cut the teachers' salary schedule twenty-four per cent.

In depression days, the Duluth Civic Symphony was formed, the outgrowth of Fred G. Bradbury's symphony orchestra which had been giving concerts in the National Guard Armory since 1925. The account of the organization meeting is one that has gained national prominence through an article by Nathan Cohen in *The Reader's Digest.* One night in the fall of 1932, about thirty musicians who played for the love of music met and later rehearsed in a reconverted barn at Fifteenth Avenue East and First Street. They climbed to the former hayloft, which had been rebuilt into a game room with a fireplace in one end, the only heat in the building. When the triangle player had his 150 bars rest, he would throw another log on the fire.

Abe Miller, one of the viola players, is now secretary of the organization. Personnel of the original orchestra who still play in the symphony are: Violins - Gustave Jackson, John Moody, Oscar Brandser, Gilbert Johnson, Roy Flaaten, and Dr. W.J. Ryan; violas - Joe Priley and Elliot Joelson; cello - Alphin Flaaten; bass - Elizabeth Donley; flute - Eugene Orren; oboe - Alfred Moroni; horn - Mike Fedo; trombones - Meda St. Pierre and Harry Gradin; and tuba - Floyd Brissette.

The Duluth Civic Symphony Orchestra was organized on a cooperative basis. In the spring of '33 and in the 1933-34 season, Paul Lemay, assistant conductor and principal violist of the Minneapolis Symphony, came up to direct concerts, with Walter Lange, assistant director.

Interested in the development of the Duluth organization, Lemay worked with the personnel for his expenses only. In 1934, he became permanent director, and with James G. Nye, attorney, organized the Duluth Civic Symphony Association to take over the business of the orchestra. Officers of the association were F.W. Paine, honorary president; James G. Nye, president; C.C. Blair, J.H. Jordan, and Mrs. Victor Anneke, vice presidents; Mrs. George Ingersoll, secretary; and R.W. Hotchkiss, treasurer.

Mr. Lemay served as conductor for nine years. In 1942, he entered the Army Air Corps, where he attained the rank of Lieutenant Colonel. He was killed in action overseas.

Tauno Hannikainen, Finnish conductor, headed the orchestra for the next five years. In 1947, Joseph Wagner, formerly founder and conductor of the Boston Civic Symphony, took over the baton.

The Duluth Symphony Orchestra has received national recognition through the country's leading newspapers and magazines and has been heard by millions of radio listeners through its many broadcasts over the major networks. In 1939, the orchestra played for the King and Queen of England on their visit to Fort William and Port Arthur. It has also made repeated appearances in Eau Claire, Superior and Ashland, Wisconsin, and has played in Ishpeming, Michigan.

In 1932, the Children's Theatre moved into its own quarters, a remodeled barn at 114 North Fifteenth Avenue East and produced for its first play "Aladdin and His Magic Lamp". The first organization of its kind in the country, the Children's Theatre was established by Miss Frances Hoffman and Mrs. D.K. Harris as a department of the Little Theatre in 1928. Its initial performance was "The Wizard of Oz". Artistic scenery designs, murals and original costumes were created by an art staff directed by Arne Edgar Nybak. Boys and girls of elementary, high school and college ages participated in activities. In 1935, a puppetry division was added, under the direction of Mrs. D.E. Seashore and Mrs. Carl Thorsell. The Junior League was the first sponsor of the Theatre, but in 1937 it came under civic administration and was operated by WPA. The Children's Theatre was closed in 1939.

In 1932 and again in 1939, the city charter commission, upon request of petitioners, prepared a city charter for a council-manager form of government. Both years, the proposed charter was defeated at the polls.

A news story of 1937 was the defeat of S.F. Snively as mayor of Duluth, after he had held the office for four terms. Elected was 32-year-old C.R. Berghult, Duluth's youngest mayor and the first native son to hold the office.

The present mayor, George W. Johnson, was Speaker of the House in the Minnesota State Legislature in 1935, the third Duluthian to have that honor. J.S. Wattrus had been Speaker for the first legislature after Minnesota had become a state, 1856-1857; and Col. C.H. Graves was Speaker in the twenty-sixth legislature in 1889.

Television first appeared in Duluth, December 10, 1939, at the annual fall meeting of dealers of Kelley-How-Thompson Company. A mobile television unit was used, set up in a private dining room, and receiving instruments were installed in the ballroom, where about 3,000 people saw the show.

Civil war in Spain and the Jap invasion of China were bad news in the Thirties. In 1934, Hitler began his rise to power, and there were armaments races in Europe and Japan. In spite of the Pact of Munich in 1938, which was supposed to bring "peace in our time", there was a constantly increasing demand for steel for armaments. In September, 1939, after the German blitzkrieg against Poland, England and France declared war on Germany. In December, Russia invaded Finland.

The effect of European affairs on Duluth industry was almost instantaneous. Night and day operations were begun at the steel plant, which employed more than 1,800 men. The Inter-lake Iron Company, which had closed in 1937, reopened on a 24-hour schedule. Ore-shipping reached old-time levels. Grain receipts and shipments of scrap iron were unusually high.

In the 1940 annual edition of the *News Tribune,* Richard L. Griggs, president of the Northern National Bank, summed up the year: "Undoubtedly, 1940 has seen the backbone broken of what may be regarded as America's longest and greatest depression...We would be happy indeed if it (prosperity) were based upon a sound basis of peace production rather than the very ugly business of war, which we have learned is ultimately paid for in `sweat and tears'."

The year 1940 saw the greatest peace time preparedness program in history' and the entire trade area benefited by a vast national defense program. Business gains are shown by a statistical view for the year:

	1939	1940
Water meters, Nov. 30	19,051	19,281
Gas meters, Nov. 30	23,399	23,673
Telephones, Oct. 31	25,958	27,291
Total electric consumers, Oct. 31	29,798	30,197
Residential electric consumers, Oct. 31	25,327	25,751
Bank clearings - first 11 months	$148,140,283	155,559,247
Bank debits - first 11 months	$494,445,200	546,036,700
Postal receipts - first 11 months	$ 652,830	675,240
Building permits - first 11 months	$ 1,976,757	2,793,872
New vehicle sales - first 10 months	2,215	2,617
Iron ore shipments, Duluth/Superior Harbor, (Short-tons)	26,673,842	42,302,323

The Marine Iron and Shipbuilding Company was awarded a contract for three coast guard cutters. The first one completed, the *Cactus,* slipped into the water, November 25, 1941, the first vessel of the Head of the Lakes defense fleet to be launched. National defense contracts were also awarded Coolerator, Clyde Iron Works, Hugo Manufacturing Company, Duluth Brass Works, Van Vick Paper Box Company, Klearflax Linen Looms and Western Welder Corporation.

Public schools ran night as well as day to carry on a national defense training program for adults. In one year, more than 1,500 workers were trained to meet the needs of industry. Approximately 1,200 of this group had been either unemployed or working on WPA.

It was in 1940 that the Duluth Women's Institute was founded, "to set in motion a program of civic, social and business growth such as Duluth has not seen before; to further it as a great amusement, education and commercial leader." The motto of the Institute is "Civic, social and cultural progress". The first officers were Mrs. Wildey Mitchell, president; Margaret Culkin Banning, honorary chairman; and Mrs. Marie E. Bryan, executive secretary and treasurer, a position she still holds. The insignia, designed by Alvin Holde, is a profile of modern woman against a background of the Aerial Lift Bridge.

In spite of general prosperity, there was a spirit of foreboding - the shadowed threat of war itself. More than 1,200 Duluth young men between the ages of twenty-one and thirty-five, including Mayor Berghult, registered for draft, October 16, 1940, under new selective service law requiring a year's peacetime service in military forces during the next five years. The first group of twelve registrants left on November 22 for training at Fort Snelling.

Members of the Forty-ninth and Fiftieth Divisions, Tenth Battalion, United States Naval Reserves, were mustered into service at the National Guard Armory,

November 3, 1940, the first contingent to enter a year's military training. The 140 men left by train that day for Chicago, where they boarded the *USS Paducah* for Brooklyn Navy Yard. Lieutenant A.M. Clure was in charge of the contingent on its departure, and A.O. Robideau was Commander of the *Paducah*.

The exodus of young men continued in 1941, when nearly 1,800 donned Uncle Sam's uniforms. More men volunteered through recruiting stations than were inducted through selective service. There were 350 voluntary enlistments in the Army, half of them in the Air Corps; 348 enlistments in the Navy, off to Great Lakes Naval Training Station; 32 Air Cadets, station at Wold-Chamberlain Field, Minneapolis; and 53 enlistments in the Marines, the men going to San Diego for training, and from there to Guam, the Philippines, Hawaii, Samoa, Panama and the Canal Zone.

The Red Cross enlisted twenty-three nurses from northeastern Minnesota for service with the armed forces that year.

On February 10, 1941, 600 officers and men of the seven Duluth units of the 125th Artillery Regiments were mobilized, and after brief ceremonies became part of the Army of the United States. They were billeted at the National Guard Armory and the Shrine Auditorium (the former Armory) until March, when they were stationed at Camp Claiborne, Louisiana, under Commanding Officer Col. A.C. Ott.

The shipbuilding industry was speeding up in 1941. By the end of the year, there was $34,000,000 in contracts for ships at the Head of the Lakes. In Duluth, shipbuilding companies included the Barnes-Duluth (Julius H. Barnes, president); Zenith Dredge (A.S. McDonald, president); Marine Iron and Shipbuilding (Arnold W. Leraan, president); and Inland Waterways, Inc. (S.J. Blackmore, president). Companies in Superior were the Lake Superior, Water Butler, and Globe.

The old *Robert L. Barnes of Duluth,* the first ship launched by Barnes-Duluth at Riverside in 1916, was still serving the Navy after twenty-five years. It was moored in Apra Harbor, Guam Island, at the time of the attack on Pearl Harbor and Guam, and was captured by the Japs. There was a revenge motive in shipbuilding at Barnes-Duluth after it was reopened. Barnes wanted his ship back!

Wartime ocean shipping demands took the last of the Poker Fleet ships of the Minnesota Atlantic Transit Company line from the Great Lakes, putting them in service of the Army, Navy and Maritime Commission and the Brazilian Government.

By contrast with the serious tone of affairs, there was light-hearted excitement and nonsense when the city hall was stormed and taken over in November of 1941 by the Ambassadors of the Duchy of Duluth, who carried out a coup in a high-handed and dramatic manner. This group of civic-minded gentlemen organized to carry on a good-will program for the city. The first president of the Ambassadors was Robert S. Mars, and the first Duke of the Duchy of Duluth was Dr. W.A. Coventry. Dignified and resplendent in his royal red robes, the Duke made the following appointments: Thomas G. Bell, Prince of the West; Judge Dennis F. Donovan, Prince of the East; Herman C. Matzke, Minister of the Crafts; Earl T. Bester, Minister of Shipping; Louis E. Sundby, Minister of Trade; Leo J. Burak, Minister of Sports; Mayor E.H. Hatch, Lord High Mayor; Sheriff Sam M. Owens, Lord High Sheriff; and Hollis B. Ryan, Captain of the Royal Guard. The Duchy of Duluth gives Ambassadorships Extraordinary to Emissaries from Distant Provinces. Among the first to receive these titles were Julius H. Barnes and William L. Shirer, CBS news analyst, from the Province of New York.

Laughter and nonsense ceased the following month. On December 7, 1941, the Japs attacked Pearl Harbor. Duluthians, seated at Sunday dinner, heard the radio announcement in shocked silence - and then grimly dug in to win another war.

In the Pearl Harbor attack, two Duluth men were killed. S-Sgt. Andrew A. Walczynski met death at Hickam Field and Robert C. McQuade, seaman 1st class, was killed when his ship, *USS Shaw*, a destroyer, was sunk.

The third selective service registration came in February of 1942, for men 20 to 45 years of age. In April, in the fourth registration, for men from 45 to 64, 12,208 men registered.

Rationing began in 1942, with sugar the first item to be controlled. Public school teachers at Central, Denfeld and Morgan Park registered institutional and industrial uses of sugar, April 29-30. At the elementary schools, 97,000 residents signed up for war rationing books from May 3 to 7. In November, citizens turned in all extra automobile tires at the express office and then 30,000 individuals registered for "A" gas rationing coupons. In February 1943, ration books no. 2 were distributed for processed foods, coffee, meat, cheese and butter. The homeowner, yardstick in hand, measured the cubic feet of rooms in his house to determine how many fuel oil stamps he would be allowed, and then learned to close the damper in the fireplace and draw down the window shades to help conserve fuel. Other commodities rationed were shoes, typewriters, tires, automobiles, bicycles and pressure cookers. Stores curtailed delivery service. Ceiling prices were placed on foods in restaurants in 1943. P.A. Burke was director of the Duluth-Superior district office of Price Administration. In January of 1944, merit awards and distinguished service pins were awarded 364 Duluthians who had volunteered service with the war price or rationing board. Many of these individuals had contributed from 500 to 2,000 hours of work.

A central body of women in the Duluth Civilian Defense Council was organized to direct and coordinate the many women's activities, with Mrs. John D. Jenswold, chairman. A women's volunteer office was opened in November 1941 in the Alworth building, directed by Mrs. D.W. Wheeler and her seventy-five assistants. Mrs. Jenswold and Robert S. Mars were co-chairmen of the first salvage drive, for aluminum, in July of 1941. A huge parade with floats and bands moved to Courthouse Square, where contributions were dumped into a big wire bin.

In the Women's Civilian Defense organized in 1942, Mrs. E.J. Kennedy was director, with Mrs. Wildey H. Mitchell her assistant. Mrs. A.C. Schaefer organized the Victory Aides, a corps of 1,800 women volunteer workers who canvassed their districts, house by house, on various assignments: to disseminate information on bond and salvage drives and on recreation, health and physical fitness programs; to determine items that could be obtained for temporary hospitals or emergency casualty stations; to survey for possible rooms available in case of bombing or other disasters; to get signatures on pledges of consumers in a war against inflation; and to make a market survey for the postwar era. The Victory Aides helped to make housewives aware of their part in the war.

Air Raid wardens, 2,500 of them, were organized in February, 1942, and began their training in March. James G. Nye was the first chief, followed by Frank C. Tenney. Duluth's official blackouts were held in May and August of 1943 and a statewide blackout was held in December. Air raid drills were held in schools.

Two other branches of service for civilian defense were the 324 auxiliary police and 350 auxiliary firemen.

The Arrowhead Chapter of the American Red Cross conducted first aid classes for civilian defense and hundreds of other citizens. The Red Cross accelerated its work under the chairmanship of Edward Martini, succeeded by Chester Tibbets. Headquarters were in the old city hall. Mrs. Robert S. Forbes was chairman of Volunteer Services, in which thousands of Duluthians participated. Chairman of

271

production - knitting, surgical dressings, and garments of rehabilitation - was Mrs. George Tweed. By the end of 1941, there were 1,000 women registered for knitting. Other chairmen included: Mrs. Peter Rudie and Mrs. Arthur Miller, blood bank; Miss Ellowyn Cowden, motor corps; Mrs. D.A. Rude, Gray Ladies; Mrs. Russell Anderson, canteen; Mrs. Fred Dutton, classes in instruction; Mrs. Clarence Nesgoda, staff aides; and Miss Elizabeth Congdon, recruiting of nurses for military service. William Bissonette was chairman of the Home Service Department, which helped families in getting messages to and from boys in prison camps and assisted financially men in service and their families. Mrs. Richard Northrup informed the public of services in which individuals could take part. Mrs. Frank Maghan was chairman of the Junior Red Cross in the schools, where pupils gave financial assistance and provided articles for men in service and in hospitals. During the war years, Mrs. Felix Seligman was director of the Junior Red Cross and Clinton Dennison and his successor, Evan Thompson, were managers of the Minnesota Arrowhead Chapter of Red Cross.

The British War Relief contributed thousands of articles to Great Britain.

Salvage operations conducted by the Duluth Defense Council were headed by Harry W. Clark. Over 924,000 pounds of tin cans were collected from Duluth householders in four drives. The Junior Chamber of Commerce loaded freight cars when the temperature was 32 below zero and the wind "she blew like a hurricane". The Head of the Lakes area shipped about 2,000,000 tons of scrap iron and steel. Among landmarks contributed to these drives were the old city jail cells, 541 tons of street car tracks, and the Central High School cannon from the Spanish American War. Great piles of newspapers and magazines stood in front of homes and business houses in the five paper drives which yielded about 1,800,000 pounds. Hundreds of thousands of pounds of salvage fat were turned in. A silk and nylon hosiery drive yielded 9,000 pounds of stockings to be used in the manufacture of parachutes and explosives. A clothing and rags drive resulted in eight carloads of articles and material. "Everybody cooperated," says Mr. Clark. "Housewives saved and collected material; the city, business and industrial firms loaned trucks, and members of labor unions volunteered their services."

Other organizations conducted drives for rubber, books, radio parts, old recordings, phonographs, keys, "Smokes for Yanks", and "junk jewelry". The latter, sponsored by the Junior Chamber of Commerce, brought in more than 1,000 pounds of discarded jewelry for boys in the South Pacific to use in barter.

The United States Coast Guard, made a part of the Navy in 1941, established offices in Duluth in May, 1942. The first contingent of about 350 men was assigned to waterfront patrol duty. The Cascade hotel was taken over for barracks. In the spring of 1943, two-thirds of the Coast Guard unit was transferred to sea duty, and a temporary reserve was recruited from the Twin Ports. The Harbor Patrol, with Lieutenant Fred Buck as commander, was composed of 200 men who patrolled the waters during shipping season. Active in this patrol was the United States Power Squadron, an organization of Duluth men trained in the ways of boats, who used their own boats in patrol duty. A charter had been issued the Duluth squadron on June 27, 1939. The organization is continuing today with a membership of 37, of which there is one navigator, George Barnum, and two junior navigators, Dr. A.J. Huderle and K.M. Brooks. The present local commander is Wilfred A. George.

The Volunteer Port Security Forces of 300 men, with Lieutenant C.R. McLean as commander, was the branch of the temporary reserve, which stood land watches. All men in both divisions did a tour of duty of six hours every four days, serving without pay. The reserves were disbanded in June, 1945.

In January, 1946, the Coast Guard returned to its former stations under the Treasury Department.

A Duluth USO center was organized, with Mrs. Eleanor Yenerich director. Serving at the center were 370 junior hostesses who provided weekly parties, a dancing class, beach parties and four formal dances for men in uniform. The Business Girls Club of the YWCA published a mimeographed paper, *USO Hi Lites*. There was a twenty-three weeks series of radio programs on which service men could make long distance telephone calls to their homes or their girls. The center had a lending library of fishing tackle and skates.

Again, Duluth oversubscribed the quota in each War Bond campaign. The first loan, the Defense Bonds, was handled through banks, but here is the record of War Bonds after Pearl Harbor through the Victory Bonds.

	Quota	*Sales*	*Percentage*
2nd	$ 6,700,000	11,954,676	178
3rd	13,712,000	18,379,963	134
4th	12,100,000	17,635,608	146
5th	15,000,000	17,997,224	120
6th	13,125,000	18,433,961	140
7th	13,675,000	23,105,149	169
8th	9,800,000	19,876,448	203
TOTALS	$ 84,112,000	127,383,029	151

Including sales outside the campaigns, the total Duluthians invested in war bonds reaches $151,218,248. Bond sales were directed by Fred W. Buck, succeeded by Charles Liscomb.

Shipbuilders at the Head of the Lakes made another notable contribution to the war, with a total of 355 ships - coast guard cutters, navy net tenders, navy water tenders, tankers, navy net layers, coastal cargoes, ocean-going cargoes, frigates, ocean-going tugs, sub-chasers, plane rearming boats and barges. When the Walter Butler Shipyards in Superior launched five vessels on May 9, 1943 (the largest number of ships to be launched in a single day from a single shipyard) the Dionne quintuplets came down from Canada to christen the ships.

The *USS Duluth,* a fast new Cruiser, was christened in East by Mrs. Edward Hatch, wife of the mayor. It became a part of Admiral Halsey's famous Task Force 38 and participated in the devastating action against the Japan homeland from July 10 to August 15, 1945. It was standing off Tokyo at the time of the surrender.

The Army-Navy "E" and Maritime Commission "M" were awarded to many Duluth firms for excellence in production for war.

Approximately 14,000 Duluth men were in military service in World War II, and 600 died in service. Duluth women also joined the newly organized WAVEs, WACs and SPARS, as well as Red Cross nurse units. There are thousands of stories of heroism. Two men were awarded the Congressional Medal of Honor, the nation's highest award for military valor.

Major Henry A. Courtney, Jr., United States Marine Corps, was posthumously awarded the medal, which was presented to his parents, Mr. and Mrs. Henry A. Courtney. He was killed by a hostile mortar burst in the assault on Sugar Loaf Hill on Okinawa. The History of the Sixth Marine Division says of Major Courtney in this action for which he won the medal: "Leading his men by example rather than by command, he pushed ahead with unrelenting aggressiveness, hurling grenades into cave openings on the slope with devastating effect."

Nineteen-year-old Pfc. Michael Colallilo, a member of the 100th Division of the Seventh Army in Germany, won the Congressional Medal "for risking his life to form a one-man spearhead for his unit, killing or wounding at least twenty-five Germans as he advanced on foot and then atop a rumbling American tank in the vicinity of Untergrieshiem, Germany." Mike's buddies called him a "one-man army".

This book will not attempt to give even a thumbnail history of the war itself. It is fresh in the minds of most readers - the fall of Corregidor and the death march of Bataan in the first dark days, Guadalcanal, the invasion of North Africa, the Normandy invasion, Makin, Tarawa, Saipan, Leyte, Berlin, Okinawa, the atom bomb on Hiroshima, and E Day on May 7 and J Day on September 2, both 1945. World War II was over.

Following the war, military reserve units were organized in Duluth. The Organized Reserve Program is established to furnish, in event of a national emergency, units effectively organized, trained and equipped in peacetime, for rapid mobilization, expansion and deployment. A Mobilization Day Force would be composed of the Regular Army, part of the National Guard, and such Organized Reserve Corps units and personnel as are necessary to provide an effective force with essential combat and service support.

Two units of the Organized Reserve Corps in Duluth are in category I with forty-eight training assemblies a year and the others are in category II with twenty-four training assemblies a year. Each summer, encampments are held where reservists can apply the theory they have been taught. All organizations authorized attended the 1949 encampment at Camp McCoy, Wisconsin.

Until World War II, the Reserve was largely inactive, and only one officer was stationed in Duluth between 1918 and 1940. There are now seven Regular Army instructors. The city has 118 officers and 105 enlisted men under training. The nucleus of twenty-one organizations would ultimately form organizations of 1,873 officers and enlisted men upon mobilization.

From one desk and one room in the Federal Building in 1947, the program has expanded to the entire fourth and fifth floors of the Christie Building, and it is contemplated to acquire the third floor for storage areas and an indoor rifle range.

Major S.J. Eifers, Officer in Charge, says, "Today the Atomic Age requires total preparedness. Unless there is some guarantee that the Reserve Forces can be maintained at a high level of efficiency and strength, the military future cannot be assured. The history of the ORC is not complete. It has only started. In the event of another conflagration that may ignite the world, attacks upon our own commodities may become a start reality. The country must be able to look to its own citizens for protection."

The United States Air Force Reserve Unit was activated in Duluth, January, 1948, under the jurisdiction of Colonel Don L. Wilhelm, Jr., Commanding Officer of the 2,465th Air Force Reserve Training Center, at Wold-Chamberlain Field, Minneapolis. T-Sgt. John F. Fitzpatrick, of the 2,465th AFRTC, was assigned to help coordinate the training program. The Duluth unit was designated as the 142nd Composite Squadron (Air Reserve), with Lt. Colonel Chester D. Seftenberg, vice president and trust officer of the First and American National bank, as Commanding Officer.

The first of the training programs was held, February 19, 1948, in the auditorium of the Napolean-Duprey VFW post. Three training assemblies a month are now held in the ORC Armory. During the summer, all pilots of the squadron are given the opportunity of maintaining their flying proficiency through the use of aircraft sent to the municipal airport from the 2,465th AFRTC.

The squadron was re-designated the 9,703rd Volunteer Air Reserve Training Squadron, June 27, 1949. At that time, Flight "A" was also activated, with Lt. Colonel Wildey H. Mitchell Flight Commander. Its personnel is that of the former 241st Composite Squadron (Air Reserve), less the squadron headquarters staff of the 9,703rd. In addition, the former 245th Composite Squadron of Bemidji was re-designated as Flight "B", 9,703rd Volunteer Air Reserve Training Squadron, with Flight "C" at Bovey activated in August.

Sergeant Fitzpatrick, unit instructor, says that since the original activation, several of the personnel have been recalled to extended active duty to the Air Force.

"B" Company, Fourth Infantry Battalion, Organized Marine Corps Reserve was activated on April 1, 1948, with the appointment of Captain Hillford G. Bowes, USMCR, as its Commanding Officer and the First Lieutenant Thomas E. Gleason, USMC, as Inspector-Instructor. The unit is a rifle company consisting of 240 enlisted Marines and seven officers, one doctor and six corpsmen. It is a separately administered part of the Fourth Infantry Battalion stationed at the U.S. Naval Air Station in Minneapolis. The personnel are all from Duluth, Superior and adjoining areas. By January 1949 the Company had reached its authorized strength.

The unit holds drills at the Emerson School Building, where its personnel are trained in the many phases of Amphibious Tactics.

Besides training men in modern warfare, the Company places great emphasis on civilian-military relationship. It participates in civic functions and enters baseball and basketball teams in competition with other local teams.

"Within the framework of its training, social and recreational program," says Lieutenant Gleason, "the Marine Corps Reserve is striving to make better citizens of its personnel in accordance with the highest traditions of the Naval service."

The 179th Fighter Squadron, Minnesota Air National Guard, was activated September 17, 1948, with Major Ralph M. Jerome Commanding Officer. From the United States Air Force are instructors Lieutenant Colonel John S. Loisel, Master Sergeant Floyd Rush and Tech. Sergeant Walter R. Kutzli. There are about thirty-five officers. The pilots are all from World War II. Other members of the unit receive instruction in all lines of maintenance, communication, supply, armament and administration. About sixty technicians are employed full-time in maintaining equipment and records.

Training assemblies are held each Wednesday night, with one full 8-hour training assembly once a month. Flying missions are planned for weekends.

The squadron headquaters are at the municipal airport, where one of three scheduled hangars is completed. Here are the fighter aircraft: single-engine F-51 Mustangs; T-6 Texan trainers; B-26 attack bombers; and C-47 transports.

The Coast Guard, Naval Reserve and Minnesota National Guard complete the military picture in Duluth in 1949.

Construction was brisk in Duluth after the war, with much remodeling and many new buildings and homes in spite of shortages of materials. The housing problem that harassed returning veterans was partially solved by the city, which built two projects. The year 1949 was the best building year in the city's history.

Modern White Way lights are hailed as the biggest 1949 public safety achievement. More than fourteen miles of major thoroughfares have been brought up to or over the minimum required standards for safe lighting.

Reports for 1949 show 25,670 gas meters and 21,813 water meters, up 116 and 327 respectively over 1939, indicative of city development. Post office receipts were approximately $1,241,407. For the first time in the history of the post office, income for every month exceeded $100,000.

Duluth today has an estimated population of 105,000 and an area of 67.34 miles. Here are located 104 churches and missions, three hospitals and fifty-one motels, as well as twelve motion picture theatres, two "drive-ins", one amateur theatre and one summer stock company theatre. The city has six national banks, two savings banks and three state banks with total deposits of $166,404,757 and total resources $171,177,604. It has 1,750 retail outlets including nine principal department stores, with retail sales about $142,872,000 a year; 227 wholesale establishments, including two of the nation's largest wholesale hardware distributors, with sales approximately $200,000,000; and approximately 300 industries, including the only steel plant in the state.

The Duluth-Superior harbor is second in the nation in shipping, surpassed only by New York City. The record number of vessels in the harbor is on November 9, 1943, when there were 39 arrivals and 53 departures, with a minimum of 63 in the harbor at one time. Maximum commerce for a single year was 74,314,646 short tons.

The harbor has an area of nineteen square miles and a frontage of forty-nine linear miles. There are seventeen miles of dredged channels, twenty-four feet deep, behind Minnesota Point. Harbor facilities include forty-six wharves handling freight other than iron ore, coal and grain. There are twenty-one coal docks with storage capacity of 13,046,000 tons; seven ore docks with storage capacity of 819,100 gross tons; thirty grain elevators with storage capacity of 51,835,000 bushels; and one cement elevator with storage capacity of 114,000 bushels. There are 110 terminals at this port.

As "the air-conditioned" city, Duluth has a tremendous tourist trade in the summer. As "the hay fever haven of America", it has an organization for visitors who come in August and September to be free of hay fever. As a winter sports center, it attracts hundreds of sports enthusiasts.

These are the facts about Duluth. But the city of Daniel de Greysolon Sieur du Luth is more than a collection of facts. It is a city that meets its adversities with courage and clings to its dreams with stubborn tenacity. Poised on its hills, it gazes out to the lake, figuratively puts its hands on its hips, raises its chin and cries out to the world, "What next? We're ready!"

This is Duluth.

APPENDIX

MAYORS OF DULUTH

City—Aldermanic form of government
1870   J. B. Culver
1871   Clinton Markell
1872   Sidney Luce (resigned)
          Clinton Markell (appointed)
1873-1874 Vespusian Smith
1875   Peter Dean
1876   John Drew

Village
1877-1878 A. M. Miller (president)
1879   John Drew (president)
1880   Peter Dean (president, resigned)
          J. D. Ensign (appointed)
1881   J. D. Ensign (president)

City—Aldermanic form of government
1882   C. H. Graves
1883   J. B. Culver (died)
          C. H. Graves
1884   J. D. Ensign
1885   H. B. Moore
1886-1889 John B. Sutphin
1890-1891 M. J. Davis
1892-1893 Charles d'Autremount
1894-1895 Ray T. Lewis
1896-1899 Henry Truelson
1900-1903 Trevanian W. Hugo
1904-1907 Marcus B. Cullum
1908-1909 R. D. Haven
1910-1911 Marcus B. Cullum
1912   J. A. McCuen

Commission form of government
1913-1916 W. I. Prince
1917-1918 Clarence R. Magney
1919-1920 Clarence R. Magney (resigned)
          Trevanian W. Hugo (appointed)
1921-1936 S. F. Snively
1937-1940 C. R. Berghult
1941-1944 Edward H. Hatch
1945-   George W. Johnson

EARLY RECOLLECTIONS OF NEW DULUTH
by Mrs. John D. Larson

(Mrs. Larson who wrote these reminiscences in 1939 died in 1948. She left historical material on early New Duluth with the Misses Anna and Ethel Brand who graciously contributed this article.)

Looking over an old Abstract of Title, I found—

Certificate of Location
Date—January 9, 1864
Filed—March 18, 1864

Certifies that Military Bounty Land Warrant No. 43,346 in the name of John Haydock was this day located by John Smith upon Lot 1 and the S. E. ¼ of N. E. ¼ of Section 10 and Lots 1 and 3 of Section 11 Township 48, Range 15.

A patent to this land was issued by the United States government to my father, dated December 1, 1864 and recorded March 28, 1871. Some years earlier, my father homesteaded 160 acres of land at Twin Lakes in Carlton county, intending to make it his home. Some of the settlers already there were the Dunphys, Mayers, Chisholms, and an interesting character known as "Esquire" Lyons.

As carrier of the mails from Twin Lakes to Oneota, across country to Fond du Lac on foot and thence by rowboat in summer and snowshoes in winter, father became interested in the beautifully forested valley of the St. Louis river. When the opportunity came, he decided to make this site his permanent home.

There was a small log house on the property to which he built on two additional rooms of hewn logs. To this home in the wilderness he brought my mother as a bride on May 8, 1870.

No minister of the gospel resided nearer than Duluth, so the ceremony was performed by a Justice of the Peace, Peter Peterson of Fond du Lac.

Three children were born in this humble but happy home. My brother William G. died May 13, 1937; my sister Louise died at the age of seven, November 23, 1884; I am the only survivor of that pioneer family.

The nearest school was at Fond du Lac, three miles away, where we attended during fall and spring terms; but owing to severe cold weather, we were often obliged to omit the mid-winter session. No school busses in those days—and no roads! We walked the railroad track, daily cautioned by mother to "watch out for trains", of which there were many. This was then the main and only line to St. Paul.

Our nearest neighbors on the east were the Swensons, Lenroots and Ericksons, all living on farms at Spirit Lake. A half mile farther on, lived a Frenchman by the name of Marshall. I believe his farm was located on about what is now the Riverside golf course.

During the winter months, father logged off the virgin growth of pine which covered our farm, hauled the logs to the river by ox-team, and there later made them into rafts to be towed to sawmills at Oneota and Rice's Point.

I recollect the Merritts had a camp just across the river on what is now a part of Oliver. My brother and I loved to visit the camp. There was a cook named Harry—an expert on preparing savory baked beans. He also made delicious coffee bread.

Tom Sandiland, better known as "Uncle Tom", was there, too, with his unlimited fund of humorous stories. I remember vividly one that he liked to tell about an itinerant school master who came to the camp, greatly agitated, one day in mid-winter, asking for shelter. He remained several weeks, working with the crew, cutting cord wood and piling it near the river's edge. It soon became known that he had taken a sudden enforced vacation from his school because of an infatuation for one of the young ladies of the village with whom he planned an elopement. A letter from the East revealed that he already had a wife and two children. Upon learning this news, the irate father of the young lady went into action with a shot gun and drove him out of the community.

Woodsmen are inclined to relieve the monotony of work by indulging in practical jokes. They made life anything but pleasant for this philanderer. Every time anyone was seen coming down the river, they shouted, "Look out! There he comes!" and the erstwhile school teacher would duck behind a woodpile.

In closing—a tribute to the memory of that host of splendid men and women now gone on to the Better Land! They blazed the trail through the wilderness, making it possible for their children and children's children to carry on for the betterment of mankind.

ADDRESS BY JAMES PROCTOR KNOTT

given in the Congress of the United States in 1871.

Mr. Speaker, if I could be actuated by any conceivable inducement to betray the sacred trust reposed in me by those to whose generous confindence I am indebted for the honor of a seat on this floor; if I could be influenced by any possible consideration to become instrumental in giving away, in violation of their known wishes, any portion of their interests in the public domain for the mere promotion of any railroad enterprise whatever, I should certainly feel a strong inclination to give this measure my most earnest and hearty support, for I am assured that its success would materially enhance the pecuniary prosperity of some of the most valued friends I have on earth, friends for whose accommodation I would be willing to make almost any sacrifice not involving my personal honor or fidelity as the trustee of an express trust. And that fact of itself would be sufficient to countervail almost any objection I might entertain to the passage of this bill, not inspired by an imperative and inexorable sense of public duty.

But independent of the seductive influences of private friendship, to which I admit I am, perhaps, as susceptible as any of the gentlemen I see around me, the intrinsic merits of the measure itself are of such an extraordinary character as to commend it most strongly to the favorable consideration of the House, myself not excepted, notwithstanding my constituents, in whose behalf alone I am acting here, would not be benefited by its passage one particle more than they would be by a project to cultivate an orange grove on the bleakest summit on Greenland's icy mountains. (Laughter.)

Now, sir, as to those great trunk lines of railroads spanning the continent from ocean to ocean, I confess my mind has never been fully made up. It is true they may afford some trifling advantages to local traffic, and they may even, in time, become the channel of a more extended commerce; yet I have never been thoroughly satisfied either of the necessity or expediency of projects promising such meager results to the great body of the people. But with regard to the transcendent merits of the gigantic enterprise contemplated in this bill I never entertained a shadow of doubt. (Laughter.) Years ago, when I first heard that there was, somewhere in the vast terra incognita, somewhere in the bleak region of the Northwest, a stream of water known to the nomadic inhabitants of the neighborhood as the River St. Croix, I became satisfied that the construction of a railroad from that raging torrent to some point in the civilized world was essential to the prosperity and happiness of the American people, if not absolutely indispensable to the perpetuity of the republican institutions on this continent. (Great laughter.) I had an abiding presentiment that some day or other the people of the whole country, irrespective of party affiliations, regardless of sectional prejudices, and "without distinction of race, color, or of previous condition of servitude," would rise in their majesty and demand an outlet for the enormous agricultural products of those vast and fertile pine barrens, drained in the rainy season by the surging waters of the turbid St. Croix. (Great laughter.)

These impressions, derived simply and solely "from the eternal fitness of things," were not only strengthened by the interesting and eloquent debate on this bill, to which I listened with so much pleasure the other day, but intensified, if possible, as I read over this morning the lively colloquy which took place on that occasion. The honorable gentleman from Minnesota, Mr. Wilson, who, I believe is managing this bill, in speaking of the character of the country through which this railroad is to pass, says this: "We want to have the timber brought to us as cheaply as possible. Now, if you tie up the lands in this way, so that no title can be obtained to them—for no settler will go on these lands, for he can not make a living—you deprive us of the benefit of that timber." Now, sir, I would not have it, by any means, inferred from this that the gentleman from Minnesota would insinuate that the people in that section desire this timber merely for the purpose of fencing up their farms so that their stock may not wander off and die of starvation among the bleak hills of the St. Croix. (Laughter). I read it for no such purpose, sir, and make no such comments on it myself. In corroboration of this statement from the gentleman from Minnesota, I find this testimony given by the honorable gentleman from Wisconsin, Mr. Washburn, who, speaking of the same lands, said: "They are generally sandy, barren lands. My friend from Gray Bay district, Mr. Sawyer, is perfectly familiar with this question, and he will bear me out in what I say, that these pine timberlands are not adapted to settlement." Now, sir, who, after listening to this emphatic and unequivocal testimony of these intelligent, competent, and ablebodied witnesses (laughter), who, that is not as incredulous as St. Thomas himself, will doubt for a moment that the Goshen of America is to be found in the sandy valleys and upon the pine-clad hills of the St. Croix? (Laughter.)

Who will have the hardihood to rise in his seat on this floor and assert that, excepting the pine bushes, the entire region would not produce vegetation enough in 10 years to fatten a grasshopper? (Great laughter.) Where is the patriot who is willing that his country shall incur the peril of remaining another day without the amplest railroad communication with such an inexhaustible mine of agricultural wealth? (Laughter.) Who will answer for the consequences of abandoning a great and warlike people in possession of a country like that to brook over the indifference and neglect of their government? (Laughter.) How long would it be before they would take to studying a declaration of independence and hatching out the damnable heresy of secession? How long before the grim demon of civil discord would rear again his horrid head in our midst, "gnash loud his iron fangs, and shake his crest of gristling bayonets"? (Laughter.) Then, sir, think of the long and painful process of reconstruction that must follow, with its concomitant amendments to the Constitution; the seventeenth, eighteenth, and nineteenth articles. The sixteenth, it is, of course, understood, is to be appropriated to those blushing damsels who are, day after day, beseeching us to let them vote, hold office, drink cocktails, ride astraddle, and do everything else the men do. (Roars of laughter.) But, above all, sir, let me implore you to reflect for a moment on the deplorable condition of our country in case of a foreign war; with all our ports blockaded; all our cities in a state of siege; the gaunt specter of famine brooding like a hungry vulture over our starving land; our commissary stores all exhausted, our famished armies withering away in the field, a helpless prey to the insatiate demon of hunger; our Navy rotting in the docks for want of provisions for our gallant seamen; and we without any railroad communication whatever with the prolific pine thickets of the St. Croix. (Great laughter.)

Ah, sir, I could well understand why my amiable friends from Pennsylvania (Mr. Meyers, Mr. Kelly, and Mr. O'Neill) should be so earnest in their support for this bill the other day, and if their honorable colleague, my friend, Mr. Randall, will pardon the remark, I will say I consider his criticism of their action on that occasion as not only unjust but ungenerous. I knew they were looking forward with far-reaching ken of enlightened statesmanship to the pitiable condition in which Philadelphia will be left unless speedily supplied with railroad connection, in some way, with this garden spot of the universe. (Laughter.) And, besides, sir, this discussion has relieved my mind of a mystery that has weighed upon it like an incubus for years. I could never understand before why there was so much excitement during the last Congress over the acquisition of Alta Vela. I could never understand why it was that some of our ablest statesmen and most distinguished patroits should entertain such dark forebodings of the untold calamities that were to befall our country unless we should take immediate possession of that desirable island. But I see now that they are laboring under the impression that the Government will need guano to manure the public lands of the St. Croix. (Great laughter.) Now, sir, I repeat, I had been satisifed for years that if there was any portion of the habitable globe absolutely in a suffering condition for a railroad, it was the teeming pine barrens of the St. Croix. (Laughter.) At what particular point on that noble stream such a road should be commenced I knew was immaterial, and so it seems to have been considered by the draftsman of this bill. It might be up at the spring or down at the foot log, or the water gate, or the fish dam, or anywhere along the bank, no matter where. (Laughter.) But in what direction it should run, or where it should terminate, were always, in my mind, questions of the most painful perplexity. I could conceive of no place on "God's green earth" in such straightened circumstances for railroad facilities as to be likely to desire or willing to accept such a connection. (Laughter.)

I know that neither Bayfield nor Superior City would have it, for they both indignantly spurned the munificence of the Government when coupled with such ignominious conditions, and let this very same land grant die on their hands years and years ago rather than submit to the degradation of direct communication by railroad with the piney woods of the St. Croix; and I know that what the enterprising inhabitants of those giant young cities refused to take would have few charms for others, whatever their necessities or the cupidity might be. (Laughter.) Hence, as I have said, sir, I was utterly at loss to determine where the terminus of this great and indispensable road should be, until I accidentally overheard some gentelmen the other day mention the name of "Duluth." (Great laughter.) "Duluth!" The word fell upon my ear with peculiar and indescribable charm, like the gentle murmur of a low fountain stealing forth in the midst of roses, or the soft sweet accents of an angel's whisper in the bright, joyous dream of sleeping innocence. Duluth! 'Twas the name for which my soul had panted for years, as a hart panteth for the waterbrooks. (Renewed laughter.) But where was Duluth? Never, in my limited reading, had my vision been gladdened by seeing the celestial word in print. (Laughter.) And I felt a profound humiliation in my ignorance that its dulcet syllables had never before ravished my delighted ear. (Roars of laughter.) I was certain the draftsman of this bill had never heard of it, or it would have been designated as one of the termini of this road. I asked my friends about it, but they knew nothing of it. I rushed to my library and examined all the maps I could find. (Laughter.) I discovered in one of them a delicate hairlike line, diverging from the Mississippi at a place marked Prescott, which I supposed was intended to represent the River St. Croix, but I could nowhere find Duluth! Nevertheless, I was confident that it existed somewhere, and that its discovery would consitute the crowning glory of the present century, if not of all modern times. (Laughter.) I knew it was bound to exist in the very nature of things; that the symmetry and perfection of our planetary system would be incomplete without it. (Renewed laughter.)

That the elements of material nature would have long since resolved themselves back into original chaos if there had been such a hiatus in creation as would have resulted from leaving out Duluth. (Roars of laughter.) In fact, sir, I was overwhelmed with the conviction that Duluth not only existed somewhere, but that, wherever it was, it was a great and glorious place. I was convinced that the greatest calamity that ever befell the benighted nations of the ancient world was in their having passed away without a knowledge of the actual existence of Duluth; that their fabled Atlantis, never seen, save by the hallowed visions of inspired poesy, was, in fact, but another name for Duluth; that the golden orchard of Hesperides was but a poetical synonym for the beer gardens in the vicinity of Duluth. (Laughter.) I was certain that Herodotus had died a miserable death because, in all his travels and all his geographical researches he had never heard of Duluth, (Laughter.) I knew that if the immortal spirit of Homer could look down from another heaven than that created by his own celestial genius, upon the long lines of pilgrims from every nation of the earth to the gushing fountain of poesy opened by the touch of his magic wand; if he could be permitted to behold the vast asesmblage of grand and glorious productions of the lyric art called into being by his own inspired strain, he would weep tears of bitter anguish that, instead of lavishing all the stores of his mighty genius upon the fall of Ilion, it had not been his more blessed lot to crystallize in deathless song the rising glories of Duluth.

Yet, sir, had it not been for this map kindly furnished me by the Legislature of Minnesota, I might have gone down to my obscure and humble grave in an agony of despair, because I could not nowhere find Duluth. (Renewed laughter.) Had such been my melancholy fate, I have no doubt but that, with the last feeble pulsation of my breaking heart, with the last faint exhalation of my fleeting breath, I should have whispered, "Where is Duluth?" (Laughter.)

But, thanks to the beneficence of that band of ministering angels who have their bright abode in the far-off capital of Minnesota, just as the agony of my anxiey was about to culminate in the frenzy of despair, this blessed map was placed in my hands, and as I unfolded it a resplendent scene of ineffable glory opened before me, such as I imagined burst upon the enraptured vision of the wandering peri through the opening gates of paradise. (Renewed laughter.) There, for the first time, my enchanted eyes rested upon the ravishing word, "Duluth." This map, sir, is intended, as it appears from its title, to illustrate the position of Duluth to the United States, but if gentlemen will examine it, I think they will concur with me in the opinion that it is far too modest in its pretensions. It not only illustrates the position of Duluth in the United States, but exhibits its relations with all created things. It even goes father than this. It lifts the shadowy veil of futurity and affords us a view of the golden prospects of Duluth far along the dim vista of ages yet to come. If gentlemen will examine it they will find Duluth not only in the center of the map but represented in a series of concentric circles 100 miles apart, and some of them as much as 4,000 miles in diameter, embracing alike in their tremendous sweep the fragrant savannas of the sunlit South and the eternal solitudes of snow that mantle the ice-bound North. (Laughter.) How the circles were produced is, perhaps, one of those primordial mysteries that the most skillful paleologists will never be able to explain. But the fact is, sir, Duluth is preeminently a central place, for I have been told by gentlemen who have been so reckless of their personal safety as to venture away in those awful regions where Duluth is supposed to be that it is so exactly in the center of the visible universe that the sky comes down precisely the same distance all around it. (Roars of laughter.) I find by reference to this map that Duluth is situated somewhere near the western end of Lake Superior, but as there is no dot or other mark indicating its exact location, I am unable to say whether it is actually confined to any particular spot or whether "It is just lying around there loose." (Renewed laughter.)

I really can not tell whether it is one of those ethereal creations of intellectual frostwork, more intangible than the rose-tinted cloud of a summer sunset; one of those airy exhalations of the speculator's brain, which I am told are ever flitting in the form of towns and cities along the lines of railroads built with Government subsidies, luring the unwary settler as the mirage of the desert lures the famishing traveler on and ever on, until it fades away on the darkening horizon, or whether it is a real, bona fide, substantial city, all "staked off," with the lots marked with their owners' names, like that proud commercial metropolis recently discovered on the desirable shore of

San Domingo. (Laughter.) But however that may be, I am satisfied Duluth is there, or thereabouts, for I see it stated here on this map that it is exactly 3,990 miles from Liverpool (laughter), though I have no doubt, for the sake of convenience, it may be moved back 10 miles so as to make the distance an even 4,000. (Renewed laughter) Then, sir, there is the climate of Duluth, unquestionably the most salubrious and delightful to be found anywhere on the Lord's earth. Now, I have always been under the impression, as I presume other gentlemen have, that, in the region around Lake Superior, it was cold enought for at least nine months in the year to freeze the smoke-stack off a locomotive. (Great laughter.) But I see it represented on this map that Duluth is situated just exactly half way between the latitudes of Paris and Venice, so that gentlemen who have inhaled the exhilerating airs of the one or basked in the golden sunshine of the other must see at a glance that Duluth must be a place of untold delights (laughter), a terrestrial paradise fanned by the balmy zephyrs of an eternal spring, clothed with gorgeous sheen of ever-blooming flowers, and vocal with the silver melody of nature's choicest slongsters. (Laughter.) In fact, sir, since I have been this map I have no doubt that Byron was vainly endeavoring to convey some faint conceptions of the delicious charms of Duluth when his poetic soul gushed forth in the rippling strains of that beautiful rhapsody—

"Know ye the land of the cedar and pine,
Where the flowers ever blossom, the beams ever shine;
Where the light wings of zephyr, oppressed with perfume
Wax faint o'er the garden of gull in her bloom;
Where the citron and olive are fairest of fruit—
And the voice of the nightingale never is mute;
Where the tints of the earth and the hues of the sky,
In color though varied, in beauty may die?"

As to the commercial resources of Duluth, sir, they are simply illimitable and inexhaustible, as is shown by this map. I see it stated here that there is a vast scope of territory, embracing an area of over 2,000,000 square miles, rich in every element of material wealth and commercial prosperity, all tributary to Duluth. Look at it, sir (pointing to the map). Here are inexhaustible mines of gold, immeasurable veins of silver, impenetrable depths of boundless forest, vast coal mines, wide extended plains of richest pasturage—all, all embraced in this vast territory, which must in the very nature of things empty the untold treasures of its commerce into the lap of Duluth. (Laughter.) Look at it, sir (pointing to the map). Do you not see these broad brown lines drawn around this immense territory, that the enterprising inhabitants of Duluth intend, some day, to inclose it all in one vast corral, so that its commerce will be bound to go there whether it would or not? (Great laughter.) And here, sir (still pointing to the map), I find, within a convenient distance, the Piegan Indians, which of all the many accessories to the glory of Duluth I consider by far the most inestimable. For, sir, I have been told that when smallpox breaks out among the women and children of that famous tribe, as it sometimes does, they afford the finest subjects in the world for strategical experiement of any enterprising military hero who desires to improve himself in the noble art of war (laughter), especially for any lieutenant general whose

"Trenchant blade, Toledo trusty,
For want of fighting has grown rusty,
And eats into itself for lack
Of somebody to hew and hack."

Sir, the great conflict now raging in the Old World has presented a phenomenon in military science unprecedented in the annals of mankind, a phenomenon that has reversed all the tradition of the past as it has disappointed all expectations of the present. A great and warlike people, renowned alike for their skill and valor, have been swept away before the advance of an inferior foe, like the autumn stubble before a hurricane of fire. For aught I know the new flash of the electric fire that shimmers along the ocean cable may tell us that Paris, with every fiber quivering with the agony of impotent despair, writhes beneath the conquering heel of her cursed invader. Ere another moon shall wax and wane the brightest star in the galaxy of nations may fall from the zenith of her glory, never to rise again. Ere the modest violet of early spring shall open her beauteous eyes, the genius of civilization may chant the unavailing requiem of the proudest nationality the world has ever seen, as she scatters her withered and tear-moistened lilies o'er the bloody tomb of butchered France. But sir, I wish to ask you if you candidly believe that the Dutch would have overrun the French in that kind of style if General Sheridan had not gone over there and told King William and Von Moltke how he managed to whip the Piegan Indians?

(Here the hammer fell.)

(Many cries, "Go on!" "Go on!")

The Speaker. Is there any objection to the gentleman from Kentucky continuing his remarks? The Chair hears none. The gentleman will proceed.

Mr. Knott. I was about remarking, sir, upon these vast "wheat fields" represented on this map in the immediate neighborhood of the buffaloes and the Piegans, and was about to say that the idea of there being these immense wheat fields in the very heart of a wilderness hundreds and hundreds of miles beyond the utmost verge of civilization may appear to some gentlemen rather incongruous—as rather too great a strain on the "blankets" of veracity. But, to my mind, there is no difficulty in the matter whatever. The phenomenon is very easily accounted for. It is evident, sir, that the Piegans sowed that wheat there and plowed it with buffalo bulls. (Great laughter.)

Now, sir, this fortunate combination of buffaloes and Piegans, considering their relative positions to each other and to Duluth, as they are arranged on the map, satisfies me that Duluth is destined to be the beef market of the world. Here you will observe (pointing to the map) are the buffaloes, directly between the Piegans and Duluth; and here, right on the road to Duluth, are the Creeks. Now, sir, when the buffaloes are sufficiently fat from grazing on these immense wheat fields, you see it will be the easiest thing in the world for the Piegans to drive them on down, stay all night with their friends the Creeks, and go into Duluth in the morning. I think I see them now, sir, a vast herd of buffaloes, with their heads down, their eyes glaring, their nostrils dilated, their tongues out, and their tails curled over their backs, tearing along toward Duluth, with about a thousand Piegans on their grassbellied ponies yelling at their heels. (Great laughter.) On they come! As they sweep past the Creeks they join in the chase, and away they all go, yelling, bellowing, ripping along amid clouds of dust, until the last buffalo is safely penned in the stockyards of Duluth. (Shouts of laughter.) Sir, I might stand here for hours and expatiate upon the gorgeous prospects of Duluth as depicted upon this map. But human life is too short and the time of this house far too valuable to allow me to linger longer upon the delightful theme. (Laughter.) I think every gentleman on this floor is as well satisfied as I am that Duluth is destined to become the commercial metropolis of the universe and that this road should be built at once. I am fully persuaded that no patriotic representative of the American people who has a proper appreciation of the associated glories of Duluth and the St. Croix will hesitate a moment to say that every able-bodied female in the land between the ages of 18 and 45 who is in favor of woman's rights should be drafted and set to work on this great work without delay. (Roars of laughter.)

Nevertheless, sir, it grieves my very soul to be compelled to say that I can not vote for the grant of lands provided for in this bill. Ah, sir, you can have no conception of the poignancy of my anguish that I am deprived of the blessed privilege. (Laughter.) There are two insuperable obstacles in the way. In the first place, my constituents, for whom I am acting here, have no more interest in this road than they have in the great question of culinary taste, now perhaps agitating the public mind of Dominica, as to whether the illustrious commissioners who recently left the Capital for that free and enlightened Republic would be better fricaseed, boiled, or roasted (great laughter); and in the second place, these lands, which I am asked to give away, alas, are not mine to bestow! My relation to them is simply that of trustee to an express trust. And shall I ever betray that trust? Never, sir! Rather perish Duluth. (Shouts of laughter.) Perish the paragon of cities! Rather let the freezing cyclones of the bleak Northwest bury it forever beneath the eddying sands of the St. Croix. (Great laughter.)

Duluth Business Firms Listed in Dun, Barlow and Company —1878 Mercantile Agency reference book containing ratings of merchants, manufacturers and traders.

Bank of Duluth — C. P. Bailey, cashier
Beckman E. — piano agent
Bell & Eyster — banking
Bulgar R. — boarding house
Burg H. — meat market
Burke Sarah E. — tobacco and cigars
Burns John — cabinet maker
Casey M. L. — restaurant
Caswell William — photographer
Christiansen Peter — tailor
Cooley, Hector & McLean — fish dealers
Costello John J. — stoves and tin
Dean Peter — general store (also N. P. R. R. junction)
Drew John — merchandise, tailor
Drohan Jas. — tavern and saloon
Duluth Electric Co.
Ebmer Alois — saloon
Farrell B. J. — tobacco and cigars
Fieberger E. — wagon maker
Fink Michael — brewer
Flynt J. H. — jeweler
Gaylord P. B. — photographer
Graves Chas. H. Co. — com'n and grain
Griggs Johnson & Foster — flour, coal, wood etc.
Gundy Morris — saloon
Haug & Manheim — restaurant
Hegardt A. B. — dry goods and groceries
Hill H. B. — florist etc.
Hokanson, John — saloon
Howard J. D. — speculator–lumber
Hughes L. G. — general store, lumber etc.
Hulett N. — restaurant
Hull J. J. — hotel and saloon
Hunter J. C. — hardware
Jacobson Wm. — cabinet maker
Jefferson E. R. — harness
Johnson Chas F. — agent—books & stat'y.
Johnson J. P. — butcher
Kaminsky J. — saloon
Kelly Lucy — tobacco, cigars, confec. etc.
Kreimer Chas. D. — feed etc.
Kugler & Dirr — meat market
LaVaque Geo. N. — paints, oils, glass etc.
Leidel E. A. — saloon
Lettan John — flour & feed
Longstreet A. M. — boarding house
Lynn Wm. — boarding house
McDaniel H. E. — furniture, undertaker
McDougall Miss Ellen — milliner
McGowan Thos. — saloon
McLaren John — blacksmith
McLean A. B. — blacksmith
McLennan & Morrison — groceries
Main Edward — groceries
Mendenhall Luther — real estate
Merrill, Miss N. — milliner
Miles A. — barber
Miller Henry — saloon
Miller A. J. & Co. — groceries & crockery
Mitchell C. H. — saloon
Munger, Markell & Co. — elevator
Munger & Gray — saw mill & lumber
Noble H. G. — groceries
O'Brien, Pratt & Co. — livery
Oppel C. H. — groceries & clothing
Osgood R. P. — butcher
Pastoret Michael — liquors, cigars
Peyton H. M. & Co. — lumber etc.
Poirier Camille — boots and shoes
Polski A. — boots and shoes
Pugsley J.—estate of — liquors
Rakowsky John G. — liquors
Ready James — poultry etc.
Rigby Mrs. T. S. — millinery, notions
Sawyer & Davis — grain
Scoville J B. — com'n.
Seip A. N. — insurance
Sherwood Geo. W. — saloon
Schoenberger J. H. — ship chandler
Silberstein B. — dry goods
Smith F. B. — drugs
Smith Geo. M. — com'n., gen. store, fish, fruit
Spalding W. W. — general store
Spalding L. M. — jewelry
Stenson O. — groceries etc.
Stone W. R. & Co. — com'n. & dock
Sullivan T. — groceries
Truelson H. — groceries
Union Improvement & Elevator Co.
Wakelin S. — hotel & saloon
Wallbank S. S. — drugs
Weber Mrs. A. N. — confectionary etc.
Weber L. — baker

Wieland C. C. & Co.	lumber, general store	Willis W. G.	clothing, fancy goods
Williams E. T. & Upham	contractors	Woodbridge W. S.	stationery

Additional firms listed in Bradstreet's—1879 Commercial reports.

Austin, Dr. James	drugs	George	
Duluth Savings Bank	John C. Hunter president, A. R. MacFarlane cashier, Pd. up cap. $25,200	McKinley and Stewart	butchers
		MacDougall Col. P.	contractor
		Mitchell R. C.	printer & publisher
Farrell James	saloon		
Hang M.	baker etc.	Petre Douglas A.	chemist, drugs
Hibbard J. J.	boat builder	Silberstein & Weiss	clothing
Hill H. B.	nursery	Weiland Ernest	tannery
Kuminski Joseph	liquors	Wheeler Martyn	fish
Larson George E.	grocer		
Lautenschlager	builder		

(Note: The above information was made available by W. J. Warren, manager of Dun and Bradstreet.)

BIBLIOGRAPHY

BOOKS

A Guidebook to Minnesota Trunk Highway No. 1—G. M. Schwartz
A Vast Empire and Its Metropolis—William F. Phelps
An Historical Review of Sacred Heart Cathedral of the Diocese of Duluth
Building Minnesota—Theodore C. Blegen
Chippewa Customs—Frances Densmore
Duluth and St. Louis County, Vol. I, II—Walter Van Brunt
Duluth-Superior Harbor Past and Present—Pauline Day
Early Days and Ways in the Old Northwest—Lindquist and Clark
The French Regime in Wisconsin and the Northwest—Louise P. Kellogg
The Geology of the Duluth Metropolitan Area—George M. Schwartz
Head of the Lakes Historical Pageant—David Wisted Post, American Legion
History of Duluth and Northern Minnesota—Judge John Carey
History of Duluth and St. Louis County, Vol. I, II—Dwight E. Woodbridge
    and John S. Pardee
Ionic Lodge No. 186—Stanley L. Mack
Minnesota, a State Guide—Federal Writer's Project
Minnesota in the Spanish-American War and the Philippine Insurrection
    —Franklin F. Holbrook
Minnesota in the War With Germany—Franklin F. Holbrook
Minnesota—The Story of a Great State—Clark and Lindquist
My Minnesota—Antoinette B. Ford
Official Road Guide, 1912—Automobile Club of Minneapolis
Old Rail Fence Corners—Daughters of the American Revolution
101 Best Stories of Minnesota—Merle Potter
Our Boys in the Spanish-American War—The Duluth Battalion
Recollections of Early Days in Duluth—Jerome Eugene Cooley
Stories of Early Minnesota—Solon J. Buck and Elizabeth Hawthorn Buck
The Story of Duluth—Jane W. Guthrie
The Story of Duluth—The fourth grade teachers of Duluth

MAGAZINE ARTICLES

American Indian Contributions to Civilization
    by Everett E. Edwards—Minnesota History, September, 1934
Daniel Greysolon DuLhut, Coureur de Bois
    by Isura Andrus-Juneau—The Wisconsin Magazine of History, June, 1941
Greysolon DuLuth: King of the Voyageurs
    by Professor Munro in the Massachusetts History Society publication

BULLETINS, PAMPHLETS

Annual Reports of the Board of Education, 1879-1949
As Others See Us—Richardson, Day and Company
The Hardy School Bulletin, 1894-95
The Maynard School Bulletin, 1896-97

UNPUBLISHED MANUSCRIPTS

Autobiography—Alfred Merritt
Daniel Greysolon, Sieur DuLuth and His Times—William E. Culkin
Diary of Edmund F. Ely
Diary of Mrs. Edmund F. Ely
Early Recollections—Mrs. John D. Larson
Games and Amusements of Ojibway—Edmund F. Ely
Geology of the Lake Superior Region—Hugh M. Roberts
Historic Site Ahead (radio series)—Gilbert Fawcett
History of Duluth—Mrs. Anne N. Dyrdahl
History of Skiing in Duluth—Harold A. Grinden
Manners and Customs of Ojibway—Edmund F. Ely
Pioneer Automobile Business—E. J. Filiatrault
Reminiscences of Ironton and Smithville—Henry J. Sullivan
Sky Harbor-Duluth—Jack C. Brockway

LOCAL HISTORICAL SKETCHES CONTRIBUTED

American Legion, David Wisted Post—Burt C. Hubbard
Aviation—Harold Lindberg and Ernest A. Bodin
"B" Company, 4th Infantry Battalion—T. E. Gleason, 1st Lieut., USMC
Bicycle Races and The First Automobile—J. R. Zweifel
Bureau of Catholic Charities of Duluth—Rev. William D. Larkin
Catholic Schools in Duluth—Sister M. Rose
City Planning Department—John Hunner
Civic Symphony Orchestra—Abe Miller
Community Chest—S. A. Bowing
Duluth District Corps of Engineers—R. S. Knowlton
Duluth Council of Churches—Rev. J. J. Runyan
Duluth Power Squadron—Wilfred A. George
Duluth Public Library—Miss Jane Morey
Duluth-Superior Harbor Development—R. S. Knowlton
Duluth-Superior Transit Company—R. B. Thompson
Duluth Telegraph History—P. D. Patterson
Duluth Telephone Development—E. C. Gladman
History of the Coast Guard and Life Saving Station—Commander R. R. Waesche,
   Jr.
KDAL—Gilbert Fawcett
Organized Reserve Program in Duluth—S. J. Eifers, Major, Infantry
Miller Memorial Hospital—(no name given)
Minnesota Power and Light Company—C. M. Baldwin
Salvation Army—Major Ernest R. Orchard
St. Louis County Historical Society—Miss Cora Colbrath
University of Minnesota, Duluth Branch—Raymond C. Gibson
War Activities of Arrowhead Chapter of the American Red Cross—Mrs. Felix
   Seligman
WEBC—Earl Henton
WREX—J. R. King
Young Men's Christian Association—(no name given)
Young Women's Christian Association—Miss Laura Huber
9703rd Volunteer Air Reserve Training Squadron—John F. Fitzpatrick T-Sgt.
   USAF

NEWSPAPERS

Files of the following newspapers have been studied: Duluth Herald,
Duluth News Tribune, Lake Superior News, Daily News, Duluth Ripsaw,
The Minnesotian, and The Morning Call.

ABOUT THE AUTHOR

Dora Mary Macdonald was born 1896 in Quincy, Illinois. After graduating from the University of Iowa she began teaching at Lincoln Junior High School in Duluth, Minnesota in 1918.

Over the next 55 years she became a well-known and esteemed figure in the Duluth area. She was a member of Delta Kappa Gamma, the American Association of University Women, and the Education Writers Association.

She won numerous awards for her work in education, including a national award for `outstanding work of interpreting education in a newspaper' from the Education Writers Association in New York City (1952), "Woman of the Year In Human Relations" (1953) and being named one of 28 outstanding women in Minnesota (1954).

Miss Macdonald also penned a weekly feature in the Cosmopolitan section of the Duluth *New-Tribune*, as well as 12 volumes of one-act and three-act plays, designed specifically for amateur production. She published "This is Duluth" in 1950.

Macdonald was the first Public Relations director for the Duluth public schools, holding this position until 1964 when she retired to Laguna Beach, California. She came back to Duluth on visits frequently until her death in 1973, at the age of seventy-six.